THE TEN COMMANDMENTS
BY

Thomas Watson

The Ten Commandments

1. INTRODUCTION

1.1 Obedience

'Take heed, and hearken, O Israel; this day thou art become the people of the Lord thy God. Thou shalt therefore obey the voice of the Lord thy God, and do his commandments.' Deut 27: 9, 10.

What is the duty which God requireth of man?

Obedience to his revealed will.

It is not enough to hear God's voice, but we must obey. Obedience is a part of the honour we owe to God. 'If then I be a Father, where is my honour?' Mal 1: 6. Obedience carries in it the life-blood of religion. 'Obey the voice of the Lord God,' and do his commandments. Obedience without knowledge is blind, and knowledge without obedience is lame. Rachel was fair to look upon, but, being barren, said, 'Give me children, or I die;' so, if knowledge does not bring forth the child of obedience, it will die. 'To obey is better than sacrifice.' I Sam 15: 22. Saul thought it was enough for him to offer sacrifices, though he disobeyed God's command; but 'to obey is better than sacrifice.' God disclaims sacrifice, if obedience be wanting. 'I spake not unto your fathers concerning burnt offerings, but this thing commanded I them, saying, Obey my voice.' Jer 7: 22. Not but that God did enjoin those religious rites of worship; but the meaning is that he looked chiefly for obedience - without which, sacrifice was but devout folly. The end why God has given us his laws, is obedience. 'Ye shall do my judgements, and keep mine ordinances.' Lev 18: 4. Why does a king publish an edict, but that it may be observed?

What is the rule of obedience?

The written word. That is proper obedience which the word requires; our obedience must correspond with the word, as the copy with the original. To seem to be zealous, if it be not according to the word, is not obedience, but will-worship. Popish traditions which have no footing in the word, are abominable; and God will say, Quis quaesivit haec? 'Who has required this at your hand?' Isa 1: I2. The apostle condemns the worshipping of angels, which had a show of humility. Col 2: 18. The Jews might say they were loath to be so bold as to go to God in their own persons; they would be more humble, and prostrate themselves before the angels, and desire them to present their petitions to God; but this show of humility was hateful to God, because there was no word to warrant it.

What are the ingredients in our obedience that make it acceptable?

(1) It must be cum animi prolubio, free and cheerful, or it is penance, not sacrifice. 'If ye be willing and obedient.' Isa 1: 19. Though we serve God with weakness, it may be with willingness. You love to see your servants go cheerfully about their work. Under the law, God will have a free-will offering. Deut 16: 10. Hypocrites obey God grudgingly, and against their will; facere bonum, but not velle [they do good but not willingly]. Cain brought his sacrifice, but not his heart. It is a true rule, Quicquid cor non facit, non fit; what the heart does not do, is not done. Willingness is the soul of obedience. God sometimes accepts of willingness without the work, but never of the work without willingness. Cheerfulness shows that there is love in the duty; and love is to our services what the sun is to fruit; it mellows and ripens them, and makes them come off with a better relish.

(2) Obedience must be devout and fervent. 'Fervent in spirit,' &c. Rom 12: 11. Quae ebullit prae ardore. As water that boils over; so the heart must boil over with hot affections in the service of God. The glorious angels, who, for burning in fervour and devotion, are called seraphims, are chosen by God to serve him in heaven. The snail under the law was unclean, because a dull, slothful creature. Obedience without fervency, is like a sacrifice without fire. Why should not our obedience be lively and fervent? God deserves the flower and strength of our affections. Domitian would not have his statue carved in wood or iron, but made of gold. Lively affections make golden services. It is fervency that makes obedience acceptable. Elijah was fervent in spirit, and his prayer opened and shut heaven; and again he prayed, and fire fell on his enemies. 2 Kings 1: 10. Elijah's prayer fetched fire from heaven, because, being fervent, it carried fire up to heaven; quicquid decorum ex fide proficiscitur. Augustine.

(3) Obedience must be extensive, it must reach to all God's commands. 'Then shall I not be ashamed (or, as it is in the Hebrew, lo Ehosh, blush), when I have respect unto all thy commandments.' Psa 119: 6. Quicquid propter Deum fit aequaliter fit [All God's requirements demand equal effort]. There is a stamp of divine authority upon all God's commands, and if I obey one precept because God commands, I must obey all. True obedience runs through all duties of religion, as the blood through all the veins, or the sun through all the signs of the zodiac. A good Christian makes gospel piety and moral equity kiss each other. Herein some discover their hypocrisy: they will obey God in some things which are more facile, and may raise their repute; but other things they leave undone. 'One thing thou lackest,' unum deest. Mark 10: 21. Herod would hear John Baptist, but not leave his incest. Some will pray, but not give alms, others will give alms, but not pray. 'Ye pay tithe of mint and anise, and have omitted the weightier matters of the law, judgement, mercy and faith.' Matt 23: 23. The badger has one foot shorter than the other; so these are shorter in some duties than in others. God likes not such partial servants, who will do some part of the work he sets them about, and leave the other

undone.

(4) Obedience must be sincere. We must aim at the glory of God in it. Finis specificat actionem; in religion the end is all. The end of our obedience must not be to stop the mouth of conscience, or to gain applause or preferment; but that we may grow more like God, and bring more glory to him. 'Do all to the glory of God.' 1 Cor 10: 31. That which has spoiled many glorious actions, and made them lose their reward, is, that men's aims have been wrong. The Pharisees gave alms, but blew a trumpet that they might have the glory of men. Matt 6: 2. Alms should shine, but not blaze. Jehu did well in destroying the Baal-worshippers, and God commended him for it; but, because his aims were not good (for he aimed at settling himself in the kingdom), God looked upon it as no better than murder. 'I will avenge the blood of Jezreel upon the house of Jehu.' Hos 1: 4. O let us look to our ends in obedience; it is possible the action may be right, and not the heart. 2 Chron 25: 2. Amaziah did that which was right in the sight of the Lord, but not with a perfect heart. Two things are chiefly to be eyed in obedience, the principle and the end. Though a child of God shoots short in his obedience, he takes a right aim.

(5) Obedience must be in and through Christ. 'He has made us accepted in the beloved.' Eph 1: 6. Not our obedience, but Christ's merits procure acceptance. In every part of worship we must present Christ to God in the arms of our faith. Unless we serve God thus, in hope and confidence of Christ's merits, we rather provoke him than please him. As, when king Uzziah would offer incense without a priest, God was angry with him, and struck him with leprosy (2 Chron 26: 20); So, when we do not come to God in and through Christ, we offer up incense to him without a priest, and what can we expect but severe rebukes?

(6) Obedience must be constant. 'Blessed [is] he that does righteousness at all times.' Psa 106: 3. True obedience is not like a high colour in a fit, but it is a right complexion. It is like the fire on the altar, which was always kept burning. Lev 6:13. Hypocrites' obedience is but for a season; it is like plastering work, which is soon washed off; but true obedience is constant. Though we meet with affliction, we must go on in our obedience. 'The righteous shall hold on his way.' Job 17: 9. We have vowed constancy; we have vowed to renounce the pomps and vanities of the world, and to fight under Christ's banner to death. When a servant has entered into covenant with his master, and the indentures are sealed, he cannot go back, he must serve out his time; so there are indentures drawn in baptism, and in the Lord's Supper the indentures are renewed and sealed on our part, that we will be faithful and constant in our obedience; therefore we must imitate Christ, who became obedient unto death. Phil 2: 8. The crown is set upon the head of perseverance. 'He that keepeth my works unto the end, I will give him the morning star.' Rev 2: 26, 28.

Use one. This condemns those who live in contradiction to the text, and have cast off the yoke of obedience. 'As for the word that thou hast spoken unto us in the name of the Lord, we will not hearken unto thee.' Jer 44: 16. God bids men pray in their family, but they live in the total neglect of it; he bids them sanctify the Sabbath, but they follow their pleasures on that day; he bids them abstain from the appearance of sin, but they do not abstain from the act; they live in the act of revenge, and in the act of uncleanness. This is a high contempt of God; it is rebellion, and rebellion is as the sin of witchcraft.

Whence is it that men do not obey God? They know their duty, but do it not.

(1) The not obeying God is for want of faith. Quis credidit? 'Who has believed our report?' Isa 53: 1: Did men believe sin were so bitter, that hell followed at the heels of it, would they go on in sin? Did they believe there was such a reward for the righteous, that godliness was gain, would they not pursue it; but they are atheists, not fully brought into the belief of these things; hence it is that they obey not. Satan's master-piece, his draw-net by which he drags millions to hell, is to keep them in infidelity; he knows, if he can but keep them from believing the truth, he is sure to keep them from obeying it.

(2) The not obeying God is for want of self-denial. God commands one thing, and men's lusts command another; and they will rather die than deny their lusts. If lust cannot be denied, God cannot be obeyed.

Use two. Obey God's voice. This is the beauty of a Christian.

What are the great arguments or incentives to obedience?

(1) Obedience makes us precious to God, his favourites. 'If ye will obey my voice, ye shall be a peculiar treasure unto me above all people;' you shall be my portion, my jewels, the apple of mine eye. Exod 19: 5. 'I will give kingdoms for your ransom.' Isa 43: 3.

(2) There is nothing lost by obedience. To obey God's will is the way to have our will. [1] Would we have a blessing in our estates? Let us obey. God. 'If thou shalt hearken to the voice of the Lord, to do all his commandments, blessed shalt thou be in the field: blessed shall be thy basket and thy store.' Deut 28: 1, 3, 5. To obey is the best way to thrive in your estates. [2] Would we have a blessing in our souls? Let us obey God. Obey, and I will be your God.' Jer 7: 23. My Spirit shall be your guide, sanctifier, and comforter. Christ 'became the author of eternal salvation unto all them that obey him.' Heb 5: 9. While we please God, we please ourselves; while we give him the duty, he gives us the dowry. We are apt to say, as Amaziah, 'What shall we do for the hundred talents?' 2 Chron 25: 9. You lose nothing by obeying. The obedient son has the inheritance settled on him. Obey, and you shall have a kingdom. 'It is your Father's good pleasure to give you the kingdom.' Luke 12: 32.

(3) What a sin is disobedience! [1] It is an irrational sin. We are not able to stand it out in defiance against God. 'Are we stronger than he?' Will the sinner go to measure arms with God? 1 Cor 10: 22. He is the Father Almighty, who can command legions. If we have no strength to

resist him, it is irrational to disobey him. It is irrational, as it is against all law and equity. We have our daily subsistence from him; in him we live and move. Is it not just that as we live by him, we should live to him? that as he gives us our allowance, so we should give him our allegiance?

[2] It is a destructive sin. 'The Lord Jesus shall be revealed from heaven with his mighty angels, in flaming fire, taking vengeance on them that obey not the gospel.' 2 Thess 1: 7, 8. He who refuses to obey God's will in commanding, shall be sure to obey his will in punishing. While the sinner thinks to slip the knot of obedience, he twists the cord of his own damnation, and he perishes without excuse. 'The servant which knew his lord's will, neither did according to his will, shall be beaten with many stripes.' Luke 12: 47. God will say, 'Why did you not obey? you knew how to do good, but did not; therefore your blood is upon your own head.'

What means shall we use that we may obey?

(1) Serious consideration. Consider, God's commands are not grievous: he commands nothing unreasonable. 1 John 5: 3. It is easier to obey the commands of God than sin. The commands of sin are burdensome - let a man be under the power of any lust, how he tires himself! what hazards he runs, even to endangering his health and soul, that he may satisfy his lusts! What tedious journeys did Antiochus Epiphanies take in persecuting the Jews! 'They weary themselves to commit iniquity;' and are not God's commands more easy to obey? Chrysostom says, virtue is easier than vice; temperance is less burdensome than drunkenness. Some have gone with less pains to heaven, than others to hell.

God commands nothing but what is beneficial. 'And now, Israel, what does the Lord require of thee, but to fear the Lord thy God, and to keep his statutes, which I command thee this day, for thy good?' Deut 10: 12, 13. To obey God, is not so much our duty as our privilege; his commands carry meat in the mouth of them. He bids us repent; and why? That our sins may be blotted out. Acts 3: 19. He commands us to believe: and why? That we may be saved. Acts 16: 31. There is love in every command: as if a king should bid one of his subjects dig in a gold mine, and then take the gold to himself.

(2) Earnest supplication. Implore the help of the Spirit to carry you on in obedience. God's Spirit makes obedience easy and delightful. If the loadstone draw the iron, it is not hard for it to move; so if God's Spirit quicken and draw the heart, it is not hard to obey. When a gale of the Spirit blows, we go full sail in obedience. Turn his promise into a prayer. 'I will put my Spirit within you, and cause you to walk in my statutes.' Ezek 36: 27. The promise encourages us, the Spirit enables us to obey.

1.2 Love

The rule of obedience being the moral law, comprehended in the Ten Commandments, the next question is:

What is the sum of the Ten Commandments?

The sum of the Ten Commandments is, to love the Lord our God with all our heart, with all our soul, with all our strength, and with all our mind, and our neighbour as ourselves.

'Thou shalt love the Lord thy God with all thine heart, and with all thy soul, and with all thy might.' Deut 6: 5. The duty called for is love, yea, the strength of love, 'with all thy heart.' God will lose none of our love. Love is the soul of religion, and that which constitutes a real Christian. Love is the queen of graces; it shines and sparkles in God's eye, as the precious stones on the breastplate of Aaron.

What is love?

It is a holy fire kindled in the affections, whereby a Christian is carried out strongly after God as the supreme good. What is the antecedent of love to God?

The antecedent of love is knowledge. The Spirit shines upon the understanding, and discovers the beauties of wisdom, holiness, and mercy in God; and these are the loadstone to entice and draw out love to God; Ignoti nulla cupido: such as know not God cannot love him; if the sun be set in the understanding, there must needs be night in the affections.

Wherein does the formal nature of love consist?

The nature of love consists in delighting in an object. Complacentia amantis in amato. [The lover's delight in his beloved] Aquinas. This is loving God, to take delight in him. 'Delight thyself also in the Lord' (Psa 37: 4), as a bride delights herself in her jewels. Grace changes a Christian's aims and delights.

How must our love to God be qualified?

(1) If it be a sincere love, we love God with all our heart. 'Thou shalt love the Lord thy God with all thy heart.' God will have the whole heart. We must not divide our love between him and sin. The true mother would not have the child divided, nor will God have the heart divided; it must be the whole heart.

(2) We must love God propter se, for himself, for his own intrinsic excellencies. We must love him for his loveliness. Meretricius est amor plus annulum quam sponsum amare: 'It is a harlot's love to love the portion more than the person.' Hypocrites love God because he gives them corn and wine: we must love God for himself; for those shining perfections which are in him. Gold is loved for itself.

(3) We must love God with all our might, in the Hebrew text, our vehemency; we must love God, quod posse, as much as we are able. Christians should be like seraphim, burning in holy love. We can never love God so much as he deserves. The angels in heaven cannot love God so much as he deserves.

(4) Love to God must be active in its sphere. Love is an industrious affection; it sets the head studying for God, hands working, feet running in the ways of his commandments. It is called the labour of love. 1 Thess 1: 3. Mary Magdalene loved Christ, and poured her ointments on him. We think we never do enough for the person whom we love.

(5) Love to God must be superlative. God is the essence of beauty, a whole paradise of delight; and he must have a priority in our love. Our love to God must be above all things besides, as the oil swims above the water. We must love God above estate and relations. Great is the love to relations. There is a story in the French Academy, of a daughter, who, when her father was condemned to die by hunger, gave him suck with her own breasts. But our love to God must be above father and mother. Matt 10: 37. We may give the creature the milk of our love, but God must have the cream. The spouse keeps the juice of her pomegranates for Christ. Cant 8: 2.

(6) Our love to God must be constant, like the fire which the Vestal virgins kept in Rome, which did not go out. Love must be like the motion of the pulse, which beats as long as there is life. 'Many waters cannot quench love,' not the waters of persecution. Cant 8: 7. 'Rooted in love.' Eph 3: 17. A branch withers that does not grow on a root; so love, that it may not die, must be well rooted.

What are the visible signs of our love to God?

If we love God, our desire will be after him. 'The desire of our soul is to thy name.' Isa 26: 8. He who loves God, breathes after communion with him. 'My soul thirsteth for the living God.' Psa 42: 2. Persons in love desire to be often conferring together. He who loves God, desires to be much in his presence; he loves the ordinances: they are the glass where the glory of God is resplendent; in the ordinances we meet with him whom our souls love; we have God's smiles and whispers, and some foretastes of heaven. Such as have no desire after ordinances, have no love to God.

The second visible sign is, that he who loves God cannot find contentment in any thing without him. Give a hypocrite who pretends to love God corn and wine, and he can be content without God; but a soul fired with love to God, cannot be without him. Lovers faint away if they have not a sight of the object loved. A gracious soul can do without health, but cannot do without God, who is the health of his countenance. Psa 43: 5. If God should say to a soul that entirely loves him, 'Take thy ease, swim in pleasure, solace thyself in the delights of the world; but thou shalt not enjoy my presence:' this would not content it. Nay, if God should say, 'I will let thee be taken up to heaven, but I will retire into another room, and thou shalt not see my face;' it would not content the soul. It is hell to be without God. The philosopher says there can be no gold without the influence of the sun; certainly there can be no golden joy in the soul without God's sweet presence and influence.

The third visible sign is that he who loves God, hates that which would separate between him and God, and that is sin. Sin makes God hide his face; it is like an incendiary, which parts chief friends; therefore, the keenness of a Christian's hatred is set against it. 'I hate every false way.' Psa 119: 128. Antipathies can never be reconciled; one cannot love health but he must hate poison; so we cannot love God but we must hate sin, which would destroy our communion with him.

The fourth visible sign is sympathy. Friends that love, grieve for the evils which befall each other. Homer, describing Agamemnon's grief, when he was forced to sacrifice his daughter, brings in all his friends weeping with him, and accompanying him to the sacrifice, in mourning. Lovers grieve together. If we have true love in our heart to God, we cannot but grieve for those things which grieve him; we shall lay to heart his dishonours; the luxury, drunkenness, contempt of God and religion. 'Rivers of waters run down mine eyes,' &c. Psa 119: 136. Some speak of the sins of others, and laugh at them; but they surely have no love to God who can laugh at that which grieves his Spirit! Does he love his father who can laugh to hear him reproached?

The fifth visible sign is, that he who loves God, labours to render him lovely to others. He not only admires God, but speaks in his praises, that he may allure and draw others to be in love with him. She that is in love will commend her lover. The lovesick spouse extols Christ, she makes a panegyrical oration of his worth, that she might persuade others to be in love with him. 'His head is as the most fine gold.' Cant 5: 11. True love to God cannot be silent, it will be eloquent in setting forth his renown. There is no better sign of loving God than to make him appear lovely, and to draw proselytes to him.

The sixth visible sign is, that he who loves God, weeps bitterly for his absence. Mary comes weeping, 'They have taken away my Lord.' John 20: 13. One cries, 'My health is gone!' another, 'My estate is gone!' but he who is a lover of God, cries out, 'My God is gone! I cannot enjoy him whom I love.' What can all worldly comforts do, when once God is absent? It is like a funeral banquet, where there is much meat, but no cheer. 'I went mourning without the sun.' Job 30: 28. If Rachel mourned greatly for the loss of her children, what vail or pencil can shadow out the sorrow of that Christian who has lost God's sweet presence? Such a soul pours forth floods of tears; and while it is lamenting, seems to say thus to God, 'Lord, thou art in heaven, hearing the melodious songs and triumph of angels; but I sit here in the valley of tears, weeping because thou art gone. Oh, when wilt thou come to me, and revive me with the light of thy countenance! Or, Lord, if thou wilt not come to me, let me come to thee, where I shall have a perpetual smile of thy face in heaven and shall never more complain, 'My beloved has withdrawn himself.'"

The seventh visible sign is, that he who loves God is willing to do and suffer for him. He subscribes to God's commands, he submits to his will. He subscribes to his commands. If God bids him mortify sin, love his enemies, be crucified to the world, he obeys. It is a vain thing for a man to say he loves God, and slight his commands. He submits to his will. If God would have him suffer for him, he does not dispute, but obeys. 'Love endureth all things.' 1 Cor 13: 7. Love made Christ suffer for us, and love will make us suffer for him. It is true that every Christian is not a martyr but he has a spirit of martyrdom in him; he has a disposition of mind to suffer, if God call him to it. 'I am ready to be offered.' 2 Tim 4: 6. Not only the sufferings were ready for Paul, but he was ready for the sufferings. Origin chose rather to live despised in Alexandria, than with Plotinus to deny the faith, and be great in the prince's favour. Rev 12: 11. Many say they love God, but will not suffer the loss of anything for him. If Christ should have said to us, 'I love you well, you are dear to me, but I cannot suffer for you, I cannot lay down my life for you,' we should have questioned his love very much; and may not the Lord question ours, when we pretend love to him, but will endure nothing for his sake?

Use one. What shall we say to those who have not a drachm of love in their hearts to God? They have their life from him, yet do not love him. He spreads their table every day, yet they do not love him. Sinners dread God as a judge, but do not love him as a father. All the strength in the angels cannot make the heart love God; judgements will not do it; omnipotent grace only can make a stony heart melt in love. How sad is it to be void of love to God. When the body is cold, and has no heat, it is a sign of death; so he is spiritually dead who has no heat of love in his heart to God. Shall such live with God that do not love him? Will God lay an enemy in his bosom? They shall be bound in chains of darkness who will not be drawn with cords of love.

Use two. Let us be persuaded to love God with all our heart and might. O let us take our love off from other things, and place it upon God. Love is the heart of religion, the fat of the offering; it is the grace which Christ inquires most after. 'Simon lovest thou me?' John 21: 15. Love makes all our services acceptable, it is the musk that perfumes them. It is not so much duty, as love to duty, God delights in; therefore serving and loving God are put together. Isa 56: 6. It is better to love him than to serve him; obedience without love, is like wine without the spirit. O then, be persuaded to love God with all your heart and might.

(1) It is nothing but your love that God desires. The Lord might have demanded your children to be offered in sacrifice; he might have bid you cut and lance yourselves, or lie in hell awhile; but he only desires your love, he would only have this flower. Is it a hard request, to love God? Was ever any debt easier paid than this? Is it any labour for the wife to love her husband? Love is delightful. Non potest amor esse, et dulcis non esse [Love must by definition be sweet]. Bernard. What is there in our love that God should desire it? Why should a king desire the love of a woman that is in debt and diseased? God does not need our love. There are angels enough in heaven to adore and love him. What is God the better for our love? It adds not the least cubit to his essential blessedness. He does not need our love, and yet he seeks it. Why does he desire us to give him our heart? Prov 23: 26. Not that he needs our heart, but that he may make it better.

(2) Great will be our advantage if we love God. He does not court our love that we should lose by it. 'Eye has not seen, nor ear heard, the things which God has prepared for them that love him.' I Cor 2: 9. If you will love him, you shall have such a reward as exceeds your faith. He will betroth you to himself in the dearest love. 'I will betroth thee unto me for ever, in loving kindness and in mercies.' Hos 2: 19. 'The Lord thy God will rest in his love, he will joy over thee with singing.' Zeph 3: 17. If you love God, he will interest you in all his riches and dignities, he will give you heaven and earth for your dowry, he will set a crown on your head. Vespasian the emperor gave a great reward to a woman who came to him, and professed she loved him; but God gives a crown of life to them that love him. James 1: 12.

(3) Love is the only grace that shall live with us in heaven. In heaven we shall need no repentance, because we shall have no sin; no faith, because we shall see God face to face; but love to God shall abide for ever. 'Love never faileth.' I Cor 13: 8. How should we nourish this grace which shall outlive all the graces, and run parallel with eternity!

(4) Our love to God is a sign of his love to us. 'We love him because he first loved us.' I John 4: 19. By nature we have no love to God; we have hearts of stone. Ezek 36: 26. And how can any love be in hearts of stone? Our loving him is from his loving us. If the glass burn, it is because the sun has shone on it; so if our hearts burn in love, it is a sign the Sun of Righteousness has shone upon us.

What shall we do in order to love God aright?

(1) Wait on the preaching of the word. As faith comes by hearing, so does love. The word sets forth God in his incomparable excellencies; it deciphers and pencils him out in all his glory, and a sight of his beauty inflames love.

(2) Beg of God that he will give you a heart to love him. When king Solomon asked wisdom of God, it pleased the Lord. I Kings 3: 10. So, when thou criest to God, Lord give me a heart to love thee, it is my grief I can love thee no more; surely this prayer will please the Lord, and he will pour out his Spirit upon thee. His golden oil will make the lamp of thy love burn bright.

(3) You who have love to God, keep it flaming upon the altar of your heart. Love, like fire, is ever ready to go out. 'Thou hast left thy first love.' Rev 2: 4. Through neglect of duty, or too much love of the world, our love to God will cool. O preserve your love to him. As you would be careful to preserve the natural heat in your body, so be careful to preserve the heat of love to God in your soul. Love is like oil to the wheels, it quickens us in God's service. When you find love abate and cool, use all means to quicken it. When the fire is going out, you throw on fuel; so when the flame of love is going out, make use of the ordinances as sacred fuel to keep the fire of your love burning.

1.3 The Preface to the Commandments

'And God spake all these words, saying, I am the LORD thy God,' &c. Exod 20: 1, 2.

What is the preface to the Ten Commandments?

The preface to the Ten Commandments is, 'I am the Lord thy God.'

The preface to the preface is, 'God spake all these words, saying,' &c. This is like the sounding of a trumpet before a solemn proclamation. Other parts of the Bible are said to be uttered by the mouth of the holy prophets (Luke 1: 70), but here God spake in his own person.

How are we to understand that, God spake, since he has no bodily parts or orgasms of speech?

God made some intelligible sound, or fanned a voice in the air, which, to the Jews was as though God himself was speaking to them. Observe:

(1) The lawgiver. 'God spake.' There are two things requisite in a lawgiver. [1] Wisdom. Laws are founded upon reason; and he must be wise that makes laws. God, in this respect, is most fit to be a lawgiver: 'he is wise in heart.' Job 9: 4. He has a monopoly of wisdom. 'The only wise God.' 1 Tim 1: 17. Therefore he is the fittest to enact and constitute laws. [2] Authority. If a subject makes laws, however wise they may be, they want the stamp of authority. God has the supreme power in his hand: he gives being to all; and he who gives men their lives, has most right to give them their laws.

(2) The law itself. 'All these words.' That is, all the words of the moral law, which is usually styled the decalogue, or ten commandments. It is called the moral law because it is the rule of life and manners. The Scripture, as Chrysostom says, is a garden, and the moral law is the chief flower in it: it is a banquet, and the moral law is the chief dish in it.

The moral law is perfect. 'The law of the Lord is perfect.' Psa 19: 7. It is an exact model and platform of religion; it is the standard of truth, the judge of controversies, the pole-star to direct us to heaven. 'The commandment is a lamp.' Prov 6: 23. Though the moral law be not a Christ to justify us, it is a rule to instruct us.

The moral law is unalterable; it remains still in force. Though the ceremonial and judicial laws are abrogated, the moral law delivered by God's own mouth is of perpetual use in the church. It was written in tables of stone, to show its perpetuity.

The moral law is very illustrious and full of glory. God put glory upon it in the manner of its promulgation. [1] The people, before the moral law was delivered, were to wash their clothes, whereby, as by a type, God required the sanctifying of their ears and hearts to receive the law. Exod 19: 10. [2] There were bounds set that none might touch the mount, which was to produce in the people reverence to the law. Exod 19: 12. [3] God wrote the law with his own finger, which was such an honour put upon the moral law, as we read of no other such writing. Exod 31: 18. God by some mighty operation, made the law legible in letters, as if it had been written with his own finger. [4] God's putting the law in the ark to be kept was another signal mark of honour put upon it. The ark was the cabinet in which He put the ten commandments, as ten jewels. [5] At the delivery of the moral law, many angels were in attendance. Deut 33: 2. A parliament of angels was called, and God himself was the speaker.

Use one. Here we may notice God's goodness, who has not left us without a law. He often sets down the giving his commandments as a demonstration of his love. 'He has not dealt so with any nation: and as for his judgements they have not known them.' Psa 147: 20. 'Thou gavest them true laws, good statutes and commandments.' Neh 9: 13. What a strange creature would man be if he had no law to direct him! There would be no living in the world; we should have none born but Ishmaels - every man's hand would be against his neighbour. Man would grow wild if he had not affliction to tame him, and the moral law to guide him. The law of God is a hedge to keep us within the bounds of sobriety and piety.

Use two. If God spake all these words of the moral law, then it condemns: (1) The Marcionites and Manichees, who speak lightly, yea, blasphemously, of the moral law; who say it is below a Christian, it is carnal; which the apostle confutes, when he says, 'The law is spiritual, but I am carnal.' Rom 7: 14. (2) The Antinomians, who will not admit the moral law to be a rule to a believer. We say not that he is under the curse of the law, but the commands. We say not the moral law is a Christ, but it is a star to lead to Christ. We say not that it saves, but sanctifies. They who cast God's law behind their backs, God will cast their prayers behind his back. They who will not have the law to rule them, shall have the law to judge them. (3) The Papists, who, as if God's law were imperfect, and when he spake all these words he did not speak enough, add to it their canons and traditions. This is to tax God's wisdom, as if he knew not how to make his own law. This surely is a high provocation. 'If any man shall add to these things, God shall add unto him the plagues that are written in this book.' Rev 22: 18. As it is a great evil to add anything to a man's sealed will, so much more to add anything to the law which God himself spake, and wrote with his own fingers.

Use three. If God spake all the words of the moral law, several duties are enjoined upon us: (1) If God spake all these words, then we must hear all these words. The words which God speaks are too precious to be lost. As we would have God hear all our words when we pray, so we must hear all his words when he speaks. We must not be as the deaf adder, which stoppeth her ears: he that stops his ears when God cries, shall cry himself, and not be heard.

(2) If God spake all these words, then we must attend to them with reverence. Every word of the moral law is an oracle from heaven. God himself is the preacher, which calls for reverence. If a judge gives a charge upon the bench, all attend with reverence. In the moral law God himself

gives a charge, 'God spake all these words;' with what veneration, therefore, should we attend! Moses put off his shoes from his feet, in token of reverence, when God was about to speak to him. Exod 3: S, 6.

(3)If God spake all these words of the moral law, then we must remember them. Surely all God speaks is worth remembering; those words are weighty which concern salvation. 'It is not a vain thing for you, because it is your life.' Deut 32: 47. Our memory should be like the chest in the ark where the law was kept. God's oracles are ornaments, and shall we forget them? 'Can a maid forget her ornaments?' Jer 2: 32.

(4) If God spake all these words, then believe them. See the name of God written upon every commandment. The heathens, in order to gain credit to their laws, reported that they were inspired by the gods at Rome. The moral law fetches its pedigree from heaven. Ipse dixit. God spake all these words. Shall we not give credit to the God of heaven? How would the angel confirm the women in the resurrection of Christ? 'Lo (said he), I have told you.' Matt 28: 7. I speak in the word of an angel. Much more should the moral law be believed, when it comes to us in the word of God. 'God spake all these words.' Unbelief enervates the virtue of God's word, and makes it prove abortive. 'The word did not profit, not being mixed with faith.' Heb 4: 2. Eve gave more credit to the devil when he spake than she did to God.

(5) If God spake all these words, then love the commandments. 'Oh, how love I thy law! it is my meditation all the day.' Psa 119: 97. 'Consider how I love thy precepts.' Psa 119: 159. The moral law is the copy of God's will, our spiritual directory; it shows us what sins to avoid, what duties to pursue. The ten commandments are a chain of pearls to adorn us, they are our treasury to enrich us; they are more precious than lands of spices, or rocks of diamonds. 'The law of thy mouth is better unto me than thousands of gold and silver.' Psa 119: 72. The law of God has truth and goodness in it. Neh 9: 13. Truth, for God spake it; and goodness, for there is nothing the commandment enjoins, but it is for our good. O then, let this command our love.

(6) If God spake all these words, then teach your children the law of God. 'These words, which I command thee this day, shall be in thy heart, and thou shalt teach them diligently unto thy children.' Deut 6: 6, 7. He who is godly, is both a diamond and a loadstone: a diamond for the sparkling of his grace, and a loadstone for his attractive virtue in drawing others to the love of God's precepts. Vir bonus magis aliis prodest quam sibi [A good man benefits others more than himself]. You that are parents, discharge your duty. Though you cannot impart grace to your children, yet you may impart knowledge. Let your children know the commandments of God. 'Ye shall teach them your children.' Deut 11: 19. You are careful to leave your children a portion: leave the oracles of heaven with them; instruct them in the law of God. If God spake all these words, you may well speak them over again to your children.

(7) If God spake all these words, the moral law must be obeyed. If a king speaks, his word commands allegiance; much more, when God speaks, must his words be obeyed. Some will obey

partially, obey some commandments, not others; like a slough, which, when it comes to a stiff piece of earth, makes a baulk; but God, who spake all the words of the moral law, will have all obeyed. He will not dispense with the breach of one law. Princes, indeed, for special reasons, sometimes dispense with penal statutes, and will not enforce the severity of the law; but God, who spake all these words, binds men with a subpoena to yield obedience to every law.

This condemns the church of Rome, which, instead of obeying the whole moral law, blots out one commandment, and dispenses with others. They leave the second commandment out of their catechism, because it makes against images; and to fill up the number of ten, they divide the tenth commandment into two. Thus, they incur that dreadful condemnation: 'If any man shall take away from the words of this book, God shall take away his part out of the book of life.' Rev 22: 19. As they blot out one commandment, and cut the knot which they cannot untie, so they dispense with other commandments. They dispense with the sixth commandment, making murder meritorious in case of propagating the Catholic cause. They dispense with the seventh commandment, wherein God forbids adultery; for the Pope dispenses with the sin of uncleanness, yea, incest, by paying fines and sums of money into his coffer. No wonder the Pope takes men off their loyalty to kings and princes, when he teaches them disloyalty to God. Some of the Papists say expressly in their writings, that the Pope has power to dispense with the laws of God, and can give men license to break the commandments of the Old and New Testament. That such a religion should ever again get foot in England, the Lord in mercy prevent! If God spake all the commandments, then we must obey all; he who breaks the hedge of the commandments, a serpent shall bite him.

But what man can obey all God's commandments?

To obey the law in a legal sense - to do all the law requires - no man can. Sin has cut the lock of original righteousness, where our strength lay; but, in a true gospel-sense, we may so obey the moral law as to find acceptance. This gospel obedience consists in a real endeavour to observe the whole moral law. 'I have done thy commandments' (Psa 119: 166); not, I have done all I should do, but I have done all I am able to do; and wherein my obedience comes short, I look up to the perfect righteousness and obedience of Christ, and hope for pardon through his blood. This is to obey the moral law evangelically; which, though it be not to satisfaction, yet it is to acceptation.

We come now to the preface itself, which consists of three parts: I. I am the Lord thy God'; II. 'which have brought thee out of the land of Egypt'; III. 'out of the house of bondage'.

I. I am the Lord thy God. Here we have a description of God; (1) By his essential greatness, 'I am the Lord;' (2) By his relative goodness, 'Thy God.'

[1] By his essential greatness, 'I am the Lord:' or, as it is in the Hebrew, JEHOVAH. By this great name God sets forth his majesty. Sanctius habitum fuit, says Buxtorf. The name of Jehovah

was had in more reverence among the Jews than any other name of God. It signifies God's self-sufficiency, eternity, independence, and immutability. Mal. 3: 6.

Use one. If God be Jehovah, the fountain of being, who can do what he will, let us fear him. 'That thou mayest fear this glorious and fearful name, Jehovah.' Deut 28: 58.

Use two. If God be Jehovah, the supreme Lord, the blasphemous Papists are condemned who speak after this manner: 'Our Lord God the Pope.' Is it a wonder the Pope lifts his triple crown above the heads of kings and emperors, when he usurps God's title, 'showing himself that he is God'? 2 Thess 2: 4. He seeks to make himself Lord of heaven, for he will canonise saints there; Lord of earth, for with his keys he binds and looses whom he pleases; Lord of hell, for he frees men out of purgatory. God will pull down these plumes of pride; he will consume this man of sin 'with the breath of his mouth, and the brightness of his coming.' 2 Thess 2: 8.

[2] God is described by his relative goodness; 'thy God.' Had he called himself Jehovah only, it might have terrified us, and made us flee from him; but when he says, 'thy God,' it allures and draws us to him. This, though a preface to the law, is pure gospel. The word Eloeha, 'thy God,' is so sweet, that we can never suck all the honey out of it. 'I am thy God,' not only by creation, but by election. This word, 'thy God,' though it was spoken to Israel, is a charter which belongs to all the saints. For the further explanation, here are three questions.

How comes God to be our God?

Through Jesus Christ. Christ is a middle person in the Trinity. He is Emmanuel, 'God with us.' He brings two different parties together: makes our nature lovely to God, and God's nature lovely to us; by his death, causes friendship, yea, union; and brings us within the verge of the covenant, and thus God becomes our God.

What is implied by God being our God?

It is comprehensive of all good things. God is our strong tower; our fountain of living water; our salvation. More particularly, being our God implies the sweetest relations.

(1) The relation of a father. 'I will be a Father unto you;' 2 Cor 6: 18. A father is full of tender care for his child. Upon whom does he settle the inheritance but his child? God being our God, will be a father to us; a 'Father of mercies,' 2 Cor 1: 3; 'The everlasting Father.' Isa 9: 6. If God be our God, we have a Father in heaven that never dies.

(2) It imports the relation of a husband. 'Thy Maker is thine husband.' Isa 54: 5. If God be our husband, he esteems us precious to him, as the apple of his eye. Zech 2: 8. He imparts his secrets to us. Psa 25: 14. He bestows a kingdom upon us for our dowry. Luke 12: 32.

How may we know that by covenant union, God is our God?

(1) By having his grace planted in us. Kings' children are known by their costly jewels. It is not having common gifts which shows we belong to God; many have the gifts of God without God; but it is grace that gives us a true genuine title to God. In particular, faith is vinculum unionis, the grace of union, by which we may spell out our interest in God. Faith does not, as the mariner, cast its anchor downwards, but upwards; it trusts in the mercy and blood of God, and trusting in God, engages him to be our God. Other graces make us like God, faith makes us one with him.

(2) We may know God is our God by having the earnest of his Spirit in our hearts. 2 Cor 1: 22. God often gives the purse to the wicked, but the Spirit only to such as he intends to make his heirs. Have we had the consecration of the Spirit? If we have not had the sealing work of the Spirit, have we had the healing work? 'Ye have an unction from the Holy One.' 1 John 2: 20. The Spirit, where it is, stamps the impress of its own holiness upon the heart; it embroiders and bespangles the soul, and makes it all glorious within. Have we had the attraction of the Spirit? 'Draw me, we will run after thee.' Cant 1: 4. Has the Spirit, by its magnetic virtue, drawn our hearts to God? Can we say, 'O thou whom my soul loveth?' Cant 1: 7. Is God our paradise of delight? our Segullah, or chief treasure! Are our hearts so chained to God that no other object can enchant us, or draw us away from him? Have we had the elevation of the Spirit? Has it raised our hearts above the world? 'The Spirit lifted me up.' Ezek 3:14. Has the Spirit made us, superna anhelare, seek the things above where Christ is? Though our flesh is on earth, is our heart in heaven? Though we live here, trade we above? Has the Spirit thus lifted us up? By this we may know that God is our God. Where God gives his Spirit for an earnest, there he gives himself for a portion.

(3) We may know God is our God, if he has given us the hearts of children. Have we obediential hearts? Psa 27: 8. Do we subscribe to God's commands when his commands cross our will? A true saint is like the flower of the sun, which opens and shuts with the sun: he opens to God, and shuts to sin. If we have the hearts of children, God is our Father.

(4) We may know God is ours, and we have an interest in him, by standing up for his interest. We shall appear in his cause and vindicate his truth, wherein his glory is so much concerned. Athanasius was the bulwark of truth; he stood up for it, when most of the world were Asians. In former times the nobles of Polonia, when the gospel was read, laid their hands upon their swords, signifying that they were ready to defend the faith, and hazard their lives for the gospel. There is no better sign of having an interest in God than standing up for his interest.

(5) We may know God is ours, and we have an interest in him, by his having an interest in us. 'My beloved is mine, and I am his.' Cant 2: 16. When God says to the soul, 'Thou art mine;' the soul answers, 'Lord, I am thine; all I have is at thy service; my head shall be thine to study for thee; my tongue shall be thine to praise thee.' If God be our God by way of donation, we are his by way of dedication; we live to him, and are more his than we are our own. Thus we may come to know that God is our God.

Use one. Above all things, let us get this great charter confirmed, that God is our God. Deity is not comfortable without propriety. Let us labour to get sound evidences that God is our God. We cannot call health, liberty, estate, ours; but let us be able to call God ours, and say as the church, 'God, even our own God, shall bless us.' Psa 67: 6. Let every soul labour to pronounce this Shibboleth, 'My God.' That we may endeavour to have God for our God, consider the misery of such as have not God for their God, in how sad a condition are they, when the hour of distress comes! This was Saul's case when he said 'I am sore distressed; for the Philistines make war against me, and God is departed from me.' 1 Sam 28: 15. A wicked man in time of trouble, is like a vessel tossed on the sea without an anchor, which strikes on rocks or sands. A sinner who has not God to be his God, may make a shift while health and estate last, but when these crutches on which he leaned are broken, his heart must sink. It is with him as it was with the old world when the flood came. The waters at first came to the valleys, but then the people would get to the hills and mountains; but when the waters came to the mountains, then there might be some trees on the high hills, and they would climb up to them; ay, but the waters rose above the tops of the trees; and then their hearts failed them, and all hopes of being saved were gone. So it is with a man that has not God to be his God. If one comfort be taken away, he has another; if he lose a child, he has an estate; but when the waters rise higher, death comes and takes away all, and he has nothing to help himself with, no God to go to, he must needs die in despair. How great a privilege it is to have God for our God! 'Happy is that people whose God is the Lord.' Psa 144: 15. Beatitudo hominis est Deus [Man's happiness is God himself]. Augustine. That you may see the privilege of this charter: -

(1) If God be our God, then though we may feel the stroke of evil, yet not the sting. He must needs be happy who is in such a condition, that nothing can hurt him. If he lose his name, it is written in the book of life; if he lose his liberty, his conscience is free; if he lose his estate, he is possessed of the pearl of price; if he meets with storms, he knows where to put in for harbour; God is his God, and heaven is his heaven.

(2) If God be our God, our soul is safe. The soul is the jewel, it is a blossom of eternity. 'I was grieved in my spirit in the midst of my body;' in the Chaldee, it is 'in the midst of my sheath.' Dan 7: 15. The body is but the sheath; the soul is the princely part of man, which sways the sceptre of reason; it is a celestial spark, as Damascene calls it. If God be our God, the soul is safe, as in a garrison. Death can do no more hurt to a virtuous heaven-born soul, than David did to Saul, when he cut off the skirt of his garment. The soul is safe, being hid in the promises; hid in the wounds of Christ; hid in God's decree. The soul is the pearl, and heaven is the cabinet where God will lock it up safe.

(3) If God be our God, then all that is in God is ours. The Lord says to a saint in covenant, as the king of Israel to the king of Syria, 'I am thine, and all that I have.' I Kings 20: 4. So saith God, 'I am thine:' how happy is he who not only inherits the gift of God, but inherits God himself! All that I have shall be thine; my wisdom shall be thine to teach thee; my power shall be thine to

support thee; my mercy shall be thine to save thee. God is an infinite ocean of blessedness, and there is enough in him to fill us: as if a thousand vessels were thrown into the sea, there is enough in the sea to fill them.

(4) If God be our God, he will entirely love us. Property is the ground of love. God may give men kingdoms, and not love them; but he cannot be our God, and not love us. He calls his covenanted saints, Jediduth Naphshi, 'The dearly beloved of my soul.' Jer 12: 7. He rejoiceth over them with joy, and rests in his love. Zeph 3: 17. They are his refined silver (Zech 13: 9); his jewels (Mal 3: 17); his royal diadem (Isa 62: 3). He gives them the cream and flower of his love. He not only opens his hand and fills them, but opens his heart and fills them. Psa 145: 16.

(5) If God be our God, he will do more for us than all the world besides can. What is that? [1] He will give us peace in trouble. When there is a storm without, he will make music within. The world can create trouble in peace, but God can create peace in trouble. He will send the Comforter, who, as a dove, brings an olive-branch of peace in his mouth. John 14: 16. [2] God will give us a crown of immortality. The world can give a crown of gold, but that crown has thorns in it and death in it; but God will give you a crown of glory that fadeth not away. 1 Pet. 5: 4. The garland made of the flowers of paradise never withers.

(6) If God be our God, he will bear with many infirmities. He may respite sinners awhile, but long forbearance is no acquittance; he will throw them to hell for their sins; but if he be our God, he will not for every failing destroy us; he bears with his spouse as with the weaker vessel. He may chastise. Psa 89: 32. He may use the rod and the pruning-knife, but not the bloody axe. 'He has not beheld iniquity in Jacob.' Numb 23: 21. He will not see sin in his people so as to destroy them, but their sins so as to pity them. He sees them as a physician a disease in his patient, to heal him. 'I have seen his ways, and will heal him.' Isa 57: 18. Every failing does not break the marriage-bond asunder. The disciples had great failings, they all forsook Christ and fled; but this did not break off their interest in God; therefore, says Christ, at his ascension, 'Tell my disciples, I go to my God and to their God.'

(7) If God be once our God, he is so for ever. 'This God is our God for ever and ever.' Psa 48: 14. Whatever worldly comforts we have, they are but for a season, and we must part with all. Heb 11: 25. As Paul's friends accompanied him to the ship, and there left him (Acts 20: 38), so all our earthly comforts will but go with us to the grave, and there leave us. You cannot say you have health, and shall have it for ever; you have a child, and shall have it for ever; but if God be your God, you shall have him for ever. 'This God is our God for ever and ever.' If God be our God, he will be a God to us as long as he is a God. 'Ye have taken away my gods,' said Micah. Judges 18: 14. But it cannot be said to a believer, that his God is taken away; He may lose all things else, but cannot lose his God. God is ours from everlasting in election, and to everlasting in glory.

(8) If God be our God, we shall enjoy all our godly relations with him in heaven. The great felicity on earth is to enjoy relations. A father sees his own picture in a child; and a wife sees

herself in her husband. We plant the flower of love among our relations, and the loss of them is like the pulling off a limb from the body. But if God be ours, with the enjoyment of God we shall enjoy all our pious relations in glory. The gracious child shall see his godly father, the virtuous wife shall see her religious husband in Christ's arms; and then there will be a dearer love to relations than there ever was before, though in a far different manner; then relations shall meet and never part. 'And so shall we be ever with the Lord.'

Use two. To such as can realise this covenant union we have several exhortations.

(1) If God be our God, let us improve our interest in him, let us cast all our burdens upon him: the burden of our fears, our wants and our sins. 'Cast thy burden upon the Lord.' Psa 55: 22. Wicked men who are a burden to God have no right to cast their burden upon him; but such as have God for their God are called upon to cast their burden on him. Where should the child ease all its cares but in the bosom of its parent? 'Let all thy wants lie upon me.' Judges 19: 20. So God seems to say to his children, 'Let all your wants lie upon me.' Christian, what troubles thee? Thou hast a God to pardon thy sins and to supply thy wants; therefore roll your burden on him. 'Casting all your care upon him.' 1 Pet 5: 7. Why are Christians so disquieted in their minds? They are taking care when they should be casting care.

(2) If God be our God, let us learn to be contented, though we have the less of other things. Contentment is a rare jewel, it is the cure of care. If we have God to be our God, well may we be contented. 'I know whom I have believed.' 2 Tim 1: 12. There was Paul's interest in God. 'As having nothing, and yet possessing all things.' 2 Cor 6: 10. Here was his content. That such who have covenant-union with God may be filled with contentment of spirit, consider what a rich blessing God is to the soul.

He is bonum sufficiens, a sufficient good. He who has God has enough. If a man be thirsty, bring him to a spring, and he is satisfied; in God there is enough to fill the heaven-born soul. He gives 'grace and glory.' Psa 84: 11. There is in God not only a sufficiency, but a redundancy; he is not only full as a vessel, but as a spring. Other things can no more fill the soul than a mariner's breath can fill the sails of a ship; but in God there is a cornucopia, an infinite fulness; he has enough to fill the angels, therefore enough to fill us. The heart is a triangle, which only the Trinity can fill.

God is bonum sanctificans, a sanctifying good. He sanctifies all our comforts and turn them into blessings. Health is blessed, estate is blessed. He gives with the venison a blessing. 'I will abundantly bless her provision.' Psa 132: 15. He gives us the life we have, tanquam arrhabo, as an earnest of more. He gives the little meal in the barrel as an earnest of the royal feast in paradise. He sanctifies all our crosses. They shall not be destructive punishments, but medicines; they shall corrode and eat out the venom of sin; they shall polish and refine our grace. The more the diamond is cut, the more it sparkles. When God stretches the strings of his viol, it is to make the music better.

God is bonum selectum, a choice good. All things, sub sole, are but bona scabelli, as Augustine says, the blessings of the footstool, but to have God himself to be ours, is the blessing of the throne. Abraham gave gifts to the sons of the concubines, but he settled the inheritance upon Isaac. 'Abraham gave all that he had to Isaac.' Gen 25: 5. God may send away the men of the world with gifts, a little gold and silver; but in giving us himself, he gives us the very essence, his grace, his love, his kingdom: here is the crowning blessing.

God is bonum summum, the chief good. In the chief good there must be delectability; it must have something that is delicious and sweet: and where can we suck those pure essential comforts, which ravish us with delight, but in God? In Deo quadam dulcedine delectatur anima, immo rapitur [In God's character there is a certain sweetness which fascinates or rather enraptures the soul]. 'At thy right hand there are pleasures.' Psa 16: 11: In the chief good there must be transcendence, it must have a surpassing excellence. Thus God is infinitely better than all other things. It is below the Deity to compare other things with it. Who would weigh a feather against a mountain of gold? God is fons et origo, the spring of all entities, and the cause is more noble than the effect. It is God that bespangles the creation, that puts light into the sun, that fills the veins of the earth with silver. Creatures do but maintain life, God gives life. He infinitely outshines all sublunary glory. He is better than the soul, than angels, and than heaven. In the chief good, there must be not only fulness, but variety. Where variety is wanting we are apt to nauseate. To feed only on honey would breed loathing; but in God is all variety of fulness. Col 1: 19. He is a universal good, commensurate to all our wants. He is bonum in quo omnia bona [the good in which is every good], a son, a portion, a horn of salvation. He is called the 'God of all comfort.' 2 Cor 1: 3. There is a complication of all beauties and delights in him. Health has not the comfort of beauty, nor beauty of riches, nor riches of wisdom; but God is the God of all comfort. In the chief good there must be eternity. God is a treasure that can neither be drawn low, nor drawn dry. Though the angels are continually spending what is his, he can never be spent; he abides for ever. Eternity is a flower of his crown. Now, if God be our God, there is enough to let full contentment into our souls. What need we of torchlight, if we have the sun? What if God deny the flower, if he has given us the jewel? How should a Christian's heart rest on this rock! If we say God is our God, and we are not content, we have cause to question our interest in him.

(3) If we can clear up this covenant-union, that God is our God, let it cheer and revive us in all conditions. To be content with God is not enough, but to be cheerful. What greater cordial can you have than union with Deity? When Jesus Christ was ready to ascend, he could not leave a richer consolation with his disciples than this, 'I ascend to my God and to your God.' John 20: 17. Who should rejoice, if not they who have an infinite, all-sufficient, eternal God to be their portion, who are as rich as heaven can make them? What though I want health? I have God who is the health of my countenance, and my God. Psa 42: 11. What though I am low in the world? If I have not the earth, I have him that made it. The philosopher comforted himself by saying, 'Though I have no music or vine-trees, yet here are the household gods with me;' so, though we

have not the vine or fig-tree, yet we have God with us. I cannot be poor, says Bernard, as long as God is rich; for his riches are mine. O let the saints rejoice in this covenant-union! To say God is ours, is more than to say heaven is ours, for heaven would not be heaven without him. All the stars cannot make day without the sun; all the angels, those morning stars, cannot make heaven without Christ the Sun of Righteousness. And as to have God for our God, is matter of rejoicing in life, so especially it will be at death. Let a Christian think thus, I am going to my God. A child is glad when he is going home to his father. It was Christ's comfort when he was leaving the world, 'I ascend to my God.' John 20: 17. And this is a believer's deathbed cordial, 'I am going to my God; I shall change my place, but not my kindred; I go to my God and my Father.'

(4) If God be our God, let us break forth into praise. 'Thou art my God, and I will praise thee.' Psa 118: 28. Oh, infinite, astonishing mercy, that God should take dust and ashes into so near a bond of love as to be our God! As Micah said, 'What have I more?' Judges 18: 24. So, what has God more? What richer jewel has he to bestow upon us than himself? What has he more? That God should put off most of the world with riches and honour, that he should pass over himself to us by a deed of gift, to be our God, and by virtue of this settle a kingdom upon us! O let us praise him with the best instrument, the heart; and let this instrument be screwed up to the highest pitch. Let us praise him with our whole heart. See how David rises by degrees. 'Be glad in the Lord, and rejoice, and shout for joy.' Psa 32: 11. Be glad, there is thankfulness; rejoice, there is cheerfulness; shout, there is triumph. Praise is called incense, because it is a sweet sacrifice. Let the saints be choristers in God's praises. The deepest springs yield the sweetest water; the more deeply sensible we are of God's covenant-love to us, the sweeter praises we should yield. We should begin here to eternise God's name, and do that work on earth which we shall be always doing in heaven. 'While I live will I praise the Lord.' Psa 146: 2.

(5) Let us carry ourselves as those who have God to be our God; that is, walk so that others may see there is something of God in us. Live homily. What have we to do with sin, which if it does not break, will weaken our interest? 'What have I to do any more with idols?' Hos 14: 8. So would a Christian say, 'God is my God; what have I to do any more with sin, with lust, pride, malice! Bid me commit sin! As well bid me drink poison. Shall I forfeit my interest in God? Let me rather die than willingly offend him who is the crown of my joy, the God of my salvation.'

II. Which have brought thee out of the land of Egypt. Egypt and the house of bondage are the same; only they are represented to us under different expressions. The first expression is, 'Which have brought thee out of the land of Egypt.'

Why does the Lord mention the deliverance of Israel out of Egypt?

(1) Because of the strangeness of the deliverance. God delivered his people Israel by strange signs and wonders, by sending plague after plague upon Pharaoh, blasting the fruits of the earth, and killing all the first-born in Egypt. Exod 12: 29. When Israel marched out of Egypt, God made the waters of the sea to part, and become a wall to his people, while they went on dry

ground; and he made the same sea a causeway to Israel, and a grave to Pharaoh and his chariots. Well might the Lord make mention of this strange deliverance. He wrought miracle upon miracle for the deliverance of that people.

(2) God mentions Israel's deliverance out of Egypt because of the greatness of the deliverance. He delivered Israel from the pollutions of Egypt. Egypt was a bad air to live in, it was infected with idolatry; the Egyptians were gross idolaters; they were guilty of that which the apostle speaks of in Rom 1: 23. 'They changed the glory of the uncorruptible God into an image made like to corruptible man, and to birds, and four-footed beasts, and creeping things.' The Egyptians, instead of the true God, worshipped corruptible man; they deified their king Apis, forbidding all, under pain of death, to say that he was a man. They worshipped birds, as the hawk. They worshipped beasts, as the ox. They made the image of a beast to be their god. They worshipped creeping things, as the crocodile, and the Indian mouse. God mentions it therefore as a signal favour to Israel, that he brought them out of such an idolatrous country. 'I brought thee out of the land of Egypt.'

The thing I would note is, that it is no small blessing to be delivered from places of idolatry. God speaks of it no less than ten times in the Old Testament, 'I brought you out of the land of Egypt;' an idolatrous place. Had there been no iron furnace in Egypt, yet so many altars being there, and false gods, it was a great privilege to Israel to be delivered out of Egypt. Joshua reckons it among the chief and most memorable mercies of God to Abraham, that he brought him out of Ur of the Chaldees, where Abraham's ancestors served strange gods. Josh 24: 2, 3. It is well for the plant that is set in a bad soil, to be transplanted to a better, where it may grow and flourish; so it is a mercy when any who are planted among idolaters, are removed and transplanted into Zion, where the silver drops of God's word make them grow in holiness.

Wherein does it appear to be so great a blessing to be delivered from places of idolatry?

(1) It is a great mercy, because our nature is prone to idolatry. Israel began to be defiled with the idols of Egypt. Ezek 22: 3. Dry wood is not more prone to take fire than our nature is to idolatry. The Jews made cakes to the queen of heaven, that is, to the moon. Jer 7: 15.

Why is it that we are prone to idolatry?

Because we are led much by visible objects, and love to have our senses pleased. Men naturally fancy a god that they may see; though it be such a god that cannot see them, yet they would see it. The true God is invisible; which makes the idolater worship something that he can see.

(2) It is a mercy to be delivered from idolatrous places, because of the greatness of the sin of idolatry, which is giving that glory to an image which is due to God. All divine worship God appropriates to himself; it is a flower of his crown. The fat of the sacrifice is claimed by him. Lev 3: 3. Divine worship is the fat of the sacrifice, which he reserves for himself. The idolater

devotes this worship to an idol, which the Lord will by no means endure. 'My glory will I not give to another, neither my praise to graven images.' Isa 42: 8. Idolatry is spiritual adultery. 'With their idols have they committed adultery.' Ezek 23: 37. To worship any other than God, is to break wedlock, and makes the Lord disclaim his interest in a people. 'Plead with your mother, plead: for she is not my wife.' Hos 2: 2. 'Thy people have corrupted themselves;' no more my people, but thy people. Exod 32: 7. God calls idolatry, blasphemy. 'In this your fathers have blasphemed me.' Idolatry is devil worship. Ezek 20: 27, 31. 'They sacrificed unto devils, not to God; to new gods.' Deut 32: 17. These new gods were old devils. 'And they shall no more offer their sacrifices unto devils.' Lev 17: 7. The Hebrew word La-sairim, is the hairy ones, because the devils were hairy, and appeared in the forms of satyrs and goats. How dreadful a sin is idolatry; and what a signal mercy is it to be snatched out of an idolatrous place, as Lot was snatched by the angels out of Sodom!

(3) It is a mercy to be delivered out of idolatrous places, because idolatry is such a silly and irrational religion. I may say, as Jer 8: 9: 'What wisdom is in them?' Is it not folly to refuse the best, and choose the worst? The trees in the field of Jotham's parable, despised the vine-tree, which cheers both God and man, and the olive which is full of fatness, and the fig-tree which is full of sweetness, and chose the bramble to reign over them - which was a foolish choice. Judg 9. So it is for us to refuse the living God, who has power to save us, and to make choice of an idol, that has eyes and sees not, feet but walks not. Psa 115: 6, 7. What a prodigy of madness is this? Therefore to be delivered from committing such folly is a mercy.

(4) It is a mercy to be delivered from idolatrous places, because of the sad judgements inflicted upon idolaters. This is a sin which enrages God, and makes the fury come up in his face. Ezek 38: 18. Search through the whole book of God, and you shall find no sin he has followed with more plagues than idolatry. 'Their sorrows shall be multiplied that hasten after another god.' Psa 16: 4. 'They moved him to jealousy with their graven images.' Psa 78: 58. 'When God heard this he was wrath, and greatly abhorred Israel; so that he forsook the tabernacle of Shiloh.' Verses 59, 60. Shiloh was a city belonging to the tribe of Ephraim, where God set his name. Jer 7: 12. But, for their idolatry, God forsook the place, gave his people up to the sword, caused his priests to be slain, and his ark to be carried away captive, never more to be returned. How severe was God against Israel for worshipping the golden calf! Exod 32: 27. The Jews say, that in every misery that befalls them, there is uncia aurei vituli, 'an ounce of the golden calf in it.' 'Come out of her, my people, that ye be not partakers of her sins, and that ye receive not of her plagues.' Rev. 18: 4. Idolatry, lived in, cuts men off from heaven. 1 Cor 6: 9. So then it is no small mercy to be delivered out of idolatrous places.

Use one. See the goodness of God to our nation, in bringing us out of mystic Egypt, delivering us from popery, which is Romish idolatry, and causing the light of his truth to break forth gloriously among us. In former times, and more lately in the Marian days, England was overspread with idolatry. It worshipped God after a false manner; and it is idolatry, not only to worship a false god, but the true God in a false manner. Such was our case formerly; we had purgatory, indulgences, the idolatrous mass, the Scriptures locked up in an unknown tongue, invocation of saints and angels, and image-worship. Images are teachers of lies. Hab 2: 18. Wherein do they teach lies? They represent God, who cannot be seen, in a bodily shape. 'Ye saw no similitude, only ye heard a voice.' Deut 4: 12. Quod invisibile est, pingi non potest. Ambrose. God cannot be pictured by any finger; not the soul even, being a spirit, much less God. 'To whom then will ye liken God?' Isa 40: 18. The Papists say they worship God by the image; which is a great absurdity, for if it be absurd to fall down to the picture of a king when the king himself is present, much more to bow down to the image of God when God himself is present. Jer 23: 24. What is the popish religion but a bundle of ridiculous ceremonies? Their wax, flowers, pyres, agnus Dei, cream and oil, beads, crucifixes; what are these but Satan's policy, to dress up a carnal worship, fitted to carnal minds? Oh! what cause have we to bless God for delivering us from popery! It was a mercy to be delivered from the Spanish invasion, and the powder treason; but it is a far greater to be delivered from the popish religion, which would have made God give us a bill of divorce.

Use two. If it be a great blessing to be delivered from the Egypt of popish idolatry, it shows the sin and folly of those who, being brought out of Egypt, are willing to return to it again. The apostle says, 'Flee from idolatry.' 1 Cor 10: 14. But these rather flee to idolatry; and are herein like the people of Israel, who, notwithstanding all the idolatry and tyranny of Egypt, longed to go back to Egypt. 'Let us make a captain and let us return into Egypt.' Numb 14: 4. But how shall they go back into Egypt? How shall they have food in the wilderness? Will God rain down man any more upon such rebels? How will they get over the Red Sea? Will God divide the water again by miracle, for such as leave his service, and go into idolatrous Egypt? Yet they say, 'Let us make a captain.' And are there not such spirits among us, who say, 'Let us make a captain and go back to the Romish Egypt again'? If we do, what shall we get by it? I am afraid the leeks and onions of Egypt will make us sick. Do we ever suppose that, if we drink in the cup of fornication, we shall drink in the cup of salvation? Oh! that any should so forfeit their reason, as to enslave themselves to the see of Rome; that they should be willing to hold a candle to a mass-priest, and bow down to a strange God! Let us not say we will make a captain, but rather say as Ephraim, 'What have I to do any more with idols?' Hos 14: 8.

Use three. If it be a mercy to be brought out of Egypt, it is not desirable or safe to plant one's self in an idolatrous place, where it may be a capital crime to be seen with a Bible in our hands. Some, for secular gain, thrust themselves among idolaters, and think there is no danger to live where Satan's seat is. They pray God would not lead them into temptation, but led themselves. They are in great danger of being polluted. It is hard to be as the fish, which keeps fresh in salt waters. A man cannot dwell among blackamoors, but he will be discoloured. You will sooner be corrupted by idolaters, than they will be converted by you. Joseph got no good by living in an idolatrous court; he did not teach Pharaoh to pray, but Pharaoh taught him to swear. They 'were mingled among the heathen, and served their idols.' Psalm 106: 35, 36. I fear it has been the undoing of many; that they have seated themselves amongst idolaters, for advancing their trade, and at last have not only traded with them in their commodities, but in their religion.

Use four. It is a mercy to be brought out of the land of Egypt, a defiled place, and where sin reigns. It reproaches such parents as show little love for the souls of their children, whether it be in putting them out to service, or matching them. In putting them out to service, their care is chiefly for their bodies, that they may be provided for, and they care not what becomes of their souls. Their souls are in Egypt, in houses where there is drinking, swearing, Sabbath-breaking, and where God's name is every day dishonoured. In matching their children, they look only at money. 'Be ye not unequally yoked.' 2 Cor 6: 14. If their children be equally yoked for estate, they care not whether they be unequally yoked for religion. Let such parents think how precious the soul of their child is; that it is immortal, and capable of communion with God and angels. Will you let a soul be lost by placing it in a bad family? If you had a horse you loved, you would not put him in a stable with other horses that were sick and diseased; and do you not love your child better than your horse? God has intrusted you with the souls of your children; you have a charge of souls. God says, as 1 Kings 20: 39: 'Keep this man: if he be missing, then shall thy life be for his life.' So says God, if the soul of thy child miscarry by thy negligence, his blood will I require at thy hand. Think of this, all ye parents; take heed of placing your children in Egypt, in a wicked family; do not put them in the devil's mouth. Seek for them a sober, religious family, such as Joshua's. 'As for me and my house, we will serve the Lord.' Josh 14: 15. Such a family as Cranmer's, which was palaestra pietatis, a nursery of piety, a Bethel, of which it may be said, 'The church which is in his house.' Col. 4: 15.

Use five. Let us pray that God would keep our English nation from the defilements of Egypt, that it may not be again overspread with superstition and idolatry. Oh, sad religion! not only to have our estates, our bodies enslaved, but our consciences. Pray that the true Protestant religion may still nourish among us, that the sun of the gospel may still shine in our horizon. The gospel lifts a people up to heaven, it is columna et corona regni, 'the crown and glory of the kingdom'; if this be removed, Ichabod, the glory is departed. The top of the beech tree being cut off, the whole body of the tree withers apace; so the gospel is the top of all our blessings; if this top be cut, the whole body politic will soon wither. O pray that the Lord will continue the visible tokens of his presence among us, his ordinances, that England may be called, Jehovah-shammah, 'The Lord is there.' Ezek 48: 35. Pray that righteousness and peace may kiss each other, that so glory may dwell in our land.

III. Out of the house of bondage. Egypt and the house of bondage are the same, only they are expressed under a different notion. By Egypt is meant a place of idolatry and superstition; by the house of bondage is meant a place of affliction. Israel, while in Egypt, were under great tyranny; they had cruel task-masters set over them, who put them to hard labour, and set them to make bricks, yet allowed them no straw; therefore, Egypt is called, in Deut 4: 20, the iron furnace, and here the house of bondage. From this expression, 'I brought thee out of the house of bondage,' two things are to be noted; God's children may sometimes be under sore afflictions. 'In the house of bondage.' But God will, in due time, bring them out of their afflicted state. 'I brought thee out of the house of bondage.'

God's children may sometimes be under sore afflictions, in domo servitutis, in the house of bondage. God's people have no writ of ease granted them, no charter of exemption from trouble in this life. While the wicked are kept in sugar, the godly are often kept in brine. And, indeed, how could God's power be seen in bringing them out of trouble, if he did not sometimes bring them into it? or how should God wipe away the tears from their eyes in heaven, if on earth they shed none? Doubtless, God sees there is need that his children should be sometimes in the house of bondage. 'If need be, ye are in heaviness.' 1 Peter 1: 6. The body sometimes needs a bitter portion more than a sweet one.

Why does God let his people be in the house of bondage or in an afflicted state?

He does it, (1) For probation or trial. 'Who led thee through that terrible wilderness, that he might humble thee and prove thee.' Deut 8: 15, 16. Affliction is the touch-stone of sincerity. 'Thou O God, hast proved us; thou hast tried us as silver; thou laidst affliction upon our loins.' Psa 66: 10, 11. Hypocrites may embrace the true religion in prosperity, and court this queen while she has a jewel hung at her ear; but he is a good Christian who will keep close to God in a time of suffering. 'All this is come upon us, yet have we not forgotten thee.' Psa 44: 17. To love God in heaven, is no wonder; but to love him when he chastises us, discovers sincerity. (2) For purgation; to purge our corruption. Ardet palea, purgatur aurum. 'And this is all the fruit, to take away his sin.' Isa 28: 9. The eye, though a tender part, yet when sore, we put sharp powders and waters into it to eat out the pearl; so though the people of God are dear to him, yet, when corruption begins to grow in them, he will apply the sharp powder of affliction, to eat out the pearl in the eye. Affliction is God's flail to thresh off our husks; it is a means God uses to purge out sloth, luxury, pride, and love of the world. God's furnace is in Zion. Isa 31: 5. This is not to consume, but to refine. What if we have more affliction, if by this means we have less sin!

(3) For augmentation; to increase the graces of the Spirit. Grace thrives most in the iron furnace. Sharp frosts nourish the corn; so sharp afflictions nourish grace. Grace in the saints is often as fire hid in the embers, affliction is the bellows to blow it up into a flame. The Lord makes the house of bondage a friend to grace. Then faith and patience act their part. The darkness of the night cannot hinder the brightness of a star; so, the more the diamond is cut the more it sparkles; and the more God afflicts us, the more our graces cast a sparkling lustre.

(4) For preparation; to fit and prepare the saints for glory. 2 Cor 4: 17. The stones which are cut out for a building, are first hewn and squared. The godly are called 'living stones.' 1 Pet 2: 5. God first hews and polishes them by affliction, that they may be fit for the heavenly building. The house of bondage prepares for the house not made with hands. 2 Cor 5: 1: The vessels of mercy are seasoned with affliction, and then the wine of glory is poured in.

How do the afflictions of the godly differ from the afflictions of the wicked?

(1) They are but castigations, but those on the wicked are punishments. The one come from a father, the other from a judge.

(2) Afflictions on the godly are fruits of covenant-mercy. 2 Sam 7: 17. Afflictions on the wicked are effects of God's wrath. 'He has much wrath with his sickness.' Eccl 5: 17. Afflictions on the wicked are the pledge and earnest of hell; they are like the pinioning of a malefactor, which presages his execution.

(3) Afflictions on the godly make them better, but afflictions on the wicked make them worse. The godly pray more; Psa 130: 1: The wicked blaspheme more. 'Men were scorched with great heat, and blasphemed the name of God.' Rev 16: 9. Afflictions on the wicked make them more impenitent; every plague upon Egypt increased the plague of hardness in Pharaoh's heart. To what a prodigy of wickedness do some persons come after great sickness. Affliction on the godly is like bruising spices, which are most sweet and fragrant: affliction on the wicked is like pounding weeds with a pestle, which makes them more unsavoury.

Use one. (1) We are not to wonder to see Israel in the house of bondage. 1 Pet 4: 12. The holiness of the saints will not excuse them from sufferings. Christ was the holy one of God, yet he was in the iron furnace. His spouse is a lily among thorns. Cant 2: 2. Though his sheep have the ear-mark of election upon them, yet they may have their wool fleeced off. The godly have some good in them, therefore the devil afflicts them; and some evil in them, therefore God afflicts them. While there are two seeds in the world, expect to be under the black rod. The gospel tells us of reigning, but first of suffering. 2 Tim 2: 12.

(2) Affliction is not always the sign of God's anger. Israel, the apple of God's eye, a peculiar treasure to him above all people, were in the house of bondage. Exod 19: 5. We are apt to judge and censure those who are in an afflicted state. When the barbarians saw the viper on Paul's hand, they said, 'No doubt this man is a murderer.' Acts 28: 4. So, when we see the viper of affliction fasten upon the godly, we are apt to censure them, and say, these are greater sinners than others, and God hates them; but this rash censuring is for want of wisdom. Were not Israel in the house of bondage? Was not Jeremiah in the dungeon, and Paul a night and day in the deep? God's afflicting is so far from evidencing hatred, that his not afflicting does. 'I will not punish your daughters when they commit whoredom.' Hos 4: 14. Deus maxime irascitur cum non irascitur. Bernard. God punishes most when he does not punish; his hand is heaviest when it seems to be lightest. The judge will not burn him in the hand whom he intends to execute.

(3) If God's own Israel may be in the house of bondage, then afflictions do not of themselves demonstrate a man miserable. Indeed, sin unrepented of, makes one miserable; but the cross does not. If God has a design in afflicting his children to make them happy, they are not miserable; but God's afflicting them is to make them happy, therefore they are not miserable. 'Happy is the man

whom God correcteth.' Job 5: 17. The world counts them happy who can keep out of affliction; but the Scripture calls them happy who are afflicted.

How are they happy?

Because they are more holy. Heb 12: 10. Because they are more in God's favour. Prov 3: 12. The goldsmith loves his gold when in the furnace. Because they have more of God's sweet presence. Psa 91: 15. They cannot be unhappy who have God's powerful presence in supporting, and his gracious presence in sanctifying, their affliction. Because the more affliction they have, the more degrees of glory they shall have; the lower they have been in the iron furnace, the higher they shall sit upon to throne of glory; the heavier their crosses, the heavier shall be their crown. So then, if afflictions make a Christian happy, they cannot call him miserable.

(4) See the merciful providence of God to his children. Though they may be in the house of bondage, and smart by affliction, yet they shall not be hurt by affliction. What hurt does the fan to the corn? it only separates the chaff from it; or the lance to the body? it only lets out the abscess. The house of bondage does that which sometimes ordinances will not; it humbles and reforms. 'If they be holden in cords of affliction, he openeth their ear to discipline, and commandeth that they return from iniquity.' Job 36: 8, 10. Oh! what a merciful providence is it that, though God bruise his people, yet, while he is bruising them, he is doing them good! It is as if one should throw a bag of money at another, which bruises him a little, but yet it enriches him. Affliction enriches the soul and yields the sweet fruits of righteousness. Heb. 12: 11.

(5) If Israel be in the house of bondage, if the Lord deals so with his own children, then how severely will he deal with the wicked! If he be so severe with those he loves, how severe will he be with those he hates! 'If they do these things in a green tree, what shall be done in the dry?' Luke 13: 31. If they that pray and mourn for sin be so severely dealt with, what will become of those that swear and break the Sabbath, and are unclean! If Israel be in the iron furnace, the wicked shall lie in the fiery furnace of hell. It should be the saddest news to wicked men, to hear that the people of God are afflicted. Let them think how dreadful the case of sinners will be. 'Judgement must begin at the house of God; and if it first begin at us, what shall the end be of them that obey not the gospel?' 1 Pet 4: 17. If God thresh his wheat, he will burn the chaff. If the godly suffer castigation, the wicked shall suffer condemnation. If he mingle his people's cup with wormwood he will mingle the wicked's cup with fire and brimstone.

Use two. If Israel be in the house of bondage,

(1) Do not entertain too hard thoughts of affliction. Christians are apt to look upon the cross and the iron furnace as frightful things, and do what they can to shun them. Nay, sometimes, to avoid affliction, they run themselves into sin. But do not think too hardly of affliction; do not look upon it as through the multiplying-glass of fear. The house of bondage is not hell. Consider that affliction comes from a wise God, who prescribes whatever befalls us. Persecutions are like

apothecaries: they give us the physic which God the physician prescribes. Affliction has its light side, as well as its dark one. God can sweeten our afflictions, and candy our wormwood. As our sufferings abound, so does also our consolation. 2 Cor 1: 5. Argerius dated his letters from the pleasant garden of the Leonine prison. God sometimes so revives his children in trouble, that they had rather bear their afflictions than want their comforts. Why then should Christians entertain such hard thoughts of afflictions? Do not look at its grim face, but at the message it brings, which is to enrich us with both grace and comfort.

(2) If Israel be sometimes in the house of bondage, in an afflicted state, think beforehand of affliction. Say not as Job (29: 18), 'I shall die in my nest.' In the house of mirth think of the house of bondage. You that are now Naomi, may be Mara. Ruth 1:20. How quickly may the scene turn, and the hyperbole of joy end in a catastrophe! All outward things are given to change. The forethoughts of affliction would make us sober and moderate in the use of lawful delight; it would cure a surfeit. Christ at a feast mentions his burial; a good antidote against a surfeit. The forethought of affliction would make us prepare for it; it would take us off the world; it would put us upon search of our evidences.

We should see what oil we have in our lamps, what grace we can find, that we may be able to stand in the evil day. That soldier is imprudent who has his sword to whet when he is just going to fight. He who forecasts sufferings, will have the shield of faith, and the sword of the Spirit ready, that he may not be surprised.

(3) If afflictions come, let us labour to conduct ourselves wisely as Christians, that we may adorn our sufferings: that is, let us endure with patience. 'Take, my brethren, the prophets for an example of suffering affliction and patience.' James 5: 10. Satan labours to take advantage of us in affliction, by making us either faint or murmur; he blows the coals of passion and discontent, and then warms himself at the fire. Patience adorns sufferings. A Christian should say as Jesus Christ did, 'Lord, not my will but thy will be done.' It is a sign the affliction is sanctified when the heart is brought to a sweet submissive frame. God will then remove the affliction: he will take us out of the iron furnace.

We may consider these words, 'Which brought thee out of the house of bondage,' either, [1] Literally; or [2] Spiritually and Mystically. In the letter, 'I brought thee out of the house of bondage;' that is, I delivered you out of the misery and servitude you sustained in Egypt, where you were in the iron furnace. Spiritually and mystically, by which 'I brought thee out of the house of bondage,' is a type of our deliverance by Christ from sin and hell.

[1] Literally, 'I brought thee out of the house of bondage,' out of great misery and slavery in the iron furnace. The thing I note here is that, though God brings his people sometimes into trouble, yet he will bring them out again. Israel was in the house of bondage, but at last was brought out.

We shall endeavour to show: 1. That God does deliver out of trouble. 2. In what manner. 3. At what seasons. 4. Why he delivers. 5. How the deliverances of the godly and wicked out of trouble differ.

God does deliver his children out of troubles. 'Our fathers trusted in thee; they trusted, and thou didst deliver them.' Psa 22: 4. 'And I was delivered out of the mouth of the lion,' namely, from Nero. 2 Tim 4: 17. 'Thou laidst affliction upon our loins, but thou broughtest us out into a wealthy place.' Psa 66: 11, 12. 'Weeping may endure for a night, but joy comes in the morning.' Psa 30: 5. God brought Daniel out of the lions' den, Zion out of Babylon. In his due time he gives an issue out of trouble. Psa 68: 20. The tree which in the winter seems dead, revives in the spring. Post nubila Phoebus [The sun emerges after the storms]. Affliction may leap on us as the viper did on Paul, but at last it shall be shaken off. It is called a cup of affliction. Isa 51: 17. The wicked drink a sea of wrath, the godly drink only a cup of affliction, and God will say shortly, 'Let this cup pass away.' God will give his people a gaol-delivery.

In what manner does God deliver his people out of trouble?

He does it like a God, in wisdom. (1) He does it sometimes suddenly. As the angel was caused to fly swiftly (Dan 9: 21), so God sometimes makes a deliverance fly swiftly, and on a sudden turns the shadow of death into the light of the morning. As he gives us mercies above what we can think (Eph 3: 20), so sometimes before we can think of them. 'When the Lord turned again the captivity of Zion, we were like them that dream;' it came suddenly upon us as a dream. Psa 126: 1. Joseph could not have thought of such a sudden alteration, to be the same day freed out of prison, and made the chief ruler in the kingdom. Mercy sometimes does not stick long in the birth, but comes forth on a sudden. (2) God sometimes delivers his people strangely. Thus the whale which swallowed up Jonah was the means of bringing him safe to land. He sometimes delivers his people in the very way which they think will destroy. In bringing Israel out of Egypt, he stirred up the heart of the Egyptians to hate them (Psa 105: 25), and that was the means of their deliverance. He brought Paul to shore by a contrary wind, and upon the broken pieces of the ship. Acts 27: 44.

When are the times and seasons that God usually delivers his people out of the bondage of affliction?

(1) When they are in the greatest extremity. Though Jonah was in the belly of hell, he says, 'Thou hast brought up my life from corruption.' Jonah 2: 6. When there is but a hair's breadth between the godly and death, God ushers in deliverance. When the ship was almost covered with waves Christ awoke and rebuked the wind. When Isaac was upon the altar, and the knife about to be put to his throat, the angel comes and says, 'Lay not thy hand upon the child.' When Peter began to sink, Christ took him by the hand. Cum duplicantur lateres, venit Moses: 'when the tale of brick was doubled, then Moses the temporal saviour comes. When the people of God are in the greatest danger the morning star of deliverance appears. When the patient is ready to faint the cordial is given.

(2) The second season is, when affliction has done its work upon them; when it has effected that which God sent it for. As, [1] When it has humbled them. 'Remembering my affliction, the wormwood and gall, my soul is humbled in me.' Lam 3: 19, 20. Then God's corrosive has eaten out the proud flesh. [2] When it has tamed their impatience. Before, they were proud and impatient, like froward children that struggle with their parents; but when their cursed hearts are tamed, they say, 'I will bear the indignation of the Lord, because I have sinned against him' (Micah 7: 9); and as Eli, 'It is the Lord; let him do what seemeth him good:' 'Let him hedge me with thorns, if he will plant me with grace.' 1 Sam 3: 18.

(3) When they are partakers of more holiness, and are more full of heavenly-mindedness. Heb 12: 10. When the sharp frost of affliction has brought forth the spring-flowers of grace, the cross is sanctified, and God will bring them out of the house of bondage. Luctus in laetitiam vertetur, cineres in corollas [Sorrow will turn to joy, ashes to garlands]. When the metal is refined it is taken out of the furnace. When affliction has healed us, God takes off the smarting plaister.

Why does God bring his people out of the house of bondage?

Hereby he makes way for his own glory. His glory is dearer to him than anything besides; it is a crown jewel. By raising his people he raises the trophies of his own honour; he glorifies his own attributes; his power, truth, and goodness are triumphant.

(1) His power. If God did not sometimes bring his people into trouble, how could his power be seen in bringing them out? He brought Israel out of the house of bondage, with miracle upon miracle; he saved them with an outstretched arm. 'What ailed thee, O thou sea, that thou fleddest?' &c. Psa 114: 5. Of Israel's march out of Egypt it is said, when the sea fled, and the waters were parted each from other. Here was the power of God set forth. 'Is there any thing too hard for me?' Jer 32: 27. God loves to help when things seem past hope. He creates deliverance. Psa 124: 8. He brought Isaac out of a dead womb, and the Messiah out of a virgin's womb. oh! how does his power shine forth when he overcomes seeming impossibilities, and works a cure when things look desperate!

(2) His truth. God has made promises to his people, when they are under great pressures, to deliver them; and his truth is engaged in his promise. 'Call upon me in the day of trouble, I will deliver thee.' Psa 50: 15. 'He shall deliver thee in six troubles, yea in seven.' Job 5: 19. How is the Scripture bespangled with these promises as the firmament is with stars! Either God will deliver them from death, or by death; he will make a way of escape. 1 Cor 10: 13. When promises are verified, God's truth is magnified.

(3) His goodness. God is full of compassion to such as are in misery. The Hebrew word, Racham, for mercy, signifies bowels. God has 'sounding of bowels.' Isa 63: 15. And this sympathy stirs up God to deliver. 'In his love and pity he redeemed them.' Isa 63: 9. This makes way for the triumph of his goodness. He is tender-hearted, he will not over afflict; he cuts

asunder the bars of iron, he breaks the yoke of the oppressor. Thus all his attributes ride in triumph in saving his people out of trouble.

How do the deliverance of the godly and tricked out of trouble differ?

(1) The deliverances of the godly are preservations; of the wicked reservations. 'The Lord knows how to deliver the godly, and to reserve the unjust to be punished.' 2 Pet 2: 9. A sinner may be delivered from dangerous sickness, and out of prison; but all this is but a reservation for some greater evil.

(2) God delivers the wicked, or rather spares them in anger. Deliverances to the wicked are not given as pledges of his love, but symptoms of displeasure; as quails were given to Israel in anger. But deliverances of the godly are in love. 'He delivered me because he delighted in me'. 2 Sam 22: 20. 'Thou hast in love to my soul delivered it from the pit of corruption;' or, as in the Hebrew, Chashiaqta Naphshi. Isa 38: 17. Thou hast loved me from the pit of corruption. A wicked man may say, 'Lord, thou hast delivered me out of the pit of corruption;' but a godly man may say, 'Lord, thou hast loved me out of the pit of corruption.' It is one thing to have God's power deliver us, and another thing to have his love deliver us. 'O,' said Hezekiah, 'Thou hast in love to my soul, delivered me from the pit of corruption.'

How may it be known that a deliverance comes in love?

(1) When it makes our heart boil over in love to God. 'I love the Lord because he has heard my voice.' Psa 116: 1. It is one thing to love our mercies, another thing to love the Lord. Deliverance is in love when it causes love.

(2) Deliverance is in love when we have hearts to improve it for God's glory. The wicked, instead of improving their deliverance for God's glory, increase their corruption; they grow worse, as the metal when taken out of the fire grows harder; but our deliverance is in love when we improve it for God's glory. God raises us out of a low condition, and we lift him up in our praises, and honour him with our substance. Prov 3: 9. He recovers us from sickness, and we spend ourselves in his service. Mercy is not as the sun to the fire, to dull it and put it out, but as oil to the wheel, to make it move faster.

(3) Deliverance comes in love when it makes us more exemplary in holiness; and our lives are walking Bibles. A thousand praises and doxologies do not honour God so much as the mortifying of one lust. 'Upon mount Zion there shall be deliverance and holiness,' Obadiah 17. When these two go together, deliverance and holiness; when, being made monuments of mercy, we are patterns of piety; then a deliverance comes in love, and we may say as Hezekiah, 'Thou hast in love to my soul delivered it from the pit of corruption.'

Use one. If God brings his people out of bondage, let none despond in trouble. Say not 'I shall sink under this burden;' or as David, 'I shall one day perish by the hand of Saul.' God can make the text good, personally and nationally, to bring his people out of the house of bondage. When he sees a fit season, he will put forth his arm and save them; and he can do it with ease. 'Lord, it is nothing with thee to help.' 2 Chron 14: 11. He that can turn tides, can turn the times; he that raised Lazarus when he was dead, can raise thee when thou art sick. 'I looked, and there was none to help, therefore mine own arm brought salvation.' Isa 63: 5. Do not despond; believe in God's power: faith sets God to work to deliver us.

Use two. Labour, if you are in trouble, to be fitted for deliverance. Many would have deliverance, but are not fitted for it.

When are we fitted for deliverance?

When, by our afflictions, we are conformed to Christ; when we have learned obedience. 'He learned obedience by the things which he suffered;' that is, he learned sweet submission to his Father's will. Heb 5: 8. 'Not my will, but thine, be done.' Luke 22: 42. When we have thus learned obedience by our sufferings, we are willing to do what God would have us do, and be what God would have us be. We are conformed to Christ, and are fitted for deliverance.

Use three. If God has brought you at any time out of the house of bondage, out of great and eminent troubles, be much in praise. Deliverance calls for praise. 'Thou hast put off my sackcloth, and girded me with gladness; to the end that my glory may sing praise to thee.' Psa 30: 11, 12. My glory, that is, my tongue, which is the instrument of glorifying thee. The saints are temples of the Holy Ghost. 1 Cor 3: 16. Where should God's praises be sounded but in his temple? Beneficium postulat officium [Gratitude should follow a favour]. The deepest springs yield the sweetest water; and hearts deeply sensible of God's deliverances yield the sweetest praises. Moses tells Pharaoh, when he was going out of Egypt, 'We will go with our flocks and our herds.' Exod 10: 9. Why so? Because he might have sacrifices of thanksgiving ready to offer to God for their deliverance. To have a thankful heart for deliverance is a greater blessing than the deliverance itself. One of the lepers, 'when he saw that he was healed, turned back, and with a loud voice glorified God.' Luke 17: 15. The leper's thankful heart was a greater blessing than to be healed of his leprosy. Have any of you been brought out of the house of bondage - out of prison, sickness, or any death-threatening danger? Do not forget to be thankful. Be not graves, but temples. That you may be the more thankful, observe every emphasis and circumstance in your deliverance; such as to be brought out of trouble when you were in articulo mortis [at the brink of death], when there was but a hair's breadth between you and death; or, to be brought out of affliction, without sin, you did not purchase your deliverance by the ensnaring of your consciences; or, to be brought out of trouble upon the wings of prayer; or, that those who were the occasions of bringing you into trouble, should be the instruments of bringing you out. These circumstances, being well weighed, heighten a deliverance, and should heighten our thankfulness. The cutting of a stone may be of more value than the stone itself; and the circumstancing of a deliverance may be greater than the deliverance itself.

But how shall we praise God in a right manner for deliverance?

(1) Be holy persons. In the sacrifice of thanksgiving, whosoever did eat thereof with his uncleanness upon him, was to be cut off (Lev 7: 20), to typify how unpleasing their praises and thank-offerings are who live in sin.

(2) Praise God with humble hearts, acknowledge how unworthy you were of deliverance. God's mercies are not debts, but legacies; and that you should have them by legacy should make you humble. 'The elders fell upon their faces (an expression of humility) and worshipped God. Rev 11: 16.

(3) Praise God for deliverances cordially. 'I will praise the Lord with my whole heart.' Psa 111: 1. In religion there is no music but in concert, when heart and tongue join.

(4) Praise God for deliverances constantly. 'While I live will I praise the Lord.' Psa 146: 2. Some will be thankful while the memory of a deliverance is fresh, and then leave off. The Carthaginians used, at first, to send the tenth of their yearly revenue to Hercules; but by degrees they grew weary, and left off sending; but we must be constant in our Eucharistic sacrifice, or thank-offering. The motion of our praise must be like the motion of our pulse, which beats as long as life lasts. 'I will sing praises unto my God while I have any being.' Psa 146: 2.

[2] THESE words are to be understood mystically and spiritually. By Israel's deliverance from the house of bondage, is typified their spiritual deliverance from sin, Satan, and hell.

(1) From sin. The house of bondage was a type of Israel's deliverance from sin. Sin is the true bondage, it enslaves the soul. Nihil durius servitute. Cicero. 'Of all conditions, servitude is the worst.' 'I was held before conversion,' says Augustine, 'not with an iron chain, but with the obstinacy of mine own will.' Sin is the enslaver; it is called a law, because it has a binding power over a man (Rom 7: 23); it is said to reign, because it exercises a tyrannical power (Rom 6: 12); and men are said to be the servants of sin, because they are so enslaved by it. Rom 6: 17. Thus sin is the house of bondage. Israel was not so enslaved in the iron furnace as the sinner is by sin. They are worse slaves and vassals who are under the power of sin, than they are who are under the power of earthly tyrants.

Other slaves have tyrants ruling over their bodies only; but the sinner has his soul tyrannised over. That princely thing, the soul, which sways the sceptre of reason, and was once crowned with perfect knowledge and holiness, now goes on foot; it is enslaved, and made a lackey to every base lust.

Other slaves have some pity shown them: the tyrant gives them meat, and lets them have hours for their rest; but sin is a merciless tyrant, it will let men have no rest. Judas had no rest until he had betrayed Christ, and after that he had less rest than before. How does a man wear himself out in the service of sin, waste his body, break his sleep, distract his mind! A wicked man is every day doing sin's drudgery-work.

Other slaves have servile work; but it is lawful. It is lawful to work in the galley, and tug at the oar; but all the laws and commands of sin are unlawful. Sin says to one man, defraud; to another, be unchaste; to another take revenge; to another, take a false oath. Thus all sin's commands are unlawful; we cannot obey sin's law, but by breaking God's law.

Other slaves are forced against their will. Israel groaned under slavery (Exod 2: 23); but sinners are content to be under the command of sin; they are willing to be slaves; they love their chains; they will not take their freedom; they 'glory in their shame.' Phil 3: 19. They wear their sins, not as their fetters, but their ornaments; they rejoice in iniquity. Jer 11: 15.

Other slaves are brought to correction, but sin's slaves are without repentance, and are brought to condemnation. Other slaves lie in the iron furnace: sin's slaves lie in the fiery furnace. What freedom of will has a sinner to his own confusion, when he can do nothing but what sin will have him? He is enslaved. Thus sinners are in the house of bondage; but God takes his elect out of the house of bondage, he beats off the chains and fetters of sin; he rescues them from their slavery; he makes them free, by bringing them into 'the glorious liberty of the children of God.' Rom 8: 21. The law of love now rules, not the law of sin. Though the life of sin be prolonged, yet not the dominion; as those beasts in Daniel had their lives prolonged for a season, but their dominion was taken away. Dan 7: 12. The saints are made spiritual kings, to rule and conquer their corruptions, to 'bind these kings in chains.' It is matter of the highest praise and thanksgiving, to be taken out of the house of bondage, to be freed from enslaving hosts, and made kings to reign in glory for ever.

(2) The bringing Israel out of the house of bondage, was a type of the deliverance from Satan. Men naturally are in the house of bondage, they are enslaved to Satan. Satan is called the prince of this world (John 14: 30); and the god of this world (2 Cor 4: 4); because he has power to command and enslave them. Though he shall one day be a close prisoner in chains, yet now he insults and tyrannises over the souls of men. Sinners are under his rule, he exercises over them a jurisdiction such as Caesar did over the senate. He fills men's heads with error, and their hearts with malice. 'Why has Satan filled thine heart?' Act 5: 3. A sinner's heart is the devil's mansion house. 'I will return into mine house.' Matt. 12: 44. And sure that must needs be a house of bondage, which is the devil's mansion-house. Satan is a complete tyrant. He rules men's minds, he blinds them with ignorance. 'The god of this world has blinded the minds of them that believe not.' 2 Cor 4: 4. He rules their memories. They remember that which is evil, and forget that which is good. Their memories are like a strainer, that lets go all the pure liquor, and retains only the dregs. He rules their wills. Though he cannot force the will, he draws it. 'The lusts of your father you will do.' John 8: 44. He has got your hearts, and him you will obey. His strong

temptations draw men to evil more than all the promises of God can draw them to good. This is the state of every man by nature; he is in the house of bondage; the devil has him in his power. A sinner grinds in the devil's mill; he is at the command of Satan, as the ass is at the command of the driver. No wonder to see men oppress and persecute; as slaves they must do what the god of this world will have them. How could those swine but run, when the devil entered into them? Matt 8: 32. When the devil tempted Ananias to tell a lie, he could not but speak what Satan had put in his heart. Acts 5: 3. When the devil entered into Judas, and bade him betray Christ, he would do it, though he hanged himself. It is a sad and dismal case, to be in the house of bondage, under the power and tyranny of Satan. When David would curse the enemies of God, how did he pray against them? That Satan might be at their right hand. Psa 109: 6. He knew he could then lead them into any snare. If the sinner has Satan at his right hand, let him take heed that he be not at God's left hand. Is it not a case to be bewailed, to see men taken captive by Satan at his will? 2 Tim 2: 26. He leads sinners as slaves before him in triumph; he wholly possesses them. If people should see their beasts bewitched and possessed of the devil, they would be much troubled; and yet, though their souls are possessed by Satan, they are not sensible of it. What can be worse than for men to be in the house of bondage, and to have the devil hurry them on in their lusts to perdition? Sinners are willingly enslaved to Satan; they love their gaoler; are content to sit quietly under Satan's jurisdiction; they choose this bramble to rule over them, though after a while, fire will come out of the bramble to devour them. Judges 9: 15. What an infinite mercy is it when God brings poor souls out of this house of bondage, when he gives them a gaol-delivery from the prince of darkness! JESUS CHRIST redeems captives, he ransoms sinners by price, and rescues them by force. As David took a lamb out of the lion's mouth (1 Sam 17: 3 5), so Christ rescues souls out of the mouth of the roaring lion. Oh, what a mercy is it to be brought out of the house of bondage, from captives to the prince of the power of the air, to be made subjects of the Prince of Peace! This is done by the preaching of the Word. 'To turn them from the power of Satan unto God.' Acts 26: 18.

(3) The bringing of Israel out of the house of bondage was a type of their being delivered from hell. Hell is domus servitutis, a house of bondage; a house built on purpose for sinners to lie in.

There is such a house of bondage where the damned lie. 'The wicked shall be turned into hell.' Psa 9: 17. 'How can ye escape the damnation of hell?' Matt 23: 33. If any one should ask where this house of bondage is, where is the place of hell? I wish he may never know experimentally. 'Let us not so much,' says Chrysostom, 'labour to know where hell is, as how to escape it.' Yet to satisfy curiosity, it may be observed that hell is locus subterraneus, some place beneath. 'Hell beneath.' Prov 15: 24. Hesiod says, 'Hell is as far under the earth, as heaven is above it.' The devils besought Christ 'that he would not command them to go out into the deep.' Luke 8: 31. Hell is in the deep.

Why must there be this house of bondage? Why a hell? Because there must be a place for the execution of divine justice. Earthly monarchs have their prison for malefactors, and shall not

God have his? Sinners are criminals, they have offended God; and it would not consist with his holiness and justice, to have his laws infringed, and not inflict penalties.

The dreadfulness of the place. Could you but hear the groans and shrieks of the damned for one hour, it would confirm you in the truth, that hell is a house of bondage. Hell is the emphasis of misery. Besides the poena damni, 'the punishment of loss,' which is the exclusion of the soul from the gloried sight of God, which divines think the worst part of hell, there will be poena sensus,' the punishment of sense.' If, when God's wrath is kindled but a little, and a spark of it flies into a man's conscience in this life, it is so terrible (as in the case of Spira), what will hell itself be?

In hell there will be a plurality of torments, 'Bonds and chains.' 2 Pet 2: 4. There will be the worm. Mark 9: 48; This is the worm of conscience. There will be the lake of fire. Rev 20: 15. Other fire is but painted to this.

This house of hell is haunted with devils. Matt 25: 41. Anselm says, 'I had rather endure all torments, than see the devil with bodily eyes.' Such as go to hell must not only be forced to behold the devil, but must be shut up with this lion in his den; they must keep the devil company. He is full of spite against mankind; a red dragon that will spit fire in men's faces.

The torments of hell abide for ever. 'The smoke of their torment ascendeth up for ever and ever.' Rev 14: 2: Time cannot finish it, tears cannot quench it. Mark 9: 44. The wicked are salamanders, who live always in the fire of hell, and are not consumed. After they have lain millions of years in hell, their punishment is as far from ending, as it was at the beginning. If all the earth and sea were sand, and every thousandth year a bird should come, and take away one grain, it would be a long time before that vast heap would be removed; yet, if after all that time the damned might come out of hell, there would be some hope; but this word EVER breaks the heart.

How does it seem to comport with God's justice to punish a sin committed in a moment, with eternal torment?

Because there is an eternity of sin in man's nature. Because sin is crimen laesae majestatis, 'committed against an infinite majesty,' and therefore the sin itself is infinite, and proportionally the punishment must be infinite. Because a finite creature cannot bear infinite wrath, he must be eternally satisfying what he can never satisfy. If hell be such a house of bondage, what infinite cause have they to bless God who are delivered from it! Jesus 'delivered us from the wrath to come.' 1 Thess 1: 10. Jesus Christ suffered the torments of hell in his soul, that believers should not suffer them. If we are thankful, when we are ransomed out of prison, or delivered from fire, oh, how should we bless God to be preserved from the wrath to come! It may cause more thankfulness in us, seeing the most part go into the house of bondage, even to hell. To be of the number of those few that are delivered from it, is matter of infinite thankfulness. Most, I say, go to that house of bondage when they die; most go to hell. 'Broad is the way that leadeth to destruction, and many there be which go in thereat.' Matt 7: 13. The greatest part of the world lies in wickedness. 1 John 5: 19. Divide the world, says Brerewood, into thirty-one parts, nineteen parts of it are possessed by Jews and Turks, and seven parts by heathens; so that there are but five parts of Christians, and among these Christians so many seduced Papists on the one hand, and so many formal Protestants on the other, that we may conclude the major part of the world goes to hell. Scripture compares the wicked to briers. Isa 10: 17. There are but few lilies in your fields, but in every hedge thorns and briers. It compares them to 'the mire in the streets.' Isa 10: 6. Few jewels or precious stones are in the street, but you cannot go a step without meeting with mire. The wicked are as common as the dirt in the street. Look at the generality of people. How many drunkards are there for one that is sober! How many adulterers for one that is chaste! How many hypocrites for one that is sincere! The devil has the harvest, and God a few gleanings only. Oh, then, such as are delivered from the house of bondage, in hell, have infinite cause to admire and bless God. How should the vessels of mercy run over with thankfulness! When most others are carried prisoners to hell, they are delivered from the wrath to come.

How shall I know I am delivered from hell?

(1) Those whom Christ saves from hell he saves from sin. 'He shall save his people from their sins.' Matt 1: 21. Has God delivered you from the power of corruption, from pride, malice, and lust? If he has delivered you from the hell of sin, he has delivered you from the hell of torment.

(2) If you have got an interest in Christ, and are prizing, trusting, and loving him, you are delivered from hell and damnation. 'No condemnation to them that are in Christ Jesus.' Rom 8:1. If you are in Christ, he has put the garment of his righteousness over you, and hell-fire can never singe it. Pliny observes, nothing will so soon quench fire as salt and blood: the salt tears of repentance and the blood of Christ will quench the fire of hell, so that it shall never kindle upon you.

1.4 The Right Understanding of the Law

'Thou shalt have no other Gods before me.' Exod 20: 3.

Before I come to the commandments, I shall answer questions, and lay down rules respecting the moral law.

What is the difference between the moral law and the gospel?

(1) The law requires that we worship God as our Creator; the gospel, that we worship him in and through Christ. God in Christ is propitious; out of him we may see God's power, justice, and

holiness: in him we see his mercy displayed.

(2) The moral law requires obedience, but gives no strength (as Pharaoh required brick, but gave no straw), but the gospel gives strength; it bestows faith on the elect; it sweetens the law; it makes us serve God with delight.

Of what use is the moral law to us?

It is a glass to show us our sins, that, seeing our pollution and misery, we may be forced to flee to Christ to satisfy for former guilt, and to save from future wrath. 'The law was our schoolmaster to bring us unto Christ. Gal 3: 24.

But is the moral law still in force to believers; is it not abolished to them?

In some sense it is abolished to believers. (1) In respect of justification. They are not justified by their obedience to the moral law. Believers are to make great use of the moral law, but they must trust only to Christ's righteousness for justification; as Noah's dove made use of her wings to fly, but trusted to the ark for safety. If the moral law could justify, what need was there of Christ's dying? (2) The moral law is abolished to believers, in respect of its curse. They are freed from its curse and condemnatory power. 'Christ has redeemed us from the curse of the law, being made a curse for us.' Gal 3: Is.

How was Christ made a curse for us?

Considered as the Son of God, he was not made a curse, but as our pledge and surety, he was made a curse for us. Heb 7: 22. This curse was not upon his Godhead, but upon his manhood. It was the wrath of God lying upon him; and thus he took away from believers the curse of the law, by being made a curse for them. But though the moral law be thus far abolished, it remains as a perpetual rule to believers. Though it be not their Saviour, it is their guide. Though it be not foedus, a covenant of life; yet it is norma, a rule of life. Every Christian is bound to conform to it; and to write, as exactly as he can, after this copy. 'Do we then make void the law through faith? God forbid.' Rom 3: 31. Though a Christian is not under the condemning power of the law, yet he is under its commanding power. To love God, to reverence and obey him, is a law which always binds and will bind in heaven. This I urge against the Antinomians, who say the moral law is abrogated to believers; which, as it contradicts Scripture, so it is a key to open the door to all licentiousness. They who will not have the law to rule them, shall never have the gospel to save them.

Having answered these questions, I shall in the next place, lay down some general rules for the right understanding of the Decalogue, or Ten Commandments. These may serve to give us some light into the sense and meaning of the commandments.

Rule I. The commands and prohibitions of the moral law reach the heart. (1) The commands of the moral law reach the heart. The commandments require not only outward actions, but inward affections; they require not only the outward act of obedience, but the inward affection of love. 'Thou shalt love the Lord thy God with all thine heart.' Deut 6: 5.

(2) The threats and prohibitions of the moral law reach the heart. The law of God forbids not only the act of sin, but the desire and inclination; not only does it forbid adultery, but lusting (Matt 5: 28): not only stealing, but coveting (Rom 7: 7). Lex humana ligat manum, lex divina comprimit animam 'Man's law binds the hands only, God's law binds the heart.'

Rule 2. In the commandments there is a synecdoche, more is intended than is spoken. (1) Where any duty is commanded, the contrary sin is forbidden. When we are commanded to keep the Sabbath-day holy, we are forbidden to break the Sabbath. When we are commanded to live in a calling, 'Six days shalt thou labour,' we are forbidden to live idly, and out of a calling.

(2) Where any sin is forbidden, the contrary duty is commanded. When we are forbidden to take God's name in vain, the contrary duty, that we should reverence his name, is commanded. 'That thou mayest fear this glorious and fearful name, the Lord Thy God.' Deut 28: 58. Where we are forbidden to wrong our neighbour, there the contrary duty, that we should do him all the good we can, by vindicating his name and supplying his wants, is included.

Rule 3. Where any sin is forbidden in the commandment, the occasion of it is also forbidden. Where murder is forbidden, envy and rash anger are forbidden, which may occasion it. Where adultery is forbidden, all that may lead to it is forbidden, as wanton glances of the eye, or coming into the company of a harlot. 'Come not nigh the door of her house.' Prov 5: 8. He who would be free from the plague, must not come near the infected house. Under the law the Nazarite was forbidden to drink wine; nor might he eat grapes of which the wine was made.

Rule 4. In relato subintelligitur correlatum. Where one relation is named in the commandment, there another relation is included. Where the child is named, the father is included. Where the duty of children to parents is mentioned, the duty of parents to children is also included. Where the child is commanded to honour the parent, it is implied that the parent is also commanded to instruct, to love, and to provide for the child.

Rule 5. Where greater sins are forbidden, lesser sins are also forbidden. Though no sin in its own nature is little, yet one may be comparatively less than another. Where idolatry is forbidden, superstition is forbidden, or bringing any innovation into God's worship, which he has not appointed. As the sons of Aaron were forbidden to worship an idol, so to sacrifice to God with strange fire. Lev 10: 1. Mixture in sacred things, is like a dash in wine, which though it gives a colour, yet does but debase and adulterate it. It is highly provoking to God to bring any superstitious ceremony into his worship which he has not prescribed; it is to tax God's wisdom, as if he were not wise enough to appoint the manner how he will be served.

Rule 6. The law of God is entire. Lex est copulativa [The law is all connected]. The first and second tables are knit together; piety to God, and equity to our neighbour. These two tables which God has joined together, must not be put asunder. Try a moral man by the duties of the first table, piety to God, and there you will find him negligent; try a hypocrite by the duties of the second table, equity to his neighbour, and there you will find him tardy. If he who is strict in the second table neglects the first, or he who is zealous in the first, neglects the second, his heart is not right with God. The Pharisees were the highest pretenders to keeping the first table with zeal and holiness; but Christ detects their hypocrisy: 'Ye have omitted judgement, mercy and faith.' Matt 23: 23. They were bad in the second table; they omitted judgement, or being just in their dealings; mercy in relieving the poor; and faith, or faithfulness in their promises and contracts with men. God wrote both the tables, and our obedience must set a seal to both.

Rule 7. God's law forbids not only the acting of sin in our own persons, but being accessory to, or having any hand in, the sins of others.

How and in what sense may we be said to partake of, and have a hand in the sins of others?

(1) By decreeing unrighteous decrees, and imposing on others that which is unlawful. Jeroboam made the people of Israel to sin; he was accessory to their idolatry by setting up golden calves. Though David did not in his own person kill Uriah, yet because he wrote a letter to Joab, to set Uriah in the forefront of the battle, and it was done by his command, he was accessory to Uriah's death, and the murder of him was laid by the prophet to his charge. 'Thou hast killed Uriah the Hittite with the sword.' 2 Sam 12: 9.

(2) We become accessory to the sins of others by not hindering them when it is in our power. Qui non prohibit cum potest, jubet [The failure to prevent something, when it lies within your power, amounts to ordering it]. If a master of a family see his servant break the Sabbath, or hear him swear, and does not use the power he has to suppress him, he becomes accessory to his sin. Eli, for not punishing his sons when they made the offering of the Lord to be abhorred, made himself guilty. 1 Sam 3: 13, 14. He that suffers an offender to pass unpunished, makes himself an offender.

(3) By counselling, abetting, or provoking others to sin. Ahithophel made himself guilty of the fact by giving counsel to Absalom to go in and defile his father's concubines. 2 Sam 16: 21. He who shall tempt or solicit another to be drunk, though he himself be sober, yet being the occasion of another's sin, he is accessory to it. 'Woe unto him that giveth his neighbour drink, that puttest thy bottle to him.' Hab 2: 15.

(4) By consenting to another's sin. Saul did not cast one stone at Stephen, yet the Scripture says, 'Saul was consenting unto his death.' Acts 8: 1. Thus he had a hand in it. If several combined to murder a man, and should tell another of their intent, and he should give his consent to it, he would be guilty; for though his hand was not in the murder, his heart was in it; though he did not

act it, yet he approved it, and so it became his sin.

(5) By example. Vivitur exemplis [We live by example]. Examples are powerful and cogent. Setting a bad example occasions another to sin, and so a person becomes accessory. If the father swears, and the child by his example, learns to swear, the father is accessory to the child's sin; he taught him by his example. As there are hereditary diseases, so there are hereditary sins.

Rule 8. The last rule about the commandments is, that though we cannot, by our own strength, fulfil all these commandments, yet doing quod posse, what we are able, the Lord has provided encouragement for us. There is a threefold encouragement.

(1) That though we have not ability to obey any one command, yet God has in the new covenant, promised to work that in us which he requires. 'I will cause you to walk in my statutes.' Ezek 36: 27. God commands us to love him. Ah, how weak is our love! It is like the herb that is yet only in the first degree; but God has promised to circumcise our hearts, that we may love him. Deut 30: 6. He that commands us, will enable us. God commands us to turn from sin, but alas! we have not power to turn; therefore he has promised to turn us, to put his Spirit within us, and to turn the heart of stone into flesh. Ezek 36: 26. There is nothing in the command, but the same is in the promise. Therefore, Christian, be not discouraged, though thou hast no strength of thy own, God will give thee strength. The iron has no power to move, but when drawn by the loadstone it can move. 'Thou hast wrought all our works in us.' Isa 26: 12.

(2) Though we cannot exactly fulfil the moral law, yet God for Christ's sake will mitigate the rigour of the law, and accept of something less than he requires. God in the law requires exact obedience, yet will accept of sincere obedience; he will abate something of the degree, if there be truth in the inward parts. He will see the faith, and pass by the failing. The gospel remits the severity of the moral law.

(3) Wherein our personal obedience comes short, God will be pleased to accept us in our Surety. 'He has made us accepted in the Beloved.' Eph 1: 6. Though our obedience be imperfect, yet, through Christ our Surety, God looks upon it as perfect. That very service which God's law might condemn, his mercy is pleased to crown, by virtue of the blood of our Mediator. Having given you these rules about the commandments, I shall come next to the commandments themselves.

2. The Ten Commandments

2.1 The First Commandment

'Thou shalt have no other gods before me.' Exod 20: 3

Why is the commandment in the second person singular, Thou? Why does not God say, You shall have no other gods?

Because the commandment concerns every one, and God would have each one take it as spoken to him by name. Though we are forward to take privileges to ourselves, yet we are apt to shift off duties from ourselves to others; therefore the commandment is in the second person, Thou and Thou, that every one may know that it is spoken to him, as it were, by name. We come now to the commandment, 'Thou shalt have no other gods before me.' This may well lead the van, and be set in the front of all the commandments, because it is the foundation of all true religion. The sum of this commandment is, that we should sanctify God in our hearts, and give him a precedence above all created beings. There are two branches of this commandment: 1. That we must have one God. 2. That we must have but one. Or thus, 1. That we must have God for our God. 2. That we must have no other.

1. That we must have God for our God. It is manifest that we must have a God, and 'who is God save the Lord?' 2 Sam 22: 32. The Lord Jehovah (one God in three persons) is the true, living, eternal God; and him we must have for our God.

[1] To have God to be a God to us, is to acknowledge him for a God. The gods of the heathen are idols. Psa 96: 5. And 'we know that an idol is nothing' (1 Cor 8: 4); that is, it has nothing of Deity in it. If we cry, 'Help, O Idol,' an idol cannot help; the idols themselves were carried into captivity, so that an idol is nothing. Isa 46: 2. Vanity is ascribed to it, we do not therefore acknowledge it to be a god. Jer 14: 22. But we have this God to be a God to us, when, ex animo [from the heart], we acknowledge him to be God. All the people fell on their faces and said, 'The Lord he is the God! the Lord he is the God!' 1 Kings 18: 39. Yea, we acknowledge him to be the only God. 'O Lord God of Israel, which dwellest between the cherubim, thou art the God, even thou alone.' 2 Kings 19: 15. Deity is a jewel that belongs only to his crown. Further, we acknowledge there is no God like him. 'And Solomon stood before the altar of the Lord; and he said, Lord God of Israel, there is no God like thee.' 1 Kings 8: 22, 23. 'For who in the heaven can be compared unto the Lord? who among the sons of the mighty can be likened unto the Lord?' Psa 89: 6. In the Chaldee it is, 'Who among the angels?' None can do as God; he brought the world out of nothing; 'And hangeth the earth upon nothing.' Job 26: 7. It makes God to be a God to us, when we are persuaded in our hearts, and confess with our tongues, and subscribe with our hands, that he is the only true God, and that there is none comparable to him.

[2] To have God to be a God to us is to choose him. 'Choose you this day whom ye will serve: but as for me and my house we will serve the Lord:' that is, we will choose the Lord to be our God. Josh 24: 15. It is one thing for the judgement to approve of God, and another for the will to

choose him. Religion is not a matter of chance, but choice.

Before choosing God for our God, there must be knowledge. We must know him before we can choose him. Before any one choose the person he will marry, he must have some knowledge of that person; so we must know God before we can choose him for our God. 'Know thou the God of thy father.' I Chron 28: 9. We must know God in his attributes, as glorious in holiness, rich in mercy, and faithful in promises. We must know him in his Son. As the face is represented in a glass, so in Christ, as in a transparent glass, we see God's beauty and love shine forth. This knowledge must go before choosing God. Lactantius said, all the learning of the philosophers was without a head, because it wanted the knowledge of God. This choosing is an act of mature deliberation. The Christian having viewed the superlative excellences in God, and being stricken with a holy admiration of his perfections, singles him out from all other objects to set his heart upon, and says as Jacob, 'The Lord shall be my God.' Gen 28: 21. He that chooses God, devotes himself to God. 'Thy servant who is devoted to thy fear.' Psa 119: 38. As the vessels of the sanctuary were consecrated and set apart from common to holy uses, so he who has chosen God to be his God, has dedicated himself to God, and will no more be devoted to profane uses. [3] To have God to be a God to us, is to enter into solemn covenant with him, that he shall be our God. After choice the marriage-covenant follows. As God makes a covenant with us, 'I will make an everlasting covenant with you, even the sure mercies of David' (Isa 55: 3); so we make a covenant with him, 'They entered into a covenant to seek the Lord God of their fathers.' 2 Chron 15: 12. 'One shall say, I am the Lord's: and another shall subscribe with his hand unto the Lord;' like soldiers that subscribe their names in the muster roll. Isa 44: 5. This covenant, 'That God shall be our God,' we have often renewed in the Lord's Supper; which, like a seal to a bond, binds us fast to God, and so keeps us that we do not depart from him.

[4] To have God to be a God to us, is to give him adoration: which consists in reverencing him: 'God is to be had in reverence of all them that are about him.' Psa 89: 7. The seraphim, who stood about God's throne, covered their faces (Isa 6), and Elijah wrapped himself in a mantle when the Lord passed by, in token of reverence. This reverence shows the high esteem we have of God's sacred majesty. Adoration consists in bowing to him, or worshipping him. 'Worship the Lord in the beauty of holiness.' Psa 29: 2. 'They bowed their heads, and worshipped the Lord with their faces to the ground.' Neh 8: 6. Divine worship is the peculiar honour belonging to the Godhead; which God is jealous of, and will have no creature share in. 'My glory will I not give to another.' Isa 42: 8. Magistrates may have a civil respect or veneration, but God only should have a religious adoration.

[5] To have God to be a God to us, is to fear him. 'That thou mayest fear this glorious and fearful name, The Lord thy God.' Deut 28: 58. This fearing God is (1) To have him always in our eye, 'I have set the Lord always before me.' Psa 16: 8. 'Mine eyes are ever towards the Lord.' Psa 25: 15. He who fears God imagines that whatever he is doing, God looks on, and as a judge, weighs all his actions. (2) To fear God is to have such a holy awe of God upon our hearts, that we dare

not sin. 'Stand in awe and sin not.' Psa 4: 4. The wicked sin and fear not; the godly fear and sin not. 'How then can I do this great wickedness and sin against God?' Gen 39: 9. Bid me sin, and you bid me drink poison. It is a saying of Anselm, 'If hell were on one side, and sin on the other, I would rather leap into hell, than willingly sin against my God.' He who fears God will not sin, though it be ever so secret. 'Thou shalt not curse the deaf, nor put a stumbling-block before the blind, but shalt fear thy God.' Lev 19: 14. Suppose you should curse a deaf man, he could not hear you; or you were to lay a block in a blind man's way, and cause him to fall, he could not see you do it; but the fear of God will make you forsake sins which can neither be heard nor seen by men. The fear of God destroys the fear of man. The three children feared God, therefore they feared not the king's wrath. Dan 3: 16. The greater noise drowns the less; the noise of thunder drowns the noise of a river; so, when the fear of God is supreme in the soul, it drowns all other carnal fear. It makes God to be God to us when we have a holy filial fear of him.

[6] To have God to be a God to us, is to trust in him. 'Mine eyes are unto thee, O God the Lord: in thee is my trust.' Psa 141: 8. 'The God of my rock, in him will I trust.' 2 Sam 22: 3. There is none in whom we can trust but God. All creatures are a refuge of lies; they are like the Egyptian reed, too weak to support us, but strong enough to wound us. 2 Kings 18: 21. Omnis motus fit super immobili [The immovable is undisturbed by any commotion]. God only is a sufficient foundation to build our trust upon. When we trust him, we make him a God to us; when we do not trust him, we make him an idol. Trusting in God is to rely on his power as a Creator, and on his love as a Father. Trusting in God is to commit our chief treasure, our soul, to him. 'Into thy hands I commit my spirit.' Psa 31: 5. As the orphan trusts his estate with his guardian, so we trust our souls with God. Then he becomes a God to us.

But how shall we know that we trust in God aright? If we trust in God aright, we shall trust him at one time as well as another. 'Trust in him at all times.' Psa 62: 8. Can we trust him in our straits? When the fig-tree does not flourish, when our earthly crutches are broken, can we lean upon God's promise? When the pipes are cut off that used to bring us comfort, can we live upon God, in whom are all our fresh springs? When we have no bread to eat but the bread of carefulness (Ezek 12: 19), when we have no water to drink but tears, as in Psa 80: 5: 'Thou givest them tears to drink in great measure;' can we then trust in God's providence to supply us? A good Christian believes, that if God feeds the ravens, he will feed his children, he lives upon God's all-sufficiency, not only for grace, but for food. He believes if God gives him heaven, he will give daily bread; he trusts his bond: 'Verily thou shalt be fed.' Psa 37: 3. Can we trust God in our fears? When adversaries grow high can we display the banner of faith? 'What time I am afraid, I will trust in thee.' Psa 56: 3. Faith cures the trembling in heart; it gets above fear, as oil swims above the water. To trust in God, makes him to be a God to us.

[7] To have God to be a God to us, is to love him. In the godly fear and love kiss each other.

[8] To have him to be a God to us, is to obey him. Upon this I shall speak more at large in the

second commandment.

Why must use cleave to the Lord as our God?

(1) Because of its equity. It is but just that we should cleave to him from whom we receive our being. Who can have a better right to us than he that gives us our breath? For 'it is he that made us, and not we ourselves.' Psa 100 3. It is unjust, yea, ungrateful, to give away our love or worship to any but God.

(2) Because of its utility. If we cleave to the Lord as our God, then he will bless us: 'God, even our own God, shall bless us.' Psa 67: 6. He will bless us in our estate. 'Blessed shall be the fruit of thy ground: blessed shall be thy basket and thy store.' Deut 28: 4, 5. We shall not only have our sacks full of corn, but money in the mouth of the sack. He will bless us with peace. 'The Lord will bless his people with peace.' Psa 29: 11. With outward peace, which is the nurse of plenty. 'He maketh peace in thy borders.' Psa 147: 14. With inward peace, a smiling conscience, which is sweeter than the dropping of honey. God will turn all evils to our good. Rom 8: 28. He will make a treacle of poison. Joseph's imprisonment was a means for his advancement. Gen 50: 20. Out of the bitterest drug he will distil his glory and our salvation. In short, he will be our guide to death, our comfort in death, and our reward after death. The utility of it, therefore, may make us cleave to the Lord as our God. 'Happy is that people whose God is the Lord.' Psa 144: 15.

(3) Because of its necessity. If God be not our God, he will curse our blessings; and God's curse blasts wherever it comes. Mal 2: 2. If God be not our God, we have none to help us in misery. Will he help his enemies? Will he assist those who disclaim him? If we do not make God to be our God, he will make himself to be our judge; and if he condemns, there is no appealing to a higher court. There is a necessity, therefore, for having God for our God, unless we intend to be eternally espoused to misery.

Use one. If we must have the Lord Jehovah for our one God, it condemns the Atheists who have no God. 'The fool has said in his heart, There is no God.' Psa 14: 1. There is no God he believes in, or worships. Such Atheists were Diagoras and Theodorus. When Seneca reproved Nero for his impieties, Nero said, 'Dost thou think I believe there is any God, when I do such things?' The duke of Silesia was so infatuated, that he affirmed, Neque inferos, neque superos esse; that there was neither God nor devil. We may see God in the works of his fingers. The creation is a great volume in which we may read a Godhead, and he must needs put out his own eyes that denies a God. Aristotle, though a heathen, not only acknowledged God, when he cried out, 'Thou Being of beings, have mercy on me,' but he thought he that did not confess a Deity was not worthy to live. They who will not believe a God, shall feel him. 'It is a fearful thing to fall into the hands of the living God.' Heb 10: 31.

Use two. Christians are condemned who profess to own God for their God and yet do not live as if he were their God. (1) They do not believe in him as a God. When they look upon their sins, they are apt to say, Can God pardon? When they look upon their wants, they say, Can God provide, can he prepare a table in the wilderness? (2) They do not love him as a God. They do not give him the cream of their love, but are prone to love other things more than God; they say they love God, but will part with nothing for him. (3) They do not worship him as God. They do not give him that reverence, nor pray with that devotion, as if they were praying to a God. How dead are their hearts! If not dead in sin, they are dead to duty. They pray as to a god that has eyes and sees not, ears and hears not. In hearing the Word, how much distraction, and what regardless hearts have many! They are thinking of their shops and drugs. Would a king take it well at our hands, if, when speaking to us, we should be playing with a feather? When God is speaking to us in his Word, and our hearts are taken up with thoughts about the world, is not this playing with a feather? Oh, how should this humble most of us, that we do not make God to be a God to us! We do not believe in him, love him, worship him as God. Many heathens have worshipped their false gods with more seriousness and devotion than some Christians do the true God. O let us chide ourselves; did I say chide? Let us abhor ourselves for our deadness and formality in religion; how we have professed God, and yet have not worshipped him as God.

II. That we must have no other god. 'Thou shalt have no other gods before me.

What is meant by the words, Before me?

It means before my face; in conspectu meo, in my sight. 'Cursed be the man that maketh any graven image, and putteth it in a secret place.' Deut 27: 15. Some would not bow to the idol in the sight of others, but they would secretly bow to it; but though this was out of man's sight, it was not out of God's sight. 'Cursed, therefore,' says God, 'be he that puts the image in a secret place.' 'Thou shalt have no other gods.' 1. There is really no other god. 2. We must have no other.

[1] There is really no other god. The Valentinians held there were two gods; the Polytheists, that there were many; the Persian worshipped the sun; the Egyptians, the ox and elephant; the Grecians, Jupiter; but there is no other than the true God. 'Know, therefore, this day, and consider it in thy heart, that the Lord he is God in heaven above, and upon the earth beneath; there is none else.' Deut 4: 39. For, (1) There is but one First Cause, that has its being of itself, and on which all other beings depend. As in the heavens the Primum Mobile moves all the other orbs, so God is the Great Mover, he gives life and motion to everything that exists.

(2) There is but one Omnipotent Power. If there be two omnipotent, we must always suppose a contest between the two: that which one would do, the other, being equal, would oppose; and so all things would be brought into confusion. If a ship should have two pilots of equal power, one would be ever crossing the other; when one would sail the other would cast anchor; there would be confusion, and the ship would perish. The order and harmony in the world, the constant and uniform government of all things, is a clear argument that there is but one Omnipotent, one God that rules all. 'I am the first, and I am the last, and beside me there is no God.' Isa 44: 6.

[2] We must have no other god. 'Thou shalt have no other gods before me.' This commandment forbids: (1) Serving a false god, and not the true God. 'Saying to a stock, Thou art my father; and to a stone, Thou hast brought me forth.' Jer 2: 27. (2) Joining a false god with a true. 'They feared the Lord, and served their own gods.' 2 Kings 17: 33. These are forbidden in the commandment; we must adhere to the true God, and no other. 'God is a jealous God,' and he will endure no rival. A wife cannot lawfully have two husbands at once; nor may we have two gods. Thou shalt worship no other god, for the Lord is a jealous God.' Exod. 34: 14. 'Their sorrows shall be multiplied that hasten after another god.' Psa 16: 4. The Lord interprets it a 'forsaking of him' to espouse any other god. 'They forsook the Lord, and followed other gods.' Judges 2: 12. God would not have his people so much as make mention of idol gods. 'Make no mention of the name of other gods, neither let it be heard out of thy mouth.' Exod 23: 13. 'God looks upon it as breaking the marriage-covenant, to go after other gods. Therefore, when Israel committed idolatry with the golden calf, God disclaimed his interest in them. 'Thy people have corrupted themselves.' Exod 32: 7. Before, God called Israel his people; but when they went after other gods, 'Now,' saith the Lord to Moses, 'they are no more my people but thy people.' 'Plead with your mother, plead; for she is not my wife.' Hos 2: 2. She does not keep faith with me, she has stained herself with idols, therefore I will divorce her, 'she is not my wife.' To go after other gods, is what God cannot bear; it makes the fury rise up in his face. 'If thy brother, or thy son, or the wife of thy bosom or thy friend, which is as thine own soul, entice thee secretly, saying, Let us go and serve other gods, thou shalt not consent unto him, neither shall thine eye pity him; but thou shalt surely kill him; thine hand shall be first upon him to put him to death, and afterwards the hand of all the people.' Deut 13: 6, 8, 9.

What is it to have other gods besides the true God? I fear upon search, we have more idolaters among us than we are aware of.

(1) To trust in any thing more than God, is to make it a god. If we trust in our riches, we make riches our god. We may take comfort, but not put confidence in them. It is a foolish thing to trust in them. They are deceitful riches, and it is foolish to trust to that which will deceive us. Matt 13: 22. They have no solid consistency, they are like landscapes or golden dreams, which leave the soul empty when it awakes or comes to itself. They are not what they promise; they promise to satisfy our desires, and they increase them; they promise to stay with us, and they take wings. They are hurtful. 'Riches kept for the owners thereof to their hurt.' Eccl 5: 13. It is foolish to trust to that which will hurt one. Who would take hold of the edge of a razor to help him? They are often fuel for pride and lust. Ezek 28: 5. Jer 5: 7. It is folly to trust in our riches; but how many do, and make money their god! 'The rich man's wealth is his strong city.' Prov 10: 15. He makes the wedge of gold his hope. Job 31: 24. God made man of the dust of the earth, and man makes a god of the dust of the earth. Money is his creator, redeemer, comforter: his creator, for if he has money, he thinks he is made; his redeemer, for if he be in danger, he trusts to his money to redeem him; his comforter, for if he be sad, money is the golden harp to drive away the evil spirit. Thus by trusting to money, we make it a god.

If we trust in the arm of flesh, we make it a god. 'Cursed be the man that trusteth in man, and maketh flesh his arm.' Jer 17: 5. The Syrians trusted in their army, which was so numerous that it filled the country; but this arm of flesh withered. 1 Kings 20: 27, 29. What we make our trust, God makes our shame. The sheep run to the hedges for shelter, and they lose their wool; so we have run to second causes to help us, and have lost much of our golden fleece; they have not only been reeds to fail us, but thorns to prick us. We have broken our parliament-crutches, by leaning too hard upon them.

If we trust in our wisdom, we make it a god. 'Let not the wise man glory in his wisdom.' Jer 9: 23. Glorying is the height of confidence. Many a man makes an idol of his wit and parts; he deifies himself, but how often does God take the wise in their own craftiness! Job 5: 13. Ahithophel had a great wit, his counsel was as the oracle of God; but his wit brought him to the halter. 2 Sam 17: 23.

If we trust in our civility, we make it a god. Many trust to this, that none can charge them with gross sin. Civility is but nature refined and cultivated; a man may be washed, and not changed; his life may be civil, and yet there may be some reigning sin in his heart. The Pharisee could say, 'I am no adulterer' (Luke 18: 11); but he could not say, 'I am not proud.' To trust to civility, is to trust to a spider's web.

If we trust to our duties to save us, we make them a god. 'Our righteousnesses are as filthy rags;' they are fly-blown with sin. Isa 64: 6. Put gold in the fire, and much dross comes out: so our most golden duties are mixed with infirmity. We are apt either to neglect duty, or idolise it. Use duty, but do not trust to it; for then you make it a god. Trust not to your praying and hearing; they are means of salvation, but they are not saviours. If you make duties bladders to trust to, you may sink with them to hell.

If we trust in our grace, we make a god of it. Grace is but a creature; if we trust to it we make it an idol. Grace is imperfect, and we must not trust to that which is imperfect to save us. 'I have walked in my integrity: I have trusted also in the Lord.' Psa 26: 1: David walked in his integrity; but did not trust in his integrity. 'I have trusted in the Lord.' If we trust in our graces, we make a Christ of them. They are good graces, but bad Christs.

(2) To love any thing more than God, is to make it a god. If we love our estate more than God, we make it a god. The young man in the gospel loved his gold better than his Saviour; the world lay nearer his heart than Christ. Matt 19: 22. Fulgens hoc aurum praestringit oculos [This gold with its glitter blinds the eyes]. Varius. The covetous man is called an idolater. Eph 5: 5. Why so? Because he loves his estate more than God, and so makes it his god. Though he does not bow down to an idol, if he worships the graven image in his coins, he is an idolater. That which has most of the heart, we make a god of.

If we love our pleasure more than God, we make a god of it. 'Lovers of pleasures more than lovers of God.' 2 Tim 3: 4. Many let loose the reins, and give themselves up to all manner of sensual delights; they idolise pleasure. 'They take the timbrel, and the harp, and rejoice at the sound of the organ. They spend their days in mirth.' Job 21: 12, 13, (mg). I have read of a place in Africa, where the people spend all their time in dancing and making merry; and have not we many who make a god of pleasure, who spend their time in going to plays and visiting ball-rooms, as if God had made them like the leviathan, to play in the water? Psa 104: 26. In the country of Sardinia there is a herb like balm, that if any one eats too much of it, he will die laughing: such a herb is pleasure, if any one feeds immoderately on it, he will go laughing to hell. Let such as make a god of pleasure read but these two Scriptures. 'The heart of fools is in the house of mirth.' Eccl 7: 4. 'How much she has lived deliciously, so much torment give her.' Rev 18: 7. Sugar laid in a damp place turns to water; so all the sugared joys and pleasures of sinners will turn to the water of tears at last.

If we love our belly more than God, we make a god of it. 'Whose god is their belly.' Phil 3: 19. Clemens Alexandrinus writes of a fish that had its heart in its belly; an emblem of epicures, whose heart is in their belly; they seek sacrificare lari, their belly is their god, and to this god they pour drink offerings. The Lord allows what is fitting for the recruiting of nature. 'I will send grass, that thou mayest eat and be full.' Deut 11: 15. But to mind nothing but the indulging of the appetite, is idolatry. 'Whose god is their belly.' What pity is it, that the soul, that princely part, which sways the sceptre of reason and is akin to angels, should be enslaved to the brutish part!

If we love a child more than God, we make a god of it. How many are guilty in this kind? They think of their children, and delight more in them than in God; they grieve more for the loss of their first-born, than for the loss of their first love. This is to make an idol of a child, and to set it in God's room. Thus God is often provoked to take away our children. If we love the jewel more than him that gave it, God will take away the jewel, that our love may return to him again.

Use one. It reproves such as have other gods, and so renounce the true God. (1) Such as set up idols. 'According to the number of thy cities are thy gods, O Judah.' Jer 2: 28. 'Their altars are as heaps in the furrows of the field.' Hos 12: 11. (2) Such as seek to familiar spirits. This is a sin condemned by the law of God. 'There shall not be found among you a consulted with familiar spirits.' Deut 18: 11. Ordinarily, if people have lost any of their goods, they send to wizards and soothsayers, to know how they may come by them again. What is this but to make a god of the devil, by consulting with him, and putting their trust in him? What! because you have lost your goods will you lose your souls too? 2 Kings 1: 6. Is it not because you think there is not a God in heaven, that you ask counsel of the devil? If any be guilty, be humbled.

Use two. It sounds a retreat in our ears. Let it call us off from idolising any creature, and lead us to renounce other gods, and cleave to the true God and his service. If we go away from God, we know not where to mend ourselves.

(1) It is honourable to serve the true God. Servire Deo est regnare [To serve God is to reign]. It is

more honour to serve God, than to have kings serve us. (2) Serving the true God is delightful. 'I will make them joyful in my house of prayer.' Isa 56: 7. God often displays the banner of his love in an ordinance, and pours the oil of gladness into the heart. All God's ways are pleasantness, his paths are strewed with roses. Prov 3: 17. (3) Serving the true God is beneficial. Men have great gain here, the hidden manna, inward peace, and a great reward to come. They that serve God shall have a kingdom when they die, and shall wear a crown made of the flowers of paradise. Luke 12: 32; 1 Pet 5: 4. To serve the true God is our true interest. God has twisted his glory and our salvation together. He bids us believe; and why? That we may be saved. Therefore, renouncing all others, let us cleave to the true God. (4) You have covenanted to serve the true JEHOVAH, renouncing all others. When one has entered into covenant with his master, and the indentures are drawn and sealed, he cannot go back, but must serve out his time. We have covenanted in baptism, to take the Lord for our God, renouncing all others; and renewed this covenant in the Lord's Supper, and shall we not keep our solemn vow and covenant? We cannot go away from God without the highest perjury. 'If any man draw back [as a soldier that steals away from his colours] my soul shall have no pleasure in him.' Heb 10: 38. 'I will pour vials of wrath on him, and make mine arrows drunk with blood.' (5) None ever had cause to repent of cleaving to God and his service. Some have repented that they had made a god of the world. Cardinal Wolsey said, 'Oh, if I had served my God as I have served my king, he would never have left me thus!' None ever complained of serving God: it was their comfort and their crown on their death-bed.

2.2 The Second Commandment

'Thou shalt not make unto thee any graven image, or any likeness of any thing that is in heaven above, or that is in the earth beneath, or that is in the water under the earth: thou shalt not bow down thyself to them, nor serve them: for I the Lord thy God am o jealous God, visiting the iniquity of the fathers upon the children unto the third and fourth generation of then that hate me; and shewing mercy unto thousands of them that love me and keep my commandments.' Exod 20: 4-6.

I. Thou shalt not make unto thee any graven image.

In the first commandment worshipping a false god is forbidden; in this, worshipping the true God in a false manner.

'Thou shalt not make unto thee any graven image.' This forbids not making an image for civil use. 'Whose is this image and superscription? They say unto him, It is Caesar's.' Matt 22: 20, 21. But the commandment forbids setting up an image for religious use or worship.

'Nor the likeness of any thing,' &c. All ideas, portraitures, shapes, images of God, whether by effigies or pictures, are here forbidden. 'Take heed lest ye corrupt yourselves, and make the similitude of any figure.' Deut 4: 15, 16. God is to be adored in the heart, not painted to the eye.

'Thou shalt not bow down to them.' The intent of making images and pictures is to worship them. No sooner was Nebuchadnezzar's golden image set up, but all the people fell down and worshipped it. Dan 3: 7. God forbids such prostrating ourselves before an idol. The thing prohibited in this commandment is image-worship. To set up an image to represent God, is debasing him. If any one should make images of snakes or spiders, saying he did it to represent his prince, would not the prince take it in disdain? What greater disparagement to the infinite God than to represent him by that which is unite; the living God, by that which is without life; and the Maker of all by a thing which is made?

[1] To make a true image of God is impossible. God is a spiritual essence and, being a Spirit, he is invisible. John 4: 24. 'Ye saw no manner of similitude on the day that the Lord spake with you out of the midst of the fire.' Deut 4: 15. How can any paint the Deity? Can they make an image of that which they never saw? Quod invisibile est, pingi non potest [There is no depicting the invisible]. Ambrose. 'Ye saw no similitude.' It is impossible to make a picture of the soul, or to paint the angels, because they are of a spiritual nature; much less can we paint God by an image, who is an infinite, untreated Spirit.

[2] To worship God by an image, is both absurd and unlawful.

(1) It is absurd and irrational; for, 'the workman is better than the work,' 'He who has builded the house has more honour than the house.' Heb 3: 3. If the workman be better than the work, and none bow to the workman, how absurd, then, is it to bow to the work of his hands! Is it not an absurd thing to bow down to the king's picture, when the king himself is present? It is more so to bow down to an image of God, when God himself is everywhere present.

(2) It is unlawful to worship God by an image; for it is against the homily of the church, which runs thus: 'The images of God, our Saviour, the Virgin Mary, are of all others the most dangerous; therefore the greatest care ought to be had that they stand not in temples and churches.' So that image-worship is contrary to our own homilies, and affronts the authority of the Church of England. Image-worship is expressly against the letter of Scripture. 'Ye shall make no graven image, neither shall ye set up any image of stone to bow down unto it.' Lev 26: 1. 'Neither shalt thou set up any image; which the Lord thy God hateth.' Deut 16: 22. 'Confounded be all they that serve graven images.' Psa 97: 7. Do we think to please God by doing that which is contrary to his mind, and that which he has expressly forbidden?

[3] Image worship is against the practice of the saints of old. Josiah, that renowned king, destroyed the groves and images. 2 Kings 23: 6, 24. Constantine abrogated the images set up in temples. The Christians destroyed images at Baste, Zurich, and Bohemia. When the Roman emperors would have thrust images upon them, they chose rather to die than deflower their

virgin profession by idolatry; they refused to admit any painter or carver into their society, because they would not have any carved state or image of God. When Seraphion bowed to an idol, the Christians excommunicated him, and delivered him up to Satan.

Use one. The Church of Rome is reproved and condemned, which, from the Alpha of its religion to the Omega, is wholly idolatrous. Romanists make images of God the Father, painting him in their church windows as an old man; and an image of Christ on the crucifix; and, because it is against the letter of this commandment, they sacrilegiously blot it out of their catechism, and divide the tenth commandment into two. Image worship must needs be very impious and blasphemous, because it is giving the religious worship to the creature which is due to God only. It is vain for Papists to say, they give God the worship of the heart, and the image only the worship of the body; for the worship of the body is due to God, as well as the worship of the heart; and to give an outward veneration to an image is to give the adoration to a creature which belongs to God only. 'My glory will I not give to another.' Isa 42: 8. The Papists say they do not worship the image, but only use it as a medium through which to worship God. Ne imagini quidem Christi in quantum est lignum sculptum, ulla debetur reverentia [Not even to a statue of Christ is any reverence owed, since it is only a piece of carved wood]. Aquinas.

(1) Where has God bidden them worship him by an effigy or image? 'Who has required this at your hands?' Isa 1: 12. The Papists cannot say so much as the devil, Scriptum est: It is written.

(2) The heathen may bring the same argument for their gross idolatry, as the Papists do for their image-worship. What heathen has been so simple as to think gold or silver, or the figure of an ox or elephant, was God? These were emblems and hieroglyphics only to represent him. They worshipped an invisible God by such visible things. To worship God by an image, God takes as done to the image itself.

But, say the Papists, images are laymen's books, and they are good to put them in mind of God. One of the Popish Councils affirmed, that we might learn more by an image than by long study of the Scriptures.

'What profiteth the graven image, the molten image, and a teacher of lies.' Hab 2: 18. Is an image a layman's book? Then see what lessons this book teaches. It teaches lies; it represents God in a visible shape, who is invisible. For Papists to say they make use of an image to put them in mind of God, is as if a woman should say she keeps company with another man to put her in mind of her husband.

But did not Moses make the image of a brazen serpent? Why, then, may not images be set tip?

That was done by God's special command. 'Make thee a brazen serpent.' Numb 21: 8. There was also a special use in it, both literal and spiritual. What! does the setting up of the image of the brazen serpent justify the setting up images in churches? What! because Moses made an image by God's appointment, may we set up an image of our own devising? Because Moses made an image to heal them that were stung, is it lawful to set up images in churches to sting them that are whole? Nay, that very brazen serpent which God himself commanded to be set up, when Israel looked upon it with too much reverence, and began to burn incense to it, Hezekiah defaced, and called it Nehushtan, mere brass; and God commended him for so doing. 2 Kings 18: 4.

But is not God represented as having hands, and eyes, and cars? Why nay we not, then, make an image to represent him, and help our devotion?

Though God is pleased to stoop to our weak capacities, and set himself out in Scripture by eyes, to signify his omniscience, and hands to signify his power, yet it is absurd, from such metaphors and figurative expressions, to bring an argument for images and pictures; for, by that rule, God may be pictured by the sun and the element of fire, and by a rock; for he is set forth by these metaphors in Scripture; and, sure, the Papists themselves would not like to have such images made of God.

If it be not lawful to make the image of God the Father, yet may we not make an image of Christ, who took upon him the nature of man?

No! Epiphanies, seeing an image of Christ hanging in a church, brake it in pieces. It is Christ's Godhead, united to his manhood, that makes him to be Christ; therefore to picture his manhood, when we cannot picture his Godhead, is a sin, because we make him to be but half Christ - we separate what God has joined, we leave out that which is the chief thing which makes him to be Christ.

But how shall we conceive of God aright, if we may not make any image or resemblance of him?

We must conceive of God spiritually. (1) In his attributes - his holiness, justice, goodness - which are the beams by which his divine nature shines forth. (2) We must conceive of him as he is in Christ. Christ is the 'Image of the invisible God' as in the wax we see the print of the seal. Col 1: 15. Set the eyes of your faith on Christ-God-man. 'He that has seen me, has seen the Father.' John 14: 9.

Use two. Take heed of the idolatry of image-worship. Our nature is prone to this sin as dry wood to take fire; and, indeed, what need of so many words in the commandment: 'Thou shalt not make any graven image, or the likeness of anything in heaven, earth, water,' sun, moon, stars, male, female, fish; 'Thou shalt not bow down to them.' I say, what need of so many words, but to show how subject we are to this sin of false worship? It concerns us, therefore, to resist this sin. Where the tide is apt to run with greater force, there we had need to make the banks higher and stronger. The plague of idolatry is very infectious. 'They were mingled among the heathen, and served their idols.' Psa 106: 35, 36. It is my advice to you, to avoid all occasions of this sin.

(1) Come not into the company of idolatrous Papists. Dare not to live under the same roof with them, or you run into the devil's mouth. John the divine would not be in the has where Cerinthus the heretic was.

(2) Go not into their chapels to see their crucifixes, or hear mass. As looking on a harlot draws to adultery, so looking on the popish gilded picture may draw to idolatry. Some go to see their idol-worship. A vagrant who has nothing to lose, cares not to go among thieves; so such as have no goodness in them, care not to what idolatrous places they come or to what temptations they expose themselves; but you who have a treasure of good principles about you, take heed the popish priests do not rob you of them, and defile you with their images.

(3) Dare not join in marriage with image-worshippers. Though Solomon was a man of wisdom, his idolatrous wives drew his heart away from God. The people of Israel entered into an oath and curse, that they would not give their daughters in marriage to idolaters. Neh 10: 30. For a Protestant and Papist to marry, is to be unequally yoked (2 Cor 6: 14); and there is more danger that the Papist will corrupt the Protestant, shall hope that the Protestant will convert the Papist. Mingle wine and vinegar, the vinegar will sooner sour the wine, than the wine will sweeten the vinegar.

(4) Avoid superstition, which is a bridge that leads over to Rome. Superstition is bringing any ceremony, fancy, or innovation into God's worship, which he never appointed. It is provoking God, because it reflects much upon his honour, as if he were not wise enough to appoint the manner of his own worship. He hates all strange fire to be offered in his temple. Lev 10: 1. A ceremony may in time lead to a crucifix. They who contend for the cross in baptism, why not have the oil, salt, and cream as well, the one being as ancient as the other? They who are for altar-worship, and will bow to the east, may in time bow to the Host. Take heed of all occasions of idolatry, for idolatry is devil-worship. Psalm 106: 37. If you search through the whole Bible, there is not one sin that God has more followed with plagues than idolatry. The Jews have a saying, that in every evil that befalls them, there is uncia aurei vituli, an ounce of the golden calf in it. Hell is a place for idolaters. 'For without are idolaters.' Rev 22: 15. Senesius calls the devil a rejoicer at idols, because the image-worshippers help to fill hell.

Use three. That you may be preserved from idolatry and image-worship. (1) Get good principles, that you may be able to oppose the gainsayer. Whence does the popish religion get ground? Not from the goodness of their cause, but from the ignorance of their people. (2) Get love to God. The wife that loves her husband is safe from the adulterer; and the soul that loves Christ is safe from the idolater. (3) Pray that God will keep you. Though it is true, there is nothing in an image to tempt (for if we pray to an image, it cannot hear, and if we pray to God by an image, he will not hear), yet we know not our own hearts, or how soon we may be drawn to vanity, if God leaves us. Therefore pray that you be not enticed by false worship, or receive the mark of the beast in your right hand or forehead. Pray, 'Hold thou me up, and I shall be safe.' Psa 119: 117.

Lord, let me neither mistake my way for want of light, nor leave the true way for want of courage. (4) Let us bless God who has given us the knowledge of his truth, that we have tasted the honey of his word, and our eyes are enlightened. Let us bless him that he has shown us the pattern of his house, the right mode of worship; that he has discovered to us the forgery and blasphemy of the Romish religion. Let us pray that God will preserve pure ordinances and powerful preaching among us. Idolatry came in at first by the want of good preaching. The people began to have golden images when they had wooden priests.

II. I the Lord thy God am a jealous God. The first reason why Israel must not worship graven images is, because the Lord is a jealous God. 'The Lord, whose name is Jealous, is a jealous God.' Exod 34: 14. Jealousy is taken, [1] In a good sense, as God is jealous for his people. [2] In a bad sense, as he is jealous of his people.

[1] In a good sense; as God is jealous for his people. 'Thus saith the Lord, I am jealous for Jerusalem, and for Zion, with a great jealousy.' Zech 1: 14. God has a dear affection for his people, they are his Hephzibah, or delight. Isa 62: 4. They are the apple of his eye, Zech 2: 8, to express how dear they are to him, and how tender he is of them, Nihil carius pupilla oculi [Nothing is dearer than the apple of the eye]. Drusius. They are his spouse, adorned with jewels of grace; they lie near his heart. He is jealous for his spouse, therefore he will be avenged on those who wrong her. 'The Lord shall stir up jealousy like a man of war; he shall roar, he shall prevail against his enemies.' Isa 42: 13. What is done to the saints, God takes as done to himself (2 Kings 19: 22); and the Lord will undo all that afflict Zion. 'I will undo all that afflict thee.' Zeph 3: 19.

[2] Jealousy is taken in a bad sense, in which God is jealous of his people. It is so taken in this commandment, 'I the Lord thy God am a jealous God.' I am jealous lest you should go after false gods, or worship the true God in a false manner; lest you defile your virgin-profession by images. God will have his spouse to keep close to him, and not go after other lovers. 'Thou shalt not be for another man' Hos 3: 3. He cannot bear a rival. Our conjugal love, a love joined with adoration and worship, must be given to God only.

Use one. Let us give God no just cause to be jealous. A good wife will be so discreet and chaste, as to give her husband no just occasion of jealousy. Let us avoid all sin, especially this of idolatry, or image-worship. It is heinous, after we have entered into a marriage covenant with God, to prostitute ourselves to an image. Idolatry is spiritual adultery, and God is a jealous God, he will avenge it. Image-worship makes God abhor a people. 'They moved him to jealousy with their graven images. When God heard this, he was wrath, and greatly abhorred Israel.' Psa 78: 58, 59. 'Jealousy is the rage of a man.' Prov 6: 34. Image-worship enrages God; it makes God divorce a people. 'Plead with your mother, plead; for she is not my wife.' Hos 2: 2. 'Jealousy is cruel as the grave.' Cant 8: 6. As the grave devours men's bodies, so God will devour image-worshippers.

Use two. If God be a jealous God, let it be remembered by those whose friends are popish idolaters, and who are hated by their friends, because they are of a different religion, and perhaps their maintenance cut off from them. Oh, remember, God is a jealous God; better move your parents to hatred, than move God to jealousy! Their anger cannot do you so much hurt as God's. If they will not provide for you, God will. 'When my father and my mother forsake me, then the Lord will take me up.' Psa 27: 10.

III. Visiting the iniquity of the fathers upon the children unto the third and fourth generation. Here is the second reason against image-worship. There is a twofold visiting. There is God's visiting in mercy. 'God will surely visit you:' that is, he will bring you into the land of Canaan, the type of heaven. Gen 50:25. Thus God has visited us with the sunbeams of his favour; he has made us swim in a sea of mercy. This is a happy visitation. There is God's visiting in anger. 'Shall I not visit for these things?' that is, God's visiting with the rod. Jer 5: 9. 'What will ye do in the day of visitation?' that is, in the day when God shall visit with his judgements. Isa 10: 3. Thus God's visiting is taken in this commandment, 'visiting iniquity,' that is, punishing iniquity. Observe here three things.

[1] That sin makes God visit. 'Visiting iniquity.' Sin is the cause why God visits with sickness, poverty, &c. 'If they keep not my commandments, then will I visit their transgressions with the rod.' Psa 89: 31, 32. Sin twists the cords which pinch us; it creates all our troubles, is the gall in our cup, and the gravel in our bread. Sin is the Trojan horse, the Phaeton that sets all on fire; it is the womb of our sorrows, and the grave of our comfort. God visits for sin.

[2] One special sin for which God's visits, is idolatry and image-worship. 'Visiting the iniquity of the fathers.' Most of his envenomed arrows have been shot among idolaters. 'Go now unto my place which was in Shiloh, where I set my name at the first, and see what I did to it.' Jer 7: 12. For Israel's idolatry he suffered their army to be routed, their priests slain, the ark taken captive, of the returns of which to Shiloh we never read any more. Jerusalem was the most famous metropolis of the world; there was the temple. 'Whither the tribes go up, the tribes of the Lord.' Psa 122: 4. But for the high places and images, that city was besieged and taken by the Chaldean forces. 2 Kings 25: 4. When images were set up in Constantinople, the chief seat of the Eastern empire, a city which in the eye of the world was impregnable, it was taken by the Turks, and many cruelly massacred. The Turks in their triumphs at that time reproached the idolatrous Christians, caused an image or crucifix to be carried through the streets in contempt, and threw dirt upon it, crying, 'This is the god of the Christians.' Here was God's visitation for their idolatry. God has set special marks of his wrath upon idolaters. At a place called Epoletium, there perished by an earthquake 350 persons, while they were offering sacrifice to idols. Idolatry brought misery upon the Eastern churches, and removed the golden candlesticks of Asia. For this iniquity God visits.

[3] Idolatrous persons are enemies not to their own souls only, but to their children. 'Visiting the

iniquity of the fathers upon their children.' As an idolatrous father entails his land of inheritance, so he entails God's anger and curse upon his children. A jealous husband, finding his wife has stained her fidelity, may justly cast her offend her children too, because they are none of his. If the father be a traitor to his prince, no wonder if all the children suffer. God may visit the iniquity of image-worshippers upon their children.

But is it not said, 'Every man shall die for his own sin; the son shall not bear the iniquity of the father?' 2 Chron 25: 4, Ezek 18: 20. How then does God say, he 'will visit the iniquity of the fathers upon the children?'

Though the son be not damned, yet he may be severely punished for his father's sin. 'God layeth up his iniquity for his children' (Job 21: 19); that is, God lays up the punishment of his iniquity for his children - the child smarts for the father's sin. Jeroboam thought to have established the kingdom by idolatrous worship, but it brought ruin upon him, and all his posterity. 1 Kings 14: 10. Ahab's idolatry wronged his posterity, which lost the kingdom, and were all beheaded. 'They took the king's sons, and slew seventy persons.' 2 Kings 10: 7. Here God visited the iniquity of the father upon the children. As a son catches an hereditary disease from his father, the stone or gout, so he catches misery from him: his father's sin ruins him.

Use one. How sad is it to be the child of an idolater! It had been sad to have been one of Gehazi's children, who had leprosy entailed upon them. 'The leprosy of Naaman shall cleave unto thee and unto thy seed for ever.' 2 Kings 5: 27. So it is sad to be a child of an idolater, or image-worshipper; for his seed are exposed to heavy judgements in this life. 'God visits the iniquity of the fathers upon their children.' Methinks I hear God speak, as in Isa 14: 21, 'Prepare slaughter for his children, for the iniquity of their fathers.'

Use two. What a privilege it is to be the children of good parents. The parents are in covenant with God, and God lays up mercy for their posterity. 'The just man walketh in his integrity, his children are blessed after him.' Prov 20: 7. A religious parent does not procure wrath, but helps to keep off wrath from his child; he seasons his child with religious principles, he prays down a blessing on it; he is a loadstone to draw his child to Christ by good counsel and example. Oh, what a privilege is it to be born of godly, religious parents! Augustine says that his mother Monica travailed with greater care and pains for his new birth, than for his natural. Wicked idolaters entail misery on their posterity; God 'visits the iniquity of the fathers upon their children;' but religious parents procure a blessing upon their children; God reserves mercy for their posterity.

IV. Of them that hate me. Another reason against image-worship is, that it is hating God. The Papists, who worship God by an image, hate God. Image-worship is a pretended love to God, but God interprets it as hating him. Quae diligit alienum odit sponsum, 'she that loves another man, hates her own husband.' An image-lover is a God hater. Idolaters are said to go a whoring from God. Exod 34: 15. How can they love God? I shall show that image-worshippers hate God, whatever love they pretend.

[1] They who go contrary to his express will hate him. He says, you shall not set up any statue, image, nor picture, to represent me; these things I hate. 'Neither shalt thou set up any image; which the Lord thy God hateth.' Deut 16: 22. Yet the idolater sets up images, and worships them. This God looks upon as hating him. How does the child love his father that does all it can to cross him?

[2] They who turned Jephthah out of doors hated him, therefore they laboured to shut him out of his father's house. Judges 11: 7. The idolater shuts the truth out of doors; he blots out the second commandment; he makes an image of the invisible God; he brings a lie into God's worship; which are clear proofs that he hates God.

[3] Though idolaters love the false image of God in a picture, they hate his true image in a believer. They pretend to honour Christ in a crucifix, and yet persecute him in his members. Such hate God.

Use one. This confutes those who plead for image-worshippers. They are very devout people; they adore images; they set up the crucifix; kiss it; light candles to it; therefore they love God. Nay, but who shall be judge of their love? God says they hate him, and give religious adoration to a creature. They hate God, and God hates them; and they shall never live with God whom he hates; he will never lay such vipers in his bosom. Heaven is kept as paradise, with a flaming sword, that they shall not enter in. He 'repayeth them that hate him to their face.' Deut. 7: 10. He will shoot all his deadly arrows among idolaters. All the plagues and curses in the book of God shall befall the idolater. The Lord repays him that hates him to his face.

Use two. Let it exhort all to flee from Romish idolatry. Let us not be among God-haters. 'Little children, keep yourselves from idols.' 1 John 5: 21. As you would keep your bodies from adultery, keep your souls from idolatry. Take heed of images, they are images of jealousy to provoke God to anger; they are damnable. You may perish by false devotions as much as by real scandal; by image-worship, as by drunkenness and whoredom. A man may die by poison as much as a pistol. We may go to hell by drinking poison in the Romish cup of fornication, as much as by being pistoled with gross and scandalous sins. To conclude, 'God is a jealous God,' who will admit of no co-rival; He will 'visit the iniquities of the fathers upon their children;' he will entail a plague upon the posterity of idolaters. He interprets idolaters to be such as hate him. He that is an image-lover is a God-hater. Therefore keep yourself pure from Romish idolatry; if you love your souls, keep yourselves from idols.

V. Showing mercy unto thousands.

Another argument against image-worship, is that God is merciful to those who do not provoke him with their images, and will entail mercy upon their posterity. 'Shewing mercy unto thousands.'

The golden sceptre of God's mercy is here displayed, 'shewing mercy to thousands.' The heathen thought they praised Jupiter enough when they called him good and great. Both excellencies of majesty and mercy meet in God. Mercy is an innate propensity in God to do good to distressed sinners. God showing mercy, makes his Godhead appear full of glory. When Moses said to God, 'I beseech thee, show me thy glory;' 'I will,' said God, 'show mercy.' Exod 33: 19. His mercy is his glory. Mercy is the name by which he will be known. 'The Lord passed by, and proclaimed, The Lord, the Lord God, merciful and gracious.' Exod 34: 6. Mercy proceeds primarily, and originally from God. He is called the 'Father of mercies' (2 Cor 1: 3), because he begets all the mercies which are in the creature. Our mercies compared with his are scarcely so much as a drop to the ocean.

What are the properties of God's mercy?

(1) It is free and spontaneous. To set up merit is to destroy mercy. Nothing can deserve mercy or force it; we cannot deserve it nor force it, because of our enmity. We may force God to punish us, but not to love us. 'I will love them freely.' Hos 14: 4. Every link in the golden chain of salvation is wrought and interwoven with free grace. Election is free. 'He has chosen us in him according to the good pleasure of his will.' Eph 1: 4. Justification is free. 'Being justified freely by his grace.' Rom 3: 24. Say not I am unworthy; for mercy is free. If God should show mercy only to such as deserve it, he must show mercy to none.

(2) The mercy which God shows is powerful. How powerful is that mercy which softens a heart of stone! Mercy changed Mary Magdalen's heart, out of whom seven devils were cast: she who was an inflexible adamant was made a weeping penitent. God's mercy works sweetly, yet irresistibly; it allures, yet conquers. The law may terrify, but mercy mollifies. Of what sovereign power and efficacy is that mercy which subdues the pride and enmity of the heart, and beats off those chains of sin in which the soul is held.

(3) The mercy which God shows is superabundant. 'Abundant in goodness and truth, keeping mercy for thousands.' Exod 34: 6. God visits iniquity 'to the third and fourth generation' only, but he shows mercy to a thousand generations. Exod 20: 5, 6. The Lord has treasures of mercy in store, and therefore is said to be 'plenteous in mercy' (Psa 86: 5), and 'rich in mercy' (Eph 2: 4). The vial of God's wrath drops only, but the fountain of his mercy runs. The sun is not so full of light as God is of love.

God has mercy of all dimensions. He has depth of mercy, it reaches as low as sinners; and height of mercy, it reaches above the clouds.

God has mercies for all seasons; mercies for the night, he gives sleep; nay, sometimes he gives a song in the night. Psa 42: 8. He has also mercies for the morning. His compassions 'are new every morning.' Lam 3: 23.

God has mercies for all sorts. Mercies for the poor: 'He raiseth up the poor out of the dust.' 1 Sam 2: 8. Mercies for the prisoner: he 'despiseth not his prisoners.' Psa 69: 33. Mercies for the dejected: 'In a little wrath I hid my face from thee but with everlasting kindness will I have mercy on thee.' Isa 54: 8. He has old mercies: 'Thy mercies have been ever of old.' Psa 25: 6. New mercies: 'He has put a new song in my mouth.' Psa 40: 3. Every time we draw our breath we suck in mercy. God has mercies under heaven, and those we taste; and mercies in heaven, and those we hope for. Thus his mercies are superabundant.

(4) The mercy of God is abiding. 'The mercy of the Lord is from everlasting to everlasting.' Psa 103: 17. God's anger to his children lasts but a while (Psa 103: 9), but his mercy lasts for ever. His mercy is not like the widow's oil, which ran awhile, and then ceased (2 Kings 4: 6), but overflowing and everflowing. As his mercy is without bounds, so is it without end. 'His mercy endureth for ever.' Psa 136. God never cuts off the entail of mercy from the elect.

In how many ways is God said to show mercy?

(1) We are all living monuments of his mercy. He shows mercy to us in daily supplying us. He supplies us with health. Health is the sauce which makes life sweeter. How would they prize this mercy who are chained to a sick-bed! God supplies us with provisions. 'God which fed me all my life long.' Gen 48: 15. Mercy spreads our tables, and carves for us every bit of bread we eat; we never drink but in the golden cup of mercy.

(2) God shows mercy in lengthening out our gospel-liberties. 1 Cor 16: 9. There are many adversaries; many would stop the waters of the sanctuary that that they should not run. We enjoy the sweet seasons of grace, we hear joyful sounds, we see the goings of God in his sanctuary, we enjoy Sabbath after Sabbath; the manna of the word falls about our tents, when in other parts of the land there is no manna. God shows mercy to us in continuing our forfeited privileges.

(3) He shows mercy in preventing many evils from invading us. 'Thou, O Lord, art a shield for me.' Psa 3: 3. God has restrained the wrath of men, and been a screen between us and danger; when the destroying angel has been abroad, and shed his deadly arrow of pestilence, he has kept off the arrow that it has not come near us.

(4) He shows mercy in delivering us. 'And I was delivered out of the mouth of the lion' (viz., Nero). 2 Tim 4: 17. He has restored us from the grave. May we not write the writing of Hezekiah, 'when he had been sick, and was recovered of his sickness?' Isa 38: 9. When we thought the sun of our life was setting God has made it return to its former brightness.

(5) He shows mercy in restraining us from sin. Lusts within are worse than lions without. The greatest sign of God's anger is to give men up to their sins. 'So I gave them up to their own

hearts' lust.' Psa 81: 12. While they sin themselves to hell, God has laid the bridle of restraining grace upon us. As he said to Abimelech, 'I withheld thee from sinning against me.' Gen 20: 6. So he has withheld us from those sins which might have made us a prey to Satan, and a terror to ourselves.

(6) God shows mercy in guiding and directing us. Is it not a mercy for one that is out of the way to have a guide? [1] There is a providential guidance. God guides our affairs for us; chalks out the way he would have us to walk in. He resolves our doubts, unties our knots, and appoints the bounds of our habitation. Acts 17: 26. [2] A spiritual guidance. 'Thou shalt guide me with thy counsel.' Psa 73: 24. As Israel had a pillar of fire to go before them, so God guides us with the oracles of his word, and the conduct of his Spirit. He guides our heads to keep us from error; and he guides our feet to keep us from scandal. Oh, what mercy is it to have God to be our guide and pilot! 'For thy name's sake, lead me and guide me.' Psa 31: 3.

(7) God shows mercy in correcting us. He is angry in love; he smites that he may save. His rod is not a rod of iron to break us, but a fatherly rod to humble us. 'He, for our profit, that we might be partakers of his holiness.' Heb 12: 10. Either he will mortify some corruption, or exercise some grace. Is there not mercy in this? Every cross, to a child of God, is like Paul's cross wind, which, though it broke the ship, it brought Paul to shore upon the broken pieces. Acts 27: 44.

(8) God shows mercy in pardoning us, 'Who is a God like unto thee, that pardoneth iniquity?' Mic 7: 18. It is mercy to feed us, rich mercy to pardon us. This mercy is spun out of the bowels of the free grace, and is enough to make a sick man well. 'The inhabitant shall not say, I am sick; the people that dwell therein shall be forgiven their iniquity.' Isa 33: 24. Pardon of sin is a mercy of the first magnitude. God seals the sinner's pardon with a kiss. This made David put on his best clothes, and anoint himself. His child was newly dead, and God had told him the sword should not depart from his house, yet he anoints himself. The reason was that God had sent him pardon by the prophet Nathan. 'The Lord has put away thy sin.' 2 Sam 12: 13. Pardon is the only fit remedy for a troubled conscience. What can give ease to a wounded spirit but pardoning mercy? Offer him the honours and pleasure of the world. It is as if flowers and music were brought to one that is condemned.

How may I know that my sins are pardoned?

Where God removes the guilt, he breaks the power of sin. 'He will have compassion: he will subdue our iniquities.' Mic 7: 19. With pardoning love God gives subduing grace.

(9) God shows his mercy in sanctifying us. 'I am the Lord which sanctify you.' Lev 20: 8. This is the partaking of the divine nature. 2 Pet 1: 4. God's Spirit is a spirit of consecration; though it sanctify us but in part, yet it is in every part. 1 Thess 5: 23. It is such a mercy that God cannot give it in anger. If we are sanctified, we are elected. 'God has chosen you to salvation through sanctification.' 2 Thess 2: 13. This prepares for happiness, as the seed prepares for harvest. When

the virgins had been anointed and perfumed, they were to stand before the king (Esth 2: 12); SO, when we have had the anointing of God, we shall stand before the King of heaven.

(10) God shows mercy in hearing our prayers. 'Have mercy upon me, and hear my prayer.' Psa 4: 1. Is it not a favour, when a man puts up a petition to the king, to have it granted? So when we pray for pardon, adoption, and the sense of God's love, it is a signal mercy to have a gracious answer. God may delay an answer, and yet not deny. You do not throw a musician money at once, because you love to hear his music. God loves the music of prayer, but does not always let us hear from him at once; but in due season gives an answer of peace. 'Blessed be God, which has not turned away my prayer, nor his mercy from me.' Psa 66: 20. If God does not turn away our prayer, he does not turn away his mercy.

(11) God shows mercy in saving us. 'According to his mercy he saved us.' Titus 3: 5. This is the top-stone of mercy, and it is laid in heaven. Here mercy displays itself in all its orient colours. Mercy is mercy indeed, when God perfectly refines us from all the lees and dregs of corruption; when our bodies are made like Christ's glorious body, and our souls like the angels. Saving mercy is crowning mercy. It is not merely to be freed from hell, but enthroned in a kingdom. In this life we desire God, rather than enjoy him; but what rich mercy will it be to be fully possessed of him, to see his smiling face, and to lay us in his bosom! This will fill us with 'joy unspeakable and full of glory.' 1 Peter 1: 8. 'I shall be satisfied, when I awake, with thy likeness.' Psa 17: 15.

Use one. Let us not despair. What an encouragement we have here to serve God. He shows mercy to thousands. Who would not be willing to serve a prince who is given to mercy and clemency? God is represented with a rainbow round about him, as an emblem of his mercy. Rev 4: 3. Acts of severity are forced from God; judgement is his strange work. Isa 28: 21. The disciples, who are not said to wonder at the other miracles of Christ, did wonder when the fig-tree was cursed and withered, because it was not his manner to put forth acts of severity. God is said to delight in mercy. Mic 7: 18. Justice is God's left hand: mercy is his right hand. He uses his right hand most; he is more used to mercy than to justice. Pronior est Deus ad parcendum quam ad puniendum [God is more inclined to mercy than to punishment]. God is said to be slow to anger (Psa 103: 8), but ready to forgive. Psa 86: 5. This may encourage us to serve him. What argument will prevail, if mercy will not? Were God all justice, it might frighten us from him, but his mercy is a loadstone to draw us to him.

Use two. Hope in God's mercies. 'The Lord taketh pleasure in them that fear him, in those that hope in his mercy.' Psa 147: 11. He counts it his glory to scatter pardons among men.

But I have been a great sinner and sure there is no mercy for me!

Not if thou goest on in sin, and art so resolved; but, if thou wilt break off thy sins, the golden sceptre of mercy shall be held forth to thee. 'Let the wicked forsake his way, and let him return unto the Lord, and he will have mercy upon him.' Isa 55: 7. Christ's blood is 'a fountain opened for sin and for uncleanness.' Zech 13: 1. Mercy more overflows in God, than sin in us. His mercy can drown great sins, as the sea covers great rocks. Some of the Jews who had their hands imbrued in Christ's blood, were saved by that blood. God loves to magnify his goodness, to display the trophies of free grace, and to set up his mercy in spite of sin. Therefore, hope in his mercy.

Use three. Labour to know that God's mercy is for you. He is 'the God of my mercy.' Psa. 59: 17. A man who was being drowned, seeing a rainbow, said, 'What am I the better, though God will not drown the world, if I am drowned?' So, what are we the better, though God is merciful, if we perish? Let us labour to know God's special mercy is for us.

How shall we know it belongs to us?

(1) If we put a high value and estimate upon it. He will not throw away his mercy on them that slight it. We prize health, but we prize adopting mercy more. This is the diamond ring; it outshines all other comforts.

(2) If we fear God, if we have a reverend awe upon us, if we tremble at sin, and flee from it, as Moses did from his rod turned into a serpent. 'His mercy is on them that fear him.' Luke 1: 50.

(3) If we take sanctuary in God's mercy, we trust in it as a man saved by catching hold of a cable. God's mercy to us is a cable let down from heaven. By taking fast hold of this by faith, we are saved. 'I trust in the mercy of God for ever.' Psa 52: 8. As a man trusts his life and goods in a garrison, so we trust our souls in God's mercy.

How shall we get a share in God's special mercy?

(1) If we would have mercy, it must be through Christ. Out of Christ no mercy is to be had. We read in the old law, that none might come unto the holy of holies, where the mercy-seat stood, but the high-priest: to signify that we have nothing to do with mercy but through Christ our High-priest; that the high-priest might not come near the mercy-seat without blood, to show that we have no right to mercy, but through the expiatory sacrifice of Christ's blood, Lev 16: 14; that the high-priest might not, upon pain of death, come near the mercy-seat without incense, Lev 16: 13, to show that there is no mercy from God without the incense of Christ's intercession. If we would have mercy, we must get a part in Christ. Mercy swims to us through Christ's blood.

(2) If we would have mercy, we must pray for it. 'Show us thy mercy, O Lord, and grant us thy salvation.' Psa 85: 7. 'Turn thee unto me, and have mercy upon me.' Psa 25: 16. Lord, put me not off with common mercy; give me not only mercy to feed and clothe me, but mercy to pardon me; not only sparing mercy, but saving mercy. Lord, give me the cream of thy mercies; let me have mercy and loving kindness. 'Who crowneth thee with loving kindness and tender mercies.' Psa

103: 4. Be earnest suitors for mercy; let your wants quicken your importunity. We pray most fervently when we pray most feelingly.

VI. Of them that love me.

God's mercy is for them that love him. Love is a grace that shines and sparkles in his eye, as the precious stone upon Aaron's breastplate. Love is a holy expansion or enlargement of soul, by which it is carried with delight after God, as the chief good. Aquinas defines love - Complacentia amantis in amato; a complacent delight in God, as our treasure. Love is the soul of religion; it is a momentous grace. If we had knowledge as the angels, or faith of miracles, yet without love it would profit nothing. 1 Cor 13: 2. Love is 'the first and great commandment.' Matt. 22: 38. It is so, because, if it be wanting, there can be no religion in the heart; there can be no faith, for faith works by love. Gal 5: 6. All else is but pageantry, or a devout compliment. It meliorates and sweetens all the duties of religion, it makes them savoury meat, without which God cares not to taste them. It is the first and great commandment, in respect of the excellence of this grace. Love is the queen of graces; it outshines all others, as the sun the lesser planets. In some respects it is more excellent than faith; though in one sense faith is more excellent, virtute unionis, as it unites us to Christ. It puts upon us the embroidered robe of Christ's righteousness, which is brighter than any the angels wear. In another sense it is more excellent, respectu durationis, in respect of the continuance of it: it is the most durable grace; as faith and hope will shortly cease, but love will remain. When all other graces, like Rachel, shall die in travail, love shall revive. The other graces are in the nature of a lease, for the term of life only; but love is a freehold that continues for ever. Thus love carries away the garland from all other graces, it is the most long-lived grace, it is a bud of eternity. This grace alone will accompany us in heaven.

How must our love to God be characterised?

(1) Love to God must be pure and genuine. He must be loved chiefly for himself; which the schoolmen call amor amicitiae. We must love God, not only for his benefits, but for those intrinsic excellencies with which he is crowned. We must love God not only for the good which flows from him, but for the good which is in him. True love is not mercenary, he who is deeply in love with God, needs not be hired with rewards, he cannot but love God for the beauty of his holiness; though it is not unlawful to look for benefits. Moses had an eye to the recompense of reward (Heb 11: 26); but we must not love God for his benefits only, for then it is not love of God, but self-love.

(2) Love to God must be with all the heart. 'Thou shalt love the Lord thy God with all thy heart.' Mark 12: 30. We must not love God a little, give him a drop or two of our love; but the main stream must flow to him. The mind must think of God, the will choose him, the affections pant after him. The true mother would not have the child divided, nor will God have the heart divided. We must love him with our whole heart. Though we may love the creature, yet it must be a subordinate love. Love to God must be highest, as oil swims above the water.

(3) Love to God must be flaming. To love coldly is the same as not to love. The spouse is said to be amore perculsa, 'sick of love.' Cant 2: 5. The seraphim are so called from their burning love. Love turns saints into seraphim; it makes them burn in holy love to God. Many waters cannot quench this love.

How may we know whether we love God?

(1) He who loves God desires his presence. Lovers cannot be long asunder, they soon have their fainting fits, for want of a sight of the object of their love. A soul deeply in love with God desires the enjoyment of him in his ordinances, in word, prayer, and sacraments. David was ready to faint away and die when he had not a sight of God. 'My soul fainteth for God.' Psa 84: 2. Such as care not for ordinances, but say, When will the Sabbath be over? plainly discover want of love to God.

(2) He who loves God, does not love sin. 'Ye that love the Lord, hate evil.' Psa 97: 10. The love of God, and the love of sin, can no more mix together than iron and clay. Every sin loved, strikes at the being of God; but he who loves God, has an antipathy against sin. He who would part two lovers is a hateful person. God and the believing soul are two lovers; sin parts between them, therefore the soul is implacably set against it. By this try your love to God. How could Delilah say she loved Samson, when she entertained correspondence with the Philistine, who were his mortal enemies? How can he say he loves God who loves sin, which is God's enemy?

(3) He who loves God is not much in love with anything else. His love is very cool to worldly things. His love to God moves swiftly, as the sun in the firmament; to the world it moves slowly, as the sun on the dial. The love of the world eats out the heart of religion; it chokes good affections, as earth puts out the fire. The world was a dead thing to Paul. 'The world is crucified unto me and I to the world.' Gal 6: 14. In Paul we may see both the picture and pattern of a mortified man. He that loves God, uses the world but chooses God. The world is his pension, but God is his portion. Psa 119: 57. The world engages him, but God delights and satisfies him. He says as David, 'God my exceeding joy,' the gladness or cream of my joy. Psa 43: 4.

(4) He who loves God cannot live without him. Things we love we cannot be without. A man can do without music or flowers, but not food; so a soul deeply in love with God looks upon himself as undone without him. 'Hide not thy face from me, lest I be like them that go down into the pit.' Psa 143: 7. He says as Job, 'I went mourning without the sun;' chap. 30: 28. I have starlight, I want the Sun of Righteousness; I enjoy not the sweet presence of my God. Is God our chief good, and we cannot live without him? Alas! how do they show they have no love to God who can do well enough without him! Let them have but corn and oil, and you shall never hear them complain of the want of God.

(5) He who loves God will be at any pains to get him. What pains the merchant takes, what hazards he runs, to have a rich return from the Indies! Extremos currit mercator ad Indos [The

merchant races to the farthest Indies]. Jacob loved Rachel, and he could endure the heat by day, and the frost by night, that he might enjoy her. A soul that loves God will take any pains for the fruition of him. 'My soul followeth hard after thee.' Psa 63: 8. Love is pondus animae [the pendulum of the soul]. Augustine. It is as the weight which sets the clock going. It is much in prayer, weeping, fasting; it strives as in agony, that he may obtain him whom his soul loves. Plutarch reports of the Gauls, an ancient people of France, that after they had tasted the sweet wine of Italy, they never rested till they had arrived at that country. He who is in love with God, never rests till he has a part in him. 'I will seek him whom my soul loveth.' Cant 3: 2. How can they say they love God, who are not industrious in the use of means to obtain him? 'A slothful man hideth his hand in his bosom.' Prov 19: 24. He is not in agony, but lethargy. If Christ and salvation would drop as a ripe fig into his mouth, he would be content to have them; but he is loath to put himself to too much trouble. Does he love his friend, who will not undertake a journey to see him?

(6) He who loves God, prefers him before estate and life. [1] Before estate. 'For whom I have suffered the loss of all things.' Phil 3: 8. Who that loves a rich jewel would not part with a flower for it? Galeacius, marquis of Vico, parted with a fair estate to enjoy God in his pure ordinances. When a Jesuit persuaded him to return to his popish religion in Italy, promising him a large sum of money, he said, 'Let their money perish with them who esteem all the gold in the world worth one day's communion with Jesus Christ and his Holy Spirit.' [2] Before life. 'They loved not their lives unto the death.' Rev 12: 2: Love to God carries the soul above the love of life and the fear of death.

(7) He who loves God loves his favourites, the saints. 1 John 5: 1. Idem est motus animi in imaginem et rem [The mind reacts to the likeness of an object just as it does to the object itself]. To love a man for his grace, and the more we see of God in him, the more we love him, is an infallible sign of love to God. The wicked pretend to love God, but hate and persecute his image. Does he love his prince who abuses his statue, or tears his picture? They seem indeed to show great reverence to saints departed; they have great reverence for St. Paul, and St. Stephen, and St. Luke; they canonise dead saints, but persecute living saints; and do they love God? Can it be imagined that he loves God who hates his children because they are like him? If Christ were alive again, he would not escape a second persecution.

(8) If we love God we cannot but be fearful of dishonouring him, as the more a child loves his father the more he is afraid to displease him, and we weep and mourn when we have offended him. 'Peter went out and wept bitterly.' Matt 26: 75. Peter might well think that Christ dearly loved him when he took him up to the mount where he was transfigured, and showed him the glory of heaven in a vision. That he should deny Christ after he had received such signal tokens of his love, broke his heart with grief 'He wept bitterly.' Are our eyes dropping tears of grief for sin against God? It is a blessed evidence of our love to God; and such shall find mercy. 'He shows mercy to thousands of them that love him.

Use. Let us be lovers of God. We love our food, and shall we not love him that gives it? All the joy we hope for in heaven is in God; and shall not he who shall be our joy then, be our love now? It is a saying of Augustine, *Annon poena satis magna est non amare te?* 'Is it not punishment enough, Lord, not to love thee?' And again, *Animam meam in odio haberem.* 'I would hate my own soul if I did not find it loving God.'

What are the incentives to provoke and inflame our love to God?

(1) God's benefits bestowed on us. If a prince bestows continual favours on a subject, and that subject has any ingenuity, he cannot but love his prince. God is constantly heaping benefits upon us, 'filling our hearts with food and gladness.' Acts 14: 17. As streams of water out of the rock followed Israel whithersoever they went, so God's blessings follow us every day. We swim in a sea of mercy. That heart is hard that is not prevailed with by all God's blessings to love him. *Magnes amoris amor* [Love attracts love]. Kindness works even on a brute: the ox knows his owner.

(2) Love to God would make duties of religion facile and pleasant. I confess that to him who has no love to God, religion must needs be a burden; and I wonder not to hear him say, 'What a weariness is it to serve the Lord!' It is like rowing against the tide. But love oils the wheels, it makes duty a pleasure. Why are the angels so swift and winged in God's service, but because they love him? Jacob thought seven years but little for the love he bare to Rachel. Love is never weary. He who loves money is not weary of telling it: and he who loves God is not weary of serving him.

(3) It is advantageous. There is nothing lost by love to God. 'Eye has not seen, &c., the things which God has prepared for them that love him.' 1 Cor 2: 9. Such glorious rewards are laid up for them that love God, that as Augustine says, 'they not only transcend our reason, but faith itself is not able to comprehend them.' A crown is the highest ensign of worldly glory; but God has promised a 'crown of life to them that love him,' and a never-fading crown. James 1: 12. 1 Pet 5: 4.

(4) By loving God we know that he loves us. 'We love him because he first loved us.' 1 John 5: 19. If ice melts, it is because the sun has shone upon it; so if the frozen heart melts in love, it is because the Sun of Righteousness has shone upon it.

What means should be used to excite our love to God?

(1) Labour to know God aright. The schoolmen say truly, *Bonum non amatur quod non cognoscitur;* 'we cannot love that which we do not know.' God is the most eligible good; all excellencies which lie scattered in the creature are united in him; he is *Optimus maximus.* Wisdom, beauty, riches, love, all concentrate in him. How fair was that tulip which had the colours of all tulips in it! All perfections and sweetnesses are eminently in God. Did we know

God more, and by the eye of faith see his orient beauty, our hearts would be fired with love to him.

(2) Make the Scriptures familiar to you. Augustine says that before his conversion he took no pleasure in Scripture, but afterwards it was his chief delight. The book of God discovers God to us, in his holiness, wisdom, veracity, and truth; it represents him as rich in mercy, and encircled with promises. Augustine calls the Scripture a golden epistle, or love-letter, sent from God to us. By reading this love-letter we become more enamoured with God; as by reading lascivious books, comedies, romances, &c., lust is excited.

(3) Meditate much upon God, and this will promote love to him. 'While I was musing, the fire burned.' Psa 39: 3. Meditation is as bellows to the affections. Meditate on God's love in the gift of Christ. 'God so loved the world that he gave his only begotten Son,' &c. John 3: 16. That God should give Christ to us, and not to angels that fell, that the Sun of Righteousness should shine in our horizon, that he is revealed to us, and not to others; what wonderful love is this! 'Can one go upon hot coals, and his feet not be burned?' Prov 6: 28. Who can meditate on God's love, who can tread on these hot coals, and his heart not burn in love? Beg a heart to love God. The affection of love is natural, but not the grace of love. Gal 5: 22. This fire of love is kindled from heaven; beg that it may burn upon the altar of your heart. Surely the request is pleasing to God, and he will not deny such a prayer as 'Lord, give me a heart to love thee.'

VII. And keep my commandments.

Love and obedience, like two sisters, must go hand and hand. 'If ye love me, keep my commandments.' John 14: 15. Probatio delectionis est exhibitio operis [We show our love by performing the work]. The son that loves his father will obey him. Obedience pleases God. 'To obey is better than sacrifice.' 1 Sam 15: 22. In sacrifice, a dead beast only is offered; in obedience, a living soul; in sacrifice, only a part of the fruit is offered; in obedience, fruit and tree and all; man offers himself up to God. 'Keep my commandments.' It is not said, God shows mercy to thousands that know his commandments, but that keep them. Knowing his commandments, without keeping them, does not entitle any to mercy. The commandment is not only a rule of knowledge, but of duty. God gives us his commandments, not only as a landscape to look upon, but as his will and testament, which we are to perform. A good Christian, like the sun, not only sends forth light, but makes a circuit round the world. He has not only the light of knowledge; but moves in a sphere of obedience.

[1] We should keep the commandments from faith. Our obedience ought, profluere a fide 'to spring from faith.' It is called, therefore, 'the obedience of faith.' Rom 16: 26. Abel, by faith, offered up a better sacrifice than Cain. Heb 11: 4. Faith is a vital principle, without which all our services are opera mortua, dead works. Heb 6: 1. It meliorates and sweetens obedience, and makes it come off with a better relish.

But why must faith be mixed with obedience to the commandments?

Because faith eyes Christ in every duty, in whom both the person and offering are accepted. The high-priest under the law laid his hand upon the head of the slain beast, which pointed to the Messiah. Exod 29: 10. So faith in every duty lays its hand upon the head of Christ. His blood expiates their guilt, and the sweet odour of his intercession perfumes our works of obedience. 'He has made us accepted in the beloved.' Eph 1: 6.

[2] Keeping the commandments must be uniform. We must make conscience of one commandment as well as of another. 'Then shall I not be ashamed, when I have respect unto all thy commandments.' Psa 119: 6. Every commandment has jus divinum, the same stamp of divine authority upon it; and if I obey one precept because God commands, by the same reason I must obey all. Some obey the commands of the first table, but are careless of the duties of the second: some of the second and not of the first. Physicians have a rule that when the body sweats in one part, and is cold in another, it is a sign of a distemper; so when men seem zealous in some duties of religion, but are cold and frozen in others, it is a sign of hypocrisy. We must have respect to all God's commandments.

But who can keep all his commandments?

There is a fulfilling God's commands, and a keeping of them. Though we cannot fulfil all, yet we may be said to keep them in an evangelical sense. We may facere, though not perficere [build, though not complete]. We keep the commandments evangelically: (1) When we make conscience of every command, when, though we come short in every duty, we dare not neglect any. (2) When our desire is to keep every commandment. 'O that my ways were directed to keep thy statutes!' Psa 119: 5. What we want in strength we make up in will. (3) When we grieve that we can do no better; weep when we fail; prefer bills of complaint against ourselves; and judge ourselves for our failings. Rom 7: 24. (4) When we endeavour to obey every commandment, elicere conatum. 'I press toward the mark.' Phil 3: 14. We strive as in agony; and, if it lay in our power, we would fully comport with every commandment. (5) When, falling short, and unable to come up to the full latitude of the law, we look to Christ's blood to sprinkle our imperfect obedience, and, with the grains of his merits cast into the scales, to make it pass current. This, in an evangelical sense, is to keep all the commandments; and though it be not to satisfaction, yet it is to acceptation.

[3] Keeping God's commandments must be voluntary. 'If ye be willing and obedient.' Isa 1: 19. God required a free-will offering. Deut 16: 10. David will run the way of God's commandments, that is freely and cheerfully. Psa 119: 32. Lawyers have a rule that adverbs are better than adjectives; that it is not the bonum, but the bene; not the doing much, but the doing well. A musician is not commended for playing long, but for playing well. Obeying God willingly is accepted. Virtus nolentium nulla est [Righteous deeds done unwillingly are worthless]. The Lord hates that which is forced; which is paying a tax rather than an offering. Cain served God

grudgingly; he brought his sacrifice, not his heart. To obey God's commandments unwillingly, is like the devils who came out of the men possessed, at Christ's command, but with reluctance, and against their will. Matt 8: 29. Obedientia praest and adest non timore poenae, sed amore Dei [Obedience is the chief thing, and this not through fear of punishment, but for love of God]. God duties must not be pressed nor beaten out of us, as the waters came from the rock, when Moses smote it with his rod, but must drop freely from us as myrrh from the tree, or honey from the comb. If a willing mind be wanting, the flower is wanting to perfume our obedience, and to make it a sweet-smelling savour to God.

That we may keep God's commandments willingly, let these things be well weighed: (1) Our willingness is more esteemed than our service. David counsels Solomon not only to serve God, but with a willing mind. 1 Chron 28: 9. The will makes sin to be worse, and duty to be better. To obey willingly shows we do it with love; and this crowns all our services.

(2) There is that in the law-giver which may make us willing to obey the commandments, which is God's indulgence to us. [1] God does not require the summum jus as absolutely necessary to salvation; he expects not perfect obedience, he requires sincerity only. Do but act from a principle of love, and aim at honouring God in your obedience, and it is accepted. [2] In the gospel a surety is admitted. The law would not favour us so far; but now God so indulges us, that what we cannot do of ourselves we may do by proxy. Jesus Christ is 'a Surety of a better testament.' Heb 7: 22. We fall short in everything, but God looks upon us in our Surety; and Christ having fulfilled all righteousness, it is as if we had fulfilled the law in our own persons. [3] God gives strength to do what he requires. The law called for obedience, but though it required brick, it gave no straw; but in the gospel, God, with his commands, gives power. 'Make ye a new heart.' Ezek 18: 31. Alas! it is above our strength, we may as well make a new world. 'A new heart also will I give you.' Ezek 36: 26. God commands us to cleanse ourselves. 'Wash you, make you clean.' Isa 1: 16. But 'who can bring a clean thing out of an unclean?' Job 14: 4. Therefore the precept is turned into a promise. 'From all your filthiness will I cleanse you.' Ezek 36: 25. When the child cannot go, the nurse takes it by the hand. 'I taught Ephraim also to go, taking them by their arms.' Hos 11: 3.

(3) There is that in God's commandments which may make us willing. They are not burdensome.

[1] A Christian, so far as he is regenerate, consents to God's commands. 'I consent to the law that it is good.' Rom 7: 16. What is done with consent is no burden. If a virgin gives her consent, the match goes on cheerfully; if a subject consents to his prince's laws because he sees the equity and reasonableness of them they are not irksome. A regenerate person in his judgement approves, and in his will consents, to God's commandments and therefore they are not burdensome.

[2] God's commandments are sweetened with joy and peace. Cicero questions whether that can properly be called a burden which is carried with delight and pleasure. Utrum onus appellatur quod laetitia fertur [Is a task performed with joy rightly so called]? If a man carries a bag of

money that has been given him, it is heavy, but the delight takes off the burden. When God gives inward joy, it makes the commandments delightful. 'I will make them joyful in my house of prayer.' Isa 56: 7. Joy is like oil to the wheels, which makes a Christian run in the way of God's commandments, so that it is not burdensome.

[3] God's commandments are advantageous. They are preventive of evil; a curb-bit to check us from sin. What mischiefs should we not run into if we had not afflictions to humble us, and the commandments to restrain us! God's commandments keep us within bounds, as the yoke keeps the beast from straggling. We should be thankful to God for precepts. Had he not set his commandments as a hedge or bar in our way, we might have run to hell and never stopped. There is nothing in the commandments but what is for our good. 'To keep the commandments of the Lord, and his statutes, which I command thee for thy good.' Deut 10: 13. God commands us to read his word; and what hurt is in this? He bespangles the word with promises; as if a father should bid his son read his last will and testament, wherein he makes over a fair estate to him. He bids us pray and tells us if we 'ask, it shall be given.' Matt 7: 7. Ask power against sin, ask salvation, and it shall be given. If you had a friend who should say, 'Come when you will to me, I will supply you with money,' would you think it a trouble to visit that friend often? God commands us to fear him. 'But fear thy God.' Lev 25: 43. There is honey in the mouth of this command. 'His mercy is on them that fear him.' Luke 1: 50. God commands us to believe, and why so? 'Believe, and thou shalt be saved.' Acts 16: 31. Salvation is the crown set upon the head of faith. Good reason then have we to obey God's commands willingly, since they are for our good, and are not so much our duty as our privilege.

[4] God's commandments are ornamental. Omnia quae praestari jubet Deus, non onerant nos sed ornant. Salvianus. 'God's commandments do not burden us, but adorn us.' It is an honour to be employed in a king's service; and much more to be employed in his 'by whom kings reign.' To walk in God's commandments proves us to be wise. 'Behold, I have taught you statutes: keep, therefore, and do them; for this your wisdom.' Deut 4: 5, 6. To be wise is a great honour. We may say of every commandment of God, as Prov 4: 9: It 'shall give to thy head an ornament of grace.'

[5] The commands of God are infinitely better than the commands of sin, which are intolerable. Let a man be under the command of any lust, and how he tires himself! What hazards he runs to endangering his health and soul, that he may satisfy his lust! 'They weary themselves to commit iniquity.' Jer 9: 5. And are not God's commandments more equal, facile, pleasant, than the commands of sin? Chrysostom says true, 'To act virtue is easier than to act vice.' Temperance is less troublesome than drunkenness; meekness is less troublesome than passion and envy. There is more difficulty in the contrivance and pursuit of a wicked design than in obeying the commands of God. Hence a sinner is said to travail with iniquity. Psa 7: 14. A woman while she is in travail is in pain - to show what pain and trouble a wicked man has in bringing forth sin. Many have gone with more pains to hell, than others have to heaven. This may make us obey the

commandments willingly.

[6] Willingness in obedience makes us resemble the angels. The cherubim, types representing the angels, are described with wings displayed, to show how ready the angels are to serve God. God no sooner speaks the word, but they are ambitious to obey. How are they ravished with joy while praising God! In heaven we shall be as the angels, and by our willingness to obey God's commands, we should be like them here. We pray that God's will may be done by us on earth as it is in heaven; and is it not done willingly there? It is also done constantly. 'Blessed is he who does righteousness at all times.' Psa 106: 3. Our obedience to the command must be as the fire of the altar, which never went out. Lev 6: 13. It must be as the motion of the pulse, always beating. The wind blows off the fruit; but the fruits of our obedience must not be blown off by any wind of persecution. 'I have chosen you that ye should go and bring forth fruit, and that your fruit should remain.' John 15: 16.

Use. They are reproved who live in a wilful breach of God's commandments, in malice, uncleanness, intemperance; and walk antipodes to the commandments. To live in a wilful breach of the commandment is:

(1) Against reason. Are we able to stand out against God? 'Do we provoke the Lord, are we stronger than he?' 1 Cor 10: 22. Can we measure arms with God? Can impotence stand against omnipotence? A sinner acts against reason.

(2) It is against equity. We have our being from God; and is it not just that we should obey him who gives us our being? We have all our subsistence from him; and is it not fitting, that as he gives us our allowance, we should give him our allegiance? If a general gives his soldiers pay, he expects them to march at his command; so for us to live in violation of the divine commands, is manifestly unjust.

(3) It is against nature. Every creature in its kind obeys God's law. [1] Animate creatures obey him. God spake to the fish, and it set Jonah ashore. Jonah 2: 10. [2] Inanimate creatures. The wind and the sea obey him. Mark 4: 41, The very stones, if God give them a commission, will cry out against the sins of men. 'The stone shall cry out of the wall, and the beam out of the timber shall answer it.' Hab 2: 11. None disobey God but wicked men and devils; and can we find no better companions?

(4) It is against kindness. How many mercies have we to allure us to obey! We have miracles of mercy; the apostle therefore joins these two together, disobedient and unthankful, which dyes sin with a crimson colour. 2 Tim 3: 2. As the sin is great, for it is a contempt of God, a hanging out of the flag of defiance against him, and rebellion is as the sin of witchcraft, so the punishment will be great. It cuts off from mercy. God's mercy is for them that keep his commandments, but there is no mercy for them that live in a wilful breach of them. All God's judgements set themselves in battle array against the disobedient: temporal judgements and eternal. Lev 26: 15,

16. Christ comes in flames of fire, to take vengeance on them that obey not God. 2 Thess 1: 8. God has iron chains to hold those who break the golden chain of his commands; chains of darkness by which the devils are held ever. Jude 6. God has time enough, as long as eternity, to reckon with all the wilful breakers of his commandments.

How shall we keep God's commandments?

Pray for the Spirit of God. We cannot do it in our strength. The Spirit must work in us both to will and to do. Phil 2: 13. When the loadstone draws, the iron moves; so, when God's Spirit draws, we run in the way of his commandments.

2.3 The Third Commandment

'Thou shalt not take the name of the Lord thy God in vain: For the Lord will not hold him guiltless that taketh his name in vain.' Exod 20: 7.

This commandment has two parts: 1. A negative expressed, that we must not take God's name in vain; that is, cast any reflections and dishonour on his name. 2. An affirmative implied. That we should take care to reverence and honour his name. Of this latter I shall speak more fully, under the first petition in the Lord's Prayer, 'Hallowed be thy name.' I shall now speak of the negative expressed in this commandment, or the prohibition, 'Thou shalt not take the name of the Lord thy God in vain.' The tongue is an unruly member. All the parts and organs of the body are defiled with sin, as every branch of wormwood is bitter; 'but the tongue is full of deadly poison.' James 3: 8. There is no one member of the body breaks forth more in God's dishonour than the tongue. We have this commandment, therefore, as a bridle for the tongue, to bind it to its good behaviour. This prohibition is backed with a strong reason, 'For the Lord will not hold him guiltless;' that is he will not hold him innocent. Men of place and eminence deem it disgraceful to have their names abused and inflict heavy penalties on the offenders. 'The Lord will not hold him guiltless that taketh his name in vain;' but looks upon him as a criminal, and will severely punish him. The thing here insisted on is, that great care must be had, that the holy and reverend name of God be not profaned by us, or taken in vain. We take God's name in vain:

[1] When we speak slightly and irreverently of his name. 'That thou mayest fear this glorious and fearful name, The Lord thy God.' Deut 28: 58. David speaks of God with reverence. 'The mighty God, even the Lord.' Psa 50: 1. 'That men may know, that thou, whose name alone is Jehovah, art the Most High over all the earth. Psa 83: 18. The disciples, when speaking of Jesus, hallowed his name. 'Jesus of Nazareth, which was a prophet mighty in deed and word before God and all the people.' Luke 24: 19. When we mention the names of kings, we give them some title of honour, as 'excellent majesty;' so should we speak of God with the sacred reverence that is due to the infinite majesty of heaven. When we speak slightly of God or his works, he interprets it as a

contempt, and taking his name in vain.

[2] When we profess God's name, but do not live answerably to it, we take it in vain. 'They profess that they know God, but in works they deny him.' Titus 1: 16. When men's tongues and lives are contrary to one another, when, under a mask of profession, they lie and cozen, and are unclean, they make use of God's name to abuse him, and take it in vain. Simulata sanctitas duplex iniquitas [Pretended holiness is merely double wickedness]. 'The name of God is blasphemed among the Gentiles through you.' Rom 2: 24. When the heathen saw the Jews, who professed to be God's people, to be scandalous, it made them speak evil of God, and hate the true religion for their sakes.

[3] When we use God's name in idle discourse. He is not to be spoken of but with a holy awe upon our hearts. To bring his name in at every turn, when we are not thinking of him, to say, 'O God!' or, 'O Christ!' or, 'As God shall save my soul' - is to take God's name in vain. How many are guilty here! Though they have God in their mouths, they have the devil in their hearts. It is a wonder that fire does not come out from the Lord to consume them, as it did Nadab and Abihu. Lev 10: 2.

[4] When we worship him with our lips, but not with our hearts. God calls for the heart, 'My son, give me thy heart.' Prov 23: 26. The heart is the chief thing in religion; it draws the will and affections after it, as the Primum Mobile draw the other orbs along with it. The heart is the incense that perfumes our holy things; is the altar that sanctifies the offering. When we seem to worship God, but withdraw our heart from him, we take his name in vain. 'This people draw near me with their mouth, and with their lips do honour me, but have removed their heart far from me.' Isa 29: 13.

(1) Hypocrites take God's name in vain: their religion is a lie; they seem to honour God, but they do not love him; their hearts go after their lusts. 'They set their heart on their iniquity.' Hos 4: 8. Their eyes are lifted up to heaven, but their hearts are rooted in the earth. Ezek 33: 31. These are devils in Samuel's mantle. (2) Superstitious persons take God's name in vain. They bring him a few ceremonies which he never appointed, bow at Christ's name and cringe to the altar, but hate and persecute God's image.

[5] When we pray to him, but do not believe in him. Faith is a grace that greatly honours God. Abraham 'was strong in faith, giving glory to God.' Rom 4: 20. But when we pray to God, but do not mix faith with our prayer, we take his name in vain. 'I may pray,' says a Christian, 'but I shall be never the better.' I question whether God ever hears or answers such. It is to dishonour God and take his name in vain; it makes him either an idol, that has ears and hears not; or a liar, who promises mercy to the penitent, but will not make good his word. 'He that believeth not God has made him a liar.' 1 John 5: 10. When the apostle says (Rom 10: 14): 'How shall they call on him in whom they have not believed?' the meaning is, How shall they call on God aright, and not believe in him? But how many do call on him who do not believe on him! They ask for pardon,

but unbelief whispers their sins are too great to be forgiven. Thus to pray and not believe, is to take God's name in vain, and highly dishonours God, as if he were not such a God as the word represents him. 'Plenteous in mercy unto all them that call upon him.' Psa 86: 5.

[6] When in any way we profane and abuse his word. The word of God is profaned, in general, when profane men meddle with it. It is unseemly and unbecoming a wicked man to talk of sacred things, of God's providence, and the decrees of God and heaven. It was very distasteful to Christ to hear the devil quote Scripture, 'It is written.' To hear a wicked man who wallows in sin talk of God and religion is offensive; it is taking God's name in vain. When the word of God is in a drunkard's mouth, it is like a pearl hung upon a swine. Under the law, the lips of the leper were to be covered. Lev 13: 45. The lips of a profane, drunken minister ought to be covered; he is unfit to speak God's word, because he takes his name in vain.

More particularly they profane God's word, and take his name in vain: (1) That speak scornfully of his word. 'Where is the promise of his coming? For since the fathers fell asleep, all things continue as they were from the beginning of the creation.' 2 Pet 3: 4. As if they had said, the preachers make much ado about the day of judgement, when all must be called to account for their works; but where is the appearing of that day? We see things keep their course, and continue as they were since the creation. Thus they speak scornfully of Scripture, and take God's name in vain. If sentence be not speedily executed, men scorn and deride; but, 'Judgements are prepared for scorners.' Prov 19: 29.

(2) That speak jestingly. Such are they who sport and play with Scripture. This is playing with fire. Some cannot be merry unless they make bold with God; they make the Scripture a harp to drive away the spirit of sadness. Eusebius relates of one who made a jest of Scripture, and God struck him with frenzy. To play with Scripture shows a very profane heart. Some will rather lose their souls than lose their jests. These are guilty of taking God's name in vain. Tremble at it. Such as mock at Scripture, God will mock at their calamity. Prov 1: 26.

(3) That bring Scripture to countenance any sin. The word, which was written for the suppression of sin, is brought by some for the defence of sin. For instance, if we tell a covetous man of his sin that covetousness is idolatry, he will say, 'Has not God bid me live in a calling? Has he not said, "Six days shalt thou labour;" and "he who provides not for his family is worse than an infidel"?' Thus he endeavours to support his covetousness by Scripture. Now, it is true that God has bid us take pains in our calling, but not to hurt our neighbour; he has bid us provide for a family, but not by oppression. 'Ye shall not oppress one another.' Lev 25: 25. He has bid us look after a livelihood, but not to the neglect of the soul: he has bid us lay up treasure in heaven (Matt 6: 20); but he has commanded us to lay out, as well as lay up; to sow seeds of charity on the backs and bellies of the poor, which is neglected by such. To bring Scripture therefore to uphold us in sin, is a high profanation of Scripture, and taking God's name in vain. Again, if we tell a man of his inordinate passions - that he may be drunk with rash anger as well as wine - he will bring

Scripture to justify it by saying, 'Does not the word say, "Be ye angry and sin not"?' Eph 4: 26. True, anger is good when mixed with holy zeal. Anger is without sin when it is against sin: but to sin in anger, to speak unadvisedly with the lips, is to have the tongue set on fire of hell. To bring Scripture to defend any sin is to profane it, and to take God's name in vain.

(4) That adulterate the word, and wrest it in a wrong sense. Such are heretics, who put their own gloss upon Scripture, and make it speak that which the Holy Ghost never meant. As, for instance, when they expound those texts literally, which were meant figuratively. Thus the Pharisees, because God said in the law, 'Thou shalt bind them (the commandments) for a sign upon thy hand, and they shall be as frontlets between thine eyes' (Deut 6: 8), took it in a literal sense, got two scrolls of parchment, wherein they wrote the two tables, putting one on their left arms and binding the other to their eyebrows; and thus wrested that Scripture, and took God's name in vain. It was intended to be understood spiritually, of meditating on God's law, and putting it in practice. The Papists expound the words, 'This is my body,' literally, of the very body of Christ; as though, when Christ gave the bread, he had two bodies, one in the bread, and the other out of the bread, whereas he meant it figuratively as a sign of his body. Again, when those Scriptures are expounded figuratively and allegorically which the Holy Ghost meant literally. For example, Christ said to Peter, 'Launch out into the deep, and make a draught,' Luke 5: 4. This text was spoken in a plain, literal sense of launching out the ship, but the Papists take it in a mystic and allegorical sense. 'It proves,' say they, 'that the Pope, who is Peter's successor, shall launch forth, and catch the ecclesiastical and political power over the western parts of the world;' but I think the Papists have launched out too far beyond the meaning of the text. When men strain their wits to wrest the word to such a sense as pleases them, they profane God's word, and take his name in vain.

[7] When we swear by God's name. Many seldom mention God's name but in oaths, for which sin the land mourns. 'Swear not at all,' that is, rashly and sinfully, so as to take God's name in vain. Matt 5: 34. Not but in some cases it is lawful to take an oath before a magistrate. 'Thou shalt fear the Lord thy God and serve him, and swear by his name.' Deut 6: 13. 'An oath for confirmation is the end of all strife.' Heb 6: 16. When Christ says, 'Swear not at all;' he forbids such swearing as takes God's name in vain. There is a threefold swearing forbidden:

(1) Vain swearing, as when men in their ordinary discourse, let fly oaths. Some excuse their swearing. It is a coarse wool that will take no dye, and a bad sin indeed that has no excuse.

Excuse 1. I swear little trifling oaths; as Faith, or, By the mass. The devil has two false glasses, which he sets before men's eyes; the one is a little glass, in which the sin appears so small that it can hardly be seen, which the devil sets before men's eyes when they are going to commit sin; the other is a great magnifying glass, wherein sin appears so big that it cannot be forgiven, which the devil sets before men's eyes when they have sinned. Thou that sayest, sin is small, when God shall open the eye of thy conscience, thou wilt see it to be great, and be ready to despair. Thou sayest, they are but small oaths; but Christ forbids vain oaths. 'Swear not at all.' If God will reckon with us for idle words, will not idle oaths be put in the account?

Excuse 2. I swear to the truth. See how this harlot-sin would paint itself with an excuse. Though it be true, yet, if it be a rash oath, it is sinful. Besides, he that swears commonly, must sometimes swear to more than is true. Where much water runs, some gravel or mud will pass along with it; so, where there is much swearing, some lies will run along with it.

Excuse 3. I shall not be believed unless I seal up my words with an oath. A man that is honest will be believed without an oath; his bare word carries authority with it, and is as good as letters testimonial. Again, the more a man swears, the less others will believe him. Juris credit minus [Less trust is placed in his oaths. Thou art a swearer. Another thinks an oath weighs very light with him, and he cares not what he swears to, so that the more he swears the less others believe him. He will trust thy bond, but not thy oath.

Excuse 4. It is a custom of swearing I have got, and I hope God will forgive me. Though among men custom has influence, and is pleadable in law, yet it is not so in the case of sin; here custom is no plea. Thou hast got a habit of swearing, and canst not leave it off, is this an excuse? Is a thing well done because it is commonly done? This is so far from being an excuse that it is an aggravation of sin. As if one that had been accused of killing a man, should plead with the judge to spare him because it was his custom to murder. Would not this be an aggravation of the offence? So it is here. Therefore, all excuses for this sin of vain-swearing are taken away. Dare not to live in this sin, for it is taking God's name in vain.

(2) Vile swearing, horrid, prodigious oaths not to be named. Swearers, like mad dogs, fly in the face of heaven; and when they are angered, spue out their blasphemous venom on God's sacred majesty. Some in gaming, when things go cross and the dice runs against them, run against God in oaths and curses. Tell them of their sin, seek to bring home these asses from going astray, and it is but pouring oil on the flame; they will swear the more. Augustine says, 'They do no less sin who blaspheme Christ now in heaven, than the Jews did who crucified him on earth.' Swearers profane Christ's blood, and tear his name. A woman told her husband, that of her three sons, one of them only was his: the father dying, desired the executors to find out which was the true natural son, and bequeath all his estate to him. The father being dead, the executors set up his corpse against a tree and delivered to every one of these three sons a bow and arrows, telling them, that he who could shoot nearest the father's heart should have the whole of the estate. Two sons shot as near as they could to his heart, but the third felt nature so to work in him, that he refused to shoot; whereupon the executors judged him to be the true son, and gave him all the estate. Such as are the true children of God, fear to shoot at him; but such as are bastards, and not sons, care not though they shoot at him in heaven with their oaths and curses. That which makes swearing yet more heinous, is, that when men have resolved upon any wicked action, they bind themselves with an oath to do it. Such were they who bound themselves with an oath and curse

to kill Paul. Acts 23: 12. To commit sin is bad enough; but to swear to commit sin, is a high profanation of God's name, and as it were, calls God to approve our sin.

(3) Forswearing, which is a heaven-daring sin. 'Ye shall not swear by my name falsely, neither shalt thou profane my name.' Lev 19: 12. Perjury is calling God to witness to a lie. It is said of Philip of Macedon, he would swear and unswear, as might stand best with his interest. 'Thou shalt swear, The Lord liveth, in truth, in judgement, and in righteousness.' Jer 4: 2. In righteousness, therefore, it must not be an unlawful oath. In judgement therefore it must not be a rash oath. In truth, therefore, it must not be a false oath. Among the Scythians, if a man did forswear himself, he was to have his head stricken off; because, if perjury were allowed, there would be no living in a commonwealth; it would take away all faith and truth from among men. The perjurer is in as bad a case as the witch; for, by a false oath, he binds his soul fast to the devil. In forswearing, or taking a false oath in a court, there are many sins linked together; plurima peccata in uno [many sins in one]; for, besides taking God's name in vain, the perjurer is a thief; by his false oath he robs the innocent of his right; he is a perverter of justice; he not only sins himself, but occasions the jury to give a false verdict, and the judge to pass an unrighteous sentence. Surely God's judgements will find him out. When God's flying-roll, or curse, goes over the face of the earth, into whose house does it enter? 'Into the house of him that sweareth falsely by my name; and it shall consume the timber and stones thereof.' Zech 5: 4. Beza relates of a perjurer, that he had no sooner taken a false oath, than he was immediately struck with apoplexy, never spake more, and died. Oh, tremble at such horrid impiety!

[8] When we prefix God's name to any wicked action. Mentioning God in connection with a wicked design, is taking his name in vain. 'I pray,' said Absalom, 'let me pay my vow, which I have vowed unto the Lord, in Hebron.' 2 Sam 15: 7. This pretence of paying his vow made to God, was only to cover his treason. 'As soon as ye hear the sound of the trumpet ye shall say, Absalom reigneth;' chap. 15: 10. When any wicked action is baptised with the name of religion, it is taking God's name in vain. Herein the Pope is highly guilty, when he sends out his bulls of excommunication, or curses against the Christian; he begins with, In nomine Dei 'in the name of God.' What a provoking sin is this! It is to do the devil's work, and put God's name to it.

[9] When we use our tongues any way to the dishonour of God's name. As when we use railing, or curse in our passions; especially when we wish a curse upon ourselves if a thing be not so, when we know it to be false. I have read of one who wished his body might rot, if that which he said was not true; and soon after his body rotted, and he became a loathsome spectacle.

[10] When we make rash and unlawful vows. It is a good vow when a man binds himself to do that which the word binds him to; as, if he be sick, he vows if God restore him, he will live a more holy life. 'I will pay thee my vows which my lips have uttered when I was in trouble.' Psa 66: 13,14. But Voveri non debet quod Deo displicet; 'such a vow should not be made as is displeasing to God;' as to vow voluntary poverty, as friars; or to vow to live in nunneries.

Jephthah's vow was rash and unlawful; he vowed to the Lord to sacrifice that to him which he met with next, and it was his daughter. Judges 11: 31. He did ill to make the vow, and worse to keep it; he became guilty of the breach of the third and sixth commandments.

[11] When we speak evil of God. 'The people spake against God.' Numb 21: 5.

How do we speak against God?

When we murmur at his providences, as if he had dealt hardly with us. Murmuring accuses God's justice. 'Shall not the judge of all the earth do right?' Gen 18: 25. Murmuring springs from a bitter root, it comes from pride and discontent; it reproaches God and thus takes his name in vain. It is a sin that God cannot bear. 'How long shall I bear with this evil congregation which murmur against me?' Numb. 14: 27.

[12] When we falsify our promise; as when we say, if God spare our life we will do a certain thing, and never intend it. Our promise should be sacred and inviolable; but, if we make a promise, and mention God's name in it, but never intend to keep it, it is a double sin; it is telling a lie, and taking God's name in vain.

Use. Take heed of taking God's name in vain in any of these ways. Remember the combination and threatening in the text, 'The Lord will not hold him guiltless.' Here is a meiosis; less is said, and more intended. 'He will not hold him guiltless;' that is, he will be severely avenged on such a one. 'The Lord will not hold him guiltless.' Here the Lord speaks after the manner of a judge, who holds the court assize. The judge here, is God himself; the accusers, Satan, and a man's own conscience; the charge is, 'Taking God's name in vain;' the accused is found guilty, and condemned: 'The Lord will not hold him guiltless.' Methinks these words, 'The Lord will not hold him guiltless,' should put a lock upon our lips, and make us afraid of speaking anything that may bring dishonour upon God, or may be taking his name in vain. It may be that men may hold such guiltless, when they curse, swear, speak irreverently of God, may let them alone, and not punish them. If one takes away another's good name, he shall be sure to be punished; but if he takes away God's good name, where is he that punishes him? He that robs another of his goods shall be put to death, but he that robs God of his glory, by oaths and curses, is spared; but God himself will take the matter into his own hand, and he will punish him who takes his name in vain.

(1) Sometimes God punishes swearing and blasphemy in this life. In the county of Samurtia, when there arose a great tempest of thunder and lightning, a soldier burst forth into swearing; but the tempest tore up a great tree by the root, which fell upon him, and crushed him to pieces. German history tells of a youth, who was given to swearing, and inventing new oaths; the Lord sent a cancer into his mouth, which ate out his tongue and from which he died. If a man blasphemed God, the Lord caused him to be stoned to death. 'The Israelitish woman's son blasphemed the name of the Lord, and cursed. And Moses spake to the children of Israel, that

they should bring forth him that had cursed, and stone him with stones.' Lev. 24: 11, 23. Olympias, an Arian bishop, reproached and blasphemed the sacred Trinity; whereupon he was suddenly struck with three flashes of lighting, which burned him to death. Felix, an officer of Julia, seeing the holy vessels which were used in the sacrament, said, in scorn of Christ, 'See what precious vessels the Son of Mary is served withal.' Soon after, he was taken with vomiting of blood from his blasphemous mouth, of which he died.

(2) If God should not execute judgement on the profaners of his name in this life, their doom is to come. He will not remit their guilt, but deliver them to Satan the gaoler, to torment them for ever. If God justify a man, who shall condemn him? But if God condemn him, who shall justify him? If God lay a man in prison, where shall he get bail? God will take his full blow at the sinner in hell. 'It is a fearful thing to fall into the hands of the living God.' Heb 10: 31.

2.4 The Fourth Commandment

'Remember the Sabbath-day to keep it holy. Six days shalt thou labour, and do all thy work: but the seventh day is the Sabbath of the Lord thy God; in it thou shalt not do any work, thou, nor thy son, nor thy daughter, thy manservant, nor thy maid-servant, nor thy cattle, nor thy stranger that is within thy gates. For in six days the Lord made heaven and earth, the sea, and all that in them is, and rested the seventh day; wherefore the Lord blessed the Sabbath-day and hallowed it. Exod 20: 8 - 11.

This commandment was engraven in stone by God's own finger, and it will be our comfort to have it engraven in our hearts.

The Sabbath-day is set apart for God's solemn worship; it is his own enclosure, and must not be alienated to common uses. As a preface to this commandment, he has put a memento to it, 'Remember to keep the Sabbath day holy.' This word, 'remember,' shows that we are apt to forget Sabbath holiness; therefore we need a memorandum to put us in mind of sanctifying the day.

I. There is in these words a solemn command. 'Remember the Sabbath-day to keep it holy.'

[1] The matter of it. The sanctifying the Sabbath, which Sabbath sanctification consists in two things, in resting from our own works, and in a conscientious discharge of our religious duty.

[2] The persons to whom the command of sanctifying the Sabbath is given. Either superiors, and they are, more private, as parents and masters; or more public, as magistrates; or inferiors, as natives, children, and servants, 'Thy son, and thy daughter, thy man-servant, and thy maidservant;' or foreigners, 'thy stranger that is within thy gates.'

II. The arguments to obey this commandment of keeping holy the Sabbath are,

[1] From the rationality of it. 'Six days shalt thou labour and do all thy work;' as if God had said, I am not a hard master, I do not grudge thee time to look after thy calling, and to get an estate. I have given thee six days, to do all thy work in, and have taken but one day for myself. I might have reserved six days for myself, and allowed thee but one; but I have given thee six days for the works of thy calling, and have taken but one day for my own service. It is just and rational, therefore, that thou shouldest set this day in a special manner apart for my worship.

[2] The second argument for sanctifying the Sabbath, is taken from the justice of it. 'The seventh day is the Sabbath of the Lord thy God;' as if God had said, The Sabbath-day is my due, I challenge a special right in it, and no other has any claim to it. He who robs me of this day, and puts it to common uses, is a sacrilegious person, he steals from the crown of heaven, and I will in nowise hold him guiltless.

[3] The third argument for sanctifying the Sabbath, is taken from God's own observance of it. He 'rested the seventh day;' as if the Lord should say, Will you not follow me as a pattern? Having finished all my works of creation, I rested the seventh day; so having done all your secular work on the six days, you should now cease from the labour of your calling, and dedicate the seventh day to me, as a day of holy rest.

[4] The fourth argument for Sabbath-sanctification, is taken ab utili, from the benefit which redounds from a religious observation of the Sabbath. 'The Lord blessed the seventh day and hallowed it.' God not only appointed the seventh day, but he blessed it. It is not only a day of honour to God, but a day of blessing to us; it is not only a day wherein we give God worship, but a day wherein he gives us grace. On this day a blessing drops down from heaven. God himself is not benefited by it, we cannot add one cubit to his essential glory; but we ourselves are benefited. This day, religiously observed, entails a blessing upon our souls, our estate, and our posterity. Not keeping it, brings a curse. Jer 17: 27. God curses a man's blessings. Mal 2: 2. The bread which he eats is poisoned with a curse; so the conscientious observation of the Sabbath, brings all manner of blessings with it. These are the arguments to induce Sabbath-sanctification.

The thing I would have you now observe is, that the commandment of keeping the Sabbath was not abrogated with the ceremonial law, but is purely moral, and the observation of it is to be continued to the end of the world. Where can it be shown that God has given us a discharge from keeping one day in seven?

Why has God appointed a Sabbath?

(1) With respect to himself. It is requisite that God should reserve one day in seven for his own immediate service, that thereby he might be acknowledged to be the great Plenipotentiary, or sovereign Lord, who has power over us both to command worship, and appoint the time when he will be worshipped.

(2) With respect to us. The Sabbath-day is for our interest; it promotes holiness in us. The business of week-days makes us forgetful of God and our souls: the Sabbath brings him back to our remembrance. When the falling dust of the world has clogged the wheels of our affections, that they can scarce move towards God, the Sabbath comes, and oils the wheels of our affections, and they move swiftly on. God has appointed the Sabbath for this end. On this day the thoughts rise to heaven, the tongue speaks of God, and is as the pen of a ready writer, the eyes drop tears, and the soul burns in love. The heart, which all the week was frozen, on the Sabbath melts with the word. The Sabbath is a friend to religion; it files off the rust of our graces; it is a spiritual jubilee, wherein the soul is set to converse with its Maker.

I should next show you the modes, or manner, how we should keep the Sabbath day holy; but before I come to that, we have a great question to consider.

How comes it to pass that we do not keep the seventh-day Sabbath as it was in the primitive institution, but have changed it to another day?

The old seventh-day Sabbath, which was the Jewish Sabbath, is abrogated, and in the room of it the first day of the week, which is the Christian Sabbath, succeeds. The morality or substance of the fourth commandment does not lie in keeping the seventh day precisely, but keeping one day in seven is what God has appointed.

But how comes the first day in the week to be substituted in the room of the seventh day?

Not by ecclesiastic authority. 'The church,' says Mr Perkins, 'has no power to ordain a Sabbath.'

(1) The change of the Sabbath from the last day of the week to the first was by Christ's own appointment. He is 'Lord of the Sabbath.' Mark 2: 28. And who shall appoint a day but he who is Lord of it? He made this day. 'This is the day which the Lord has made.' Psa 118: 24. Arnobius and most expositors understand it of the Christian Sabbath, which is called the 'Lord's-day.' Rev 1: 10. As it is called the 'Lord's Supper,' because of the Lord's instituting the bread and wine and setting it apart from a common to a special and sacred use; so it is called the Lord's-day, because of the Lord's instituting it, and setting it apart from common days, to his special worship and service. Christ rose on the first day of the week, out of the grave, and appeared twice on that day to his disciples, John 20: 19, 26, which was to intimate to them, as Augustine and Athanasius say, that he transferred the Jewish Sabbath to the Lord's day.

(2) The keeping of the first day was the practice of the apostles. 'Upon the first day of the week, when the disciples came together to break bread, Paul preached unto them.' Acts 20: 7; 1 Cor 16: 2. Here was both preaching and breaking of bread on this day. Augustine and Innocentius, and Isidore, make the keeping of our gospel Sabbath to be of apostolic sanction, and affirm, that by virtue of the apostles' practice, this day is to be set apart for divine worship. What the apostles did, they did by divine authority; for they were inspired by the Holy Ghost.

(3) The primitive church had the Lord's-day, which we now celebrate, in high estimation. It was a great badge of their religion to observe this day. Ignatius, the most ancient father, who lived in the time of John the apostle, has these words, 'Let every one that loveth Christ keep holy the first day of the week, the Lord's-day.' This day has been observed by the church of Christ above sixteen hundred years, as the learned Bucer notes. Thus you see how the seventh-day Sabbath came to be changed to the first-day Sabbath.

The grand reason for changing the Jewish Sabbath to the Lord's-day is that it puts us in mind of the 'Mystery of our redemption by Christ.' The reason why God instituted the old Sabbath was to be a memorial of the creation; but he has now brought the first day of the week in its room in memory of a more glorious work than creation, which is redemption. Great was the work of creation, but greater was the work of redemption. As it was said, 'The glory of this latter house shall be greater than of the former.' Hag 2: 9. So the glory of the redemption was greater than the glory of the creation. Great wisdom was seen in making us, but more miraculous wisdom in saving us. Great power was seen in bringing us out of nothing, but greater power in helping us when we were worse than nothing. It cost more to redeem than to create us. In creation it was but speaking a word (Psa 148: 5); in redeeming there was shedding of blood. 1 Pet 1: 19. Creation was the work of God's fingers, Psa 8: 3, redemption was the work of his arm. Luke 1: 51. In creation, God gave us ourselves; in the redemption, he gave us himself. By creation, we have life in Adam; by redemption, we have life in Christ. Col 3: 3. By creation, we had a right to an earthly paradise: by redemption, we have a title to a heavenly kingdom. Christ might well change the seventh day of the week into the first, as it puts us in mind of our redemption, which is a more glorious work than creation.

Use one. The use I shall make of this is, that we should have the Christian Sabbath, we now celebrate, in high veneration. The Jews called the Sabbath, 'The desire of days, and the queen of days.' This day we must call a 'delight, the holy of the Lord, honourable.' Isa 58: 13. Metal that has the king's stamp upon it is honourable, and of great value. God has set his royal stamp upon the Sabbath; it is the Sabbath of the Lord, and this makes it honourable. We should look upon this day as the best day in the week. What the phoenix is among birds, what the sun is among planets the Lord's-day is among other days. 'This is the day which the Lord has made.' Psa 118: 24. God has made all the days, but he has blessed this. As Jacob got the blessing from his brother, so the Sabbath got the blessing from all other days in the week. It is a day in which we converse in a special manner with God. The Jews called the Sabbath 'a day of light;' so on this day the Sun of Righteousness shines upon the soul. The Sabbath is the market-day of the soul, the cream of time. It is the day of Christ's rising from the grave, and the Holy Ghost's descending upon the earth. It is perfumed with the sweet odour of prayer, which goes up to heaven as incense. On this day the manna falls, that is angels' food. This is the soul's festival-day, on which the graces act their part: the other days of the week are most employed about earth, this day about heaven; then you gather straw, now pearl. Now Christ takes the soul up into the mount, and gives it transfiguring sights of glory. Now he leads his spouse into the wine-cellar, and displays the banner of his love. Now he gives her his spiced wine, and the juice of the pomegranate. Cant 2: 4, 8: 2. The Lord usually reveals himself more to the soul on this day. The apostle John was in the Spirit on the Lord's-day. Rev 1: 10. He was carried up on this day in divine raptures towards heaven. This day a Christian is in the altitudes; he walks with God, and takes as it were a turn with him in heaven. 1 John 1: 3. On this day holy affections are quickened; the stock of grace is improved; corruptions are weakened; and Satan falls like lightning before the majesty of the word. Christ wrought most of his miracles upon the Sabbath; so he does still: dead souls are raised and hearts of stone are made flesh. How highly should we esteem and reverence this day! It is more precious than rubies. God has anointed it with the oil of gladness above its fellows. On the Sabbath we are doing angels' work, our tongues are tuned to God's praises. The Sabbath on earth is a shadow and type of the glorious rest and eternal Sabbath we hope for in heaven, when God shall be the temple, and the Lamb shall be the light of it. Rev 21: 22, 23.

Use two. 'SIX days shalt thou labour.' God would not have any live out of a calling: religion gives no warrant for idleness. It is a duty to labour six days, as well as keep holy rest on the seventh day. 'We hear that there are some which walk among you disorderly, working not at all. Now, them that are such, we command and exhort by our Lord Jesus, that with quietness they work, and eat their own bread.' 2 Thess 3: 11. A Christian must not only mind heaven, but his calling. While the pilot has his eye to the star, he has his hand to the helm. Without labour the pillars of a commonwealth will dissolve, and the earth, like the sluggard's field, will be overrun with briers. Prov 24: 31. Adam in innocence, though monarch of the world, must not be idle, but must dress and till the ground. Gen 2: 15. Piety does not exclude industry. Standing water putrifies. Inanimate creatures are in motion. The sun goes its circuit, the fountain runs, and the fire sparkles. Animate creatures work. Solomon sends us to the ant and pismire to learn labour. Prov 6: 6; 30: 25. The bee is the emblem of industry; some of the bees trim the honey, others work the wax, others frame the comb, others lie sentinel at the door of the hive to keep out the drone. And shall not man much more innate himself to labour? That law in paradise was never repeated. 'In the sweat of thy face shalt thou eat bread.' Gen 3: 19. Such professors are to be disliked who talk of living by faith, but live out of a calling; they are like the lilies which 'toil not, neither do they spin.' Matt 6: 28. It is a speech of holy and learned Mr Perkins, 'Let a man be endowed with excellent gifts, and hear the word with reverence, and receive the sacrament, yet if he practice not the duties of his calling, all is but hypocrisy.' What is an idle person good for? What benefit is a ship that lies always on the shore? or armour that hangs up and rusts? To live out of a calling exposes a person to temptation. Melanchthon calls idleness the Devil's bath, because he bathes himself with delight in an idle soul. We do not sow seed in ground when it lies fallow; but Satan sows most of his seed of temptation in such persons as lie fallow, and are out of a calling. Idleness is the nurse of vice. Seneca, an old heathen, could say, Nullus mihi per otium dies exit; 'No day passes me without some labour.' An idle person stands for a cipher in the world, and God writes down no ciphers in the book of life. We read in Scripture of eating the 'bread of idleness,' and drinking the 'wine of violence.' Prov 31: 27; 4: 17. It is as much a sin to eat 'the bread of idleness,' as to 'drink the wine of violence.' An idle person can give no account of his time. Time is a talent to trade with, both in our particular and general callings. The slothful person 'hides his talent in the earth;' he does no good; his time is not lived, but lost. An idle person lives unprofitably, he cumbers the ground. God calls the slothful servant 'wicked.' 'Thou wicked and slothful servant.' Matt 25: 26. Draco, whose laws were written in blood, deprived those of their life who would not work for their living. In Hetruria they caused such persons to be banished. Idle persons live in the breach of the commandment, 'Six days shalt thou labour.' Let them take heed they be not banished from heaven. A man may as well go to hell for not working in his calling, as for not believing.

Having spoken of the reasons of sanctifying the Sabbath I come now to

III. The manner of sanctifying the Sabbath.

[1] Negatively. We must do no work in it. This is the commandment. 'In it thou shall do no manner of work.' God has set apart this day for himself; therefore we are not to use it in common, by doing any civil work. As when Abraham went to sacrifice he left his servants and the ass at the bottom of the hill; so, when we are to worship God on this day, we must leave all worldly business behind, leave the ass at the bottom of the hill. Gen 22: 5. As Joseph, when he would speak with his brethren, thrust out the Egyptians, so, when we would converse with God on this day, we must thrust out all earthly employments. The Lord's day is a day of holy rest. All secular work must be forborne and suspended, as it is a profanation of the day. 'In those days saw I in Judah some treading winepresses on the Sabbath, and bringing in sheaves, and lading asses; as also wine, grapes and figs, and all manner of burdens which they brought into Jerusalem on the Sabbath-day; and I testified against them. Then I contended with the nobles of Judah, and said unto them, "What evil thing is this that ye do, and profane the Sabbath-day?' " Neh 13: 15, 17. It is sacrilege to rob for civil work the time which God has set apart for his worship. He that devotes any time of the Sabbath to worldly business, is a worse thief than he who robs on the highway; for the one does but rob man, but the other robs God. The Lord forbade mamma to be gathered on the Sabbath. Exod 16: 26. One might think it would have been allowed, as manna was the 'staff of their life,' and the time when it fell was between five and six in the morning, so that they might have gathered it betimes, and all the rest of the Sabbath might have been employed in God's worship; and besides, they needed not to have taken any great journey for it, for it was but stepping out of their doors, and it fell about their tents: and yet they might not gather it on the Sabbath; and for purposing only to do it, God was very angry. 'There went out some of the people on the seventh day for to gather, and they found none. And the Lord said, How long refuse ye to keep my commandments and my laws?' Exod 16: 27, 28. Surely anointing Christ when he was dead was a commendable work; but, though Mary Magdalene, and Mary the mother of James, had prepared sweet ointments to anoint the dead body of Christ, they went not to the sepulchre to embalm him till the Sabbath was past. 'They rested the Sabbath-day, according to the commandment.' Luke 23: 56. The hand cannot be busied on the Lord's-day but

the heart will be defiled. The very heathen, by the light of nature, would not do any secular work in the time which they had set apart for the worship of their false gods. Clemens Alexandrinus reports of one of the emperors of Rome, who, on the day of set worship for his gods, put aside warlike affairs and spent the time in devotion. To do servile work on the Sabbath shows an irreligious heart, and greatly offends God. To do secular work on this day is to follow the devil's slough; it is to debase the soul. God made this day on purpose to raise the heart to heaven, to converse with him, to do angels' work; and to be employed in earthly work is to degrade the soul of its honour. God will not have his day entrenched upon, or defiled in the least thing. The man that gathered sticks on the Sabbath he commanded to be stoned. Numb. 15: 35. It would seem a small thing to pick up a few sticks to make a fire; but God would not have this day violated in the smallest matters. Nay, the work which had reference to a religious use might not be done on the Sabbath, as the hewing of stones for the building of the sanctuary. Bezaleel, who was to cut the stones, and carve the timber out for the sanctuary, must forbear to do it on the Sabbath. Exod 31: 15. A temple is a place of God's worship, but it was a sin to build a temple on the Lord's-day. This is keeping the Sabbath-day holy negatively, in doing no servile work.

Works of necessity and charity however may be done on this day. In these cases God will have mercy and not sacrifice. (1) It is lawful to take the necessary supplies of nature. Food is to the body as oil to the lamp. (2) It is lawful to do works of mercy, as helping a neighbour when either life or estate are in danger. Herein the Jews were too nice and precise, who would not suffer works of charity to be done on the Sabbath. If a man was sick, they thought they might not on this day use means for his recovery. Christ charges them with being angry because he had wrought a cure on the Sabbath. John 7: 23. If a house were on fire, the Jews thought they might not bring water to quench it; if a vessel leaked on this day, they thought they might not stop it. They were 'righteous overmuch;' it was seeming zeal, but wanted discretion to guide it. Except in these two cases, of necessity and charity, all secular work is to be suspended and laid aside on the Lord's-day. 'In it thou shalt do no manner of work.' This arraigns and condemns many among us who too much foul their fingers with work on that day; some in dressing great feasts, others in opening their shop-doors, and selling meat on the Sabbath. The mariner will not put to sea but on the Sabbath, and so runs full sail into the violation of this command. Others work on this day privately, put up their shop-windows, and follow their trade within doors; but though they think to hide their sin under a canopy, God sees it. 'Whither shall I flee from thy presence?' 'The darkness hideth not from thee.' Psa 139: 7, 12. Such profane the day, and God will have an action of trespass against them.

[2] Positively. We keep the Sabbath-day holy, by 'consecrating and dedicating' this day to the 'service of the high God.' It is good to rest on the Sabbath-day from the works of our calling; but if we rest from labour and do no more, the ox and the ass keep the Sabbath as well as we; for they rest from labour. We must dedicate the day to God; we must not only 'keep a Sabbath,' but 'sanctify' a Sabbath. Sabbath-sanctification consists in two things: (1) Solemn preparation for it. If a prince were to come to your house, what preparation would you make for his entertainment!

You would sweep the house, wash the floor, adorn the room with the richest tapestry and hangings, that there might be something suitable to the state and dignity of so great a person. On the blessed Sabbath, God intends to have sweet communion with you; he seems to say to you, as Christ to Zacchaeus, 'Make haste and come down, for this day I must abide at thy house.' Luke 19: 5. Now, what preparation should you make for entertaining this King of glory? When Saturday evening approaches, sound a retreat; call your minds off from the world and summon your thoughts together, to think of the great work of the approaching day. Purge out all unclean affections, which may indispose you for the work of the Sabbath. Evening preparation will be like the tuning of an instrument, it will fit the heart better for the duties of the ensuing Sabbath.

(2) The sacred observation of it. Rejoice at the approach of the day, as a day wherein we have a prize for our souls, and may enjoy much of God's presence. John 8: 56. 'Abraham rejoiced to see my day.' So, when we see the light of a Sabbath shine, we should rejoice, and 'call the Sabbath a delight:' this is the queen of days, which God has crowned with a blessing. Isa 58: 13. As there was one day in the week on which God rained manna twice as much as upon any other day, so he rains down the manna of heavenly blessings twice as much on the Sabbath as on any other. This is the day wherein Christ carries the soul into the house of wine, and displays the banner of love over it; now the dew of the Spirit falls on the soul, whereby it is revived and comforted. How many may write the Lord's day, the day of their new birth! This day of rest is a pledge and earnest of the eternal rest in heaven. Shall we not then rejoice at its approach? The day on which the Sun of Righteousness shines should be a day of gladness.

Get up betides on the Sabbath morning. Christ rose early on this day, before the sun was up. John 20: 1. Did he rise early to save us, and shall not we rise early to worship and glorify him? 'Early will I seek thee.' Psa 63: 1. Can we be up betimes on other days? The husband man is early at his slough, the traveller rises early to go his journey, and shall not we, who on this day are travelling to heaven? Certainly, if we loved God as we should, we should rise on this day betimes, that we may meet with him whom our souls love. Such as sit up late at work on the night before, are so buried in sleep, that they will hardly be up betides on a Sabbath morning.

IV. Having dressed your bodies, you must dress your souls for hearing the word. As the people of Israel were to wash themselves before the law was delivered to them, so we must wash and cleanse our souls; and that is done by reading, meditation, and prayer. Exod 19: 10.

[1] By reading the word. The word is a great means to sanctify the heart, and bring it into a Sabbath-frame. 'Sanctify them through thy truth,' &c. John 17: 17. Read not the word carelessly, but with seriousness and affection; as the oracle of heaven, the well of salvation, the book of life. David, for its preciousness, esteemed it above gold; and for its sweetness, above honey. Psa 19: 10. By reading the word aright, our hearts, when dull, are quickened; when hard, are mollified; when cold and frozen are inflamed; and we can say as the disciples, 'Did not our heart burn within us?' Some step out of their bed to hearing. The reason why many get no more good on a

Sabbath by the word preached, is because they did not breakfast with God in the morning by reading his word.

[2] Meditation. Get upon the mount of meditation, and there converse with God. Meditation is the soul's retiring within itself, that, by a serious and solemn thinking upon God, the heart may be raised up to divine affections. It is a work fit for the morning of a Sabbath. Meditate on four things.

(1) On the works of creation. This is expressed in the commandment. "The Lord made heaven and earth, the sea,' &c. The creation is a looking glass, in which we see the wisdom and power of God gloriously represented. God produced this fair structure of the world without any pre-existent matter, and with a word. 'By the word of the Lord were the heavens made.' Psa 33: 6. The disciples wondered that Christ could, with a word, calm the sea, but it was far more astounding with a word to make the sea. Matt 8: 26. On the Sabbath let us meditate on the infiniteness of the Creator. Look up to the firmament and see God's wonders in the deep.' Psa 107: 24. Look into the earth, where we may behold the nature of minerals, the power of the loadstone, the virtue of herbs, and the beauty of flowers. By meditating on these works of creation, so curiously embroidered, we shall learn to admire God and praise him. 'O Lord, how manifold are thy works, in wisdom hast thou made them all.' Psa 104: 24. By meditating on the works of creation, we shall learn to confide in God. He who can create, can provide; he that could make us when we were nothing, can raise us when we are low. 'Our help is in the name of the Lord who made heaven and earth.' Psa 124: 8.

(2) Meditate on God's holiness. 'Holy and reverend is his name.' Psa 111: 9. 'Thou art of purer eyes than to behold evil.' Hab 1: 13. God is essentially, originally, and efficiently holy. All the holiness in men and angels is but a crystal stream that runs from this glorious fountain. God loves holiness because it is his own image. A king cannot but love to see his own effigies stamped on coin. God counts holiness his glory, and the most sparkling jewel of his crown. 'Glorious unholiness.' Exod 15: 2: Here is meditation fit for the first entrance upon a Sabbath. The contemplation of this would work in us such a frame of heart as is suitable to a holy God; it would make us reverence his name and hallow his day. While musing; upon the holiness of God's nature, we shall begin to be transformed into his likeness.

(3) Meditate on Christ's love in redeeming us. Rev 1: 5. Redemption exceeds creation; the one is a monument of God's power, the other of his love. Here is fit work for a Sabbath. Oh, the infinite stupendous love of Christ in raising poor lapsed creatures from a state of guilt and damnation! That Christ who was God should die! that this glorious Sun of Righteousness should be in an eclipse! We can never admire enough this love, no, not in heaven. That Christ should die for sinners! not sinful angels, but sinful men. That such clods of earth and sin should be made bright stars of glory! Oh, the amazing love of Christ! This was Illustreamoris Christi mnemosynum. Brugensis. That Christ should not only die for sinners, but die as a sinner! 'He has made him to

be sin for us' 2 Cor 5: 21. He who was among the glorious persons of the Trinity, 'was numbered with the transgressors.' Isa 53: 12. Not that he had sin, but he was like a sinner, having our sins imputed to him. Sin did not live in him, but it was laid upon him. Here was an hyperbole of love enough to strike us with astonishment. That Christ should redeem us, when he could not expect to gain anything, or to be advantaged at all by us! Men will not lay out their money upon purchase unless it will turn to their profit; but what benefit could Christ expect in purchasing and redeeming us? We were in such a condition that we could neither deserve nor recompense Christ's love. We could not deserve it; for we were in our blood. Ezek 16: 6. We had no spiritual beauty to tempt him. Nay, we were not only in our blood, but we were in arms against him. 'When we were enemies, we were reconciled to God by the death of his Son;' Rom 5: 10. When he was shedding his blood, we were spitting out poison. As we could not deserve, so neither could we recompense it. After he had died for us, we could not so much as love him, till he made us love him. We could give him nothing in lieu of his love. 'Who has first given to him?' Rom 11: 35. We were fallen into poverty. If we have any beauty, it is from him, 'It was perfect through my comeliness which I had put upon thee.' Ezek 16: 14. If we bring forth any good fruit, it is not of our own growth, it comes from him, the true vine. 'From me is thy fruit found.' Hos 14: 8. It was nothing but pure love for Christ to lay out his blood to redeem such as he could not expect to be really bettered by. That Christ should die so willingly! 'I lay down my life.' John 10: 17. The Jews could not have taken it away if he had not laid it down. He could have called to his Father for legions of angels to be his life-guard; but what need for even that, when his own Godhead could have defended himself from all assaults? He laid down his life. The Jews did not so much thirst for his death, as he thirsted for our redemption. 'I have a baptism to be baptised with, and how am I straitened till it be accomplished?' Luke 12: 50. He called his sufferings a baptism; he was to be baptised and sprinkled with his own blood; and he thought the time long before he suffered. To show Christ's willingness to die, his sufferings are called an offering. 'Through the offering of the body of Jesus.' Heb 10: 10. His death was a free-will offering. That Christ should not grudge nor think much of all his sufferings! Though he was scourged and crucified, he was well contented with what he had done, and, if it were needful, he would do it again. 'He shall see of the travail of his soul, and shall be satisfied.' Isa 53: 11. As the mother who has had hard labour, does not repent of her pangs when she sees a child brought forth, but is well contented; so Christ, though he had hard travail upon the cross, does not think much of it; he is not troubled, but thinks his sweat and blood well bestowed, because he sees the man-child of redemption brought forth into the world. That Christ should make redemption effectual to some, and not to others! Here is surprising love. Though there is sufficiency in his merits to save all, yet some only partake of their saving virtue; all do not believe. 'There are some of you that believe not.' John 6: 64. Christ does not pray for all. John 17: 9. Some refuse him. This is 'the stone which the builders refused.' Psa 118: 22. Others deride him. Luke 16: 14. Others throw off his yoke. 'We will not have this man to reign over us.' Luke 19: 14. SO that all have not the benefit of salvation by him. Herein appears the distinguishing love of Christ, that the virtue of his death should reach some, and not others. 'Not many wise men after the flesh, not many mighty, not many noble are called.' 1 Cor 1: 26. That Christ should pass by many of birth and parts, and that the lot of free grace should fall upon thee; that he should sprinkle his blood upon thee; 'Oh, the depth of the love of Christ!' That Christ should love us with such a transcendent love! The apostle calls it 'Love which passeth knowledge.' Eph 3: 19. That he should love us more than the angels. He loves them as his friends, but believers as his spouse. He loves them with such a kind of love as God the Father bears to him. 'As the Father has loved me, so have I loved you.' John 15: 9. Oh, what an hyperbole of love does Christ show in redeeming us! That Christ's love in our redemption should be everlasting! 'Having loved his own, he loved them unto the end.' John 13: 1. As Christ's love is matchless, so it is endless. The flower of his love is sweet; and that which makes it sweeter is that it never dies. His love is eternized. Jer 31: 3. He will never divorce his elect spouse. The failings of his people cannot quite take off his love; they may eclipse it, but not wholly remove it; their failings may make Christ angry with them, but not hate them. Every failing does not break the marriagebond. Christ's love is not like the saint's love. They sometimes have strong affections towards him, at other times the fit is off, and they find little or no love stirring in them; but it is not so with Christ's love to them, it is a love of eternity. When the sunshine of Christ's electing love is once risen upon the soul, it never finally sets. Death may take away our life from us, but not Christ's love. Behold here a rare subject for meditation on a Sabbath morning. The meditation of Christ's wonderful love in redeeming us would work in us a Sabbath-frame of heart.

It would melt us in tears for our spiritual unkindness, that we should sin against so sweet a Saviour; that we should be no more affected with his love, but requite evil for good; that like the Athenians, who, notwithstanding all the good service Aristides had done them, banished him out of their city, we should banish him from our temple; that we should grieve him with our pride, rash anger, unfruitfulness, animosities, and strange factions. Have we none to abuse but our friend? Have we nothing to kick against but the bowels of our Saviour? Did not Christ suffer enough upon the cross, but we must needs make him suffer more? Do we give him more 'gall and vinegar to drink?' Oh, if anything can dissolve the heart in sorrow, and melt the eyes to tears, it is unkindness offered to Christ. When Peter thought of Christ's love to him, how he had made him an apostle, and revealed his bosom-secrets to him, and taken him to the mount of transfiguration, and yet that he should deny him; it broke his heart with sorrow; 'he went out and wept bitterly.' Matt 26: 75 What a blessed thing is it to have the eyes dropping tears on a Sabbath! and nothing would sooner fetch tears than to meditate on Christ's love to us, and our unkindness to him.

Meditating on a Lord's-day morning on Christ's love, would kindle love in our hearts to him. How can we look on his bleeding and dying for us and our hearts not be warmed with love to him? Love is the soul of religion, the purest affection. It is not rivers of oil, but sparks of love that Christ values. And sure, as David said, 'While I was musing the fire burned' (Psa 39: 3), so, while we are musing of Christ's love in redeeming us, the fire of our love will burn towards him; and then the Christian is in a blessed Sabbath-frame, when, like a seraphim, he is burning in love to Christ.

(4) On a Sabbath morning meditate on the glory of heaven. Heaven is the extract and essence of happiness. It is called a kingdom. Matt 25: 34. A kingdom for its riches and magnificence. It is set forth by precious stones, and gates of pearl. Rev 21: 19, 21. There is all that is truly glorious; transparent light, perfect love, unstained honour, unmixed joy; and that which crowns the joy of the celestial paradise is eternity. Suppose earthly kingdoms were more glorious than they are, their foundations of gold, their walls of pearl, their windows of sapphire, yet they are corruptible; but the kingdom of heaven is eternal; those rivers of pleasure run 'for evermore.' Psa 16: 11. That wherein the essence of glory consists, and makes heaven to be heaven, is the immediate sight and fruition of the blessed God. 'I shall be satisfied, when I awake, with thy likeness.' Psa 17: 15. Oh, think of the Jerusalem above!

This is proper for a Sabbath. The meditation of heaven would raise our hearts above the world. oh, how would earthly things disappear and shrink into nothing, if our minds were mounted above visible things, and we had a prospect of glory! How would the meditation of heaven make us heavenly in our Sabbath exercises! It would quicken affection, would add wings to devotion, and cause us to be 'in the Spirit on the Lord's-day.' Rev 1: 10. How vigorously does he serve God who has a crown of glory always in his eye!

[3] We dress our souls on a Sabbath-morning by prayer; 'When thou prayest, enter into thy closet,' &c. Matt 6: 6. Prayer sanctifies a Sabbath.

(1) The things we should pray for in the morning of the Sabbath. Let us beg a blessing upon the word which is to be preached; that it may be a savour of life to us; that by it our minds may be more illuminated, our corruptions more weakened, and our stock of grace more increased. Let us pray that God's special presence may be with us, that our hearts may burn within us while God speaks, that we may receive the word into meek and humble hearts, and that we may submit to it, and bring forth fruits. James 1: 21. Nor should we only pray for ourselves, but for others.

Pray for him who dispenses the word; that his tongue may be touched with a coal from God's altar; that God would warm his heart who is to help to warm others. Your prayers may be a means to quicken the minister. Some complain they find no benefit by the word preached; perhaps they did not pray for their minister as they should. Prayer is like the whetting and sharpening of an instrument, which makes it cut better. Pray with and for your family. Yea, pray for all the congregations that meet on this day in the fear of the Lord; that the dew of the Spirit may fall with the manna of the word; that some souls may be converted, and others strengthened; that gospel ordinances may be continued, and have no restraint put upon them. These are the things we should pray for. The tree of mercy will not drop its fruit, useless it be shaken by the hand of prayer.

(2) The manner of our prayer. It is not enough to say a prayer; to pray in a dull, cold manner,

which asks God to deny; but we must pray with reverence, humility, fervency, and hope in God's mercy. Luke 22: 44. Christ prayed more earnestly. That we may pray with more fervency, we must pray with a sense of our wants. He who is pinched with wants, will be earnest in craving alms. He prays most fervently who prays most feelingly. This is to sanctify the morning of a Sabbath; and it is a good preparation for the word preached. When the ground is broken up by the slough, it is fit to receive the seed; when the heart has been broken by prayer, it is fit to receive the seed of the preached word.

V. Having thus dressed your souls on a morning, for the further sanctification of the Sabbath, address yourself to the hearing of the preached word.

When you sit down in your seat, lift up your eyes to heaven for a blessing upon the word to be dispensed; for you must know that the word preached does not work as physic, by its own inherent virtue, but by a virtue from heaven, and the co-operation of the Holy Ghost. Therefore put up a short ejaculatory prayer for a blessing upon the word, that it may be made effectual to you.

The word being begun to be preached, hear it with reverence and holy attention. 'A certain woman, named Lydia, attended unto the things which were spoken of Paul.' Acts 16: 14. Constantine, the emperor, was noted for his reverent attention to the word. Christ taught daily in the temple: and 'all the people were very attentive to hear him.' Luke 19: 48. In the Greek, 'they hung upon his lip.' Could we tell men of a rich purchase, they would diligently attend; and should they not much more, when the gospel of grace is preached unto them? That we may sanctify and hallow the Sabbath by attentive hearing, beware of these two things in hearing: distraction and drowsiness.

[1] Distraction. 'That ye may attend open the Lord without distraction.' 1 Cor 7: 35. It is said of Bernard, that when he came to the church-door, he would say, 'Stay here all my earthly thoughts.' So should we say to ourselves, when we are at the door of God's house, 'Stay here all my worldly cares and wandering cogitations; I am now going to hear what the Lord will say to me.' Distraction hinders devotion. The mind is tossed with vain thoughts, and diverted from the business in hand. It is hard to make a quicksilver heart fix. Jerome complains of himself, 'Sometimes when I am about God's service, per porticus diambulo, I am walking in the galleries, and sometimes casting up accounts.' How often in hearing the word, the thoughts dance up and down; and, when the eye is upon the minister, the mind is upon other things. Distracted hearing is far from sanctifying the Sabbath. It is very sinful to give way to vain thoughts at this time; because, when we are hearing the word, we are in God's special presence. To do any treasonable action in the king's presence is high great impudence. 'Yea, in my house have I found their wickedness.' Jer 23: 11. So the Lord may say, 'In my house, while they are hearing my word, I have found wickedness; they have wanton eyes, and their soul is set on vanity.'

Whence do these roving and distracting thoughts in hearing come?

(1) Partly from Satan. The devil is sure to be present in our assemblies. If he cannot hinder us from hearing, he will hinder us in hearing. 'When the sons of God came to present themselves before the Lord, Satan came also among them.' Job 1: 6. The devil sets vain objects before the fancy to cause a diversion. His great design is to render the word fruitless. As when one is writing, another jogs him that he cannot write even, so when we are hearing, the devil will be jogging us with a temptation, that we should not attend to the word preached. 'He shewed me Joshua the high-priest standing before the angel of the Lord, and Satan standing at his right hand to resist him.' Zech 3: 1.

(2) These wandering thoughts in hearing come partly from ourselves. We must not lay all the blame upon Satan.

They come from the eye. A wandering eye causes wandering thoughts. As a thief may come into the house at a window, so vain thoughts may be at the eye. As we are bid to keep our feet when we enter into the house of God (Eccl 5: 1), so we had need make a covenant with our eyes, that we be not distracted by beholding other objects. Job 31: 1.

Wandering thoughts in hearing rise out of the heart. These sparks come out of our own furnace. Vain thoughts are the mud which the heart, as from a troubled sea, casts up. 'For from within, out of the heart of men, proceed evil thoughts.' Mark 7: 21. As the foulness of the stomach sends up fumes into the head, so the corruption of the heart sends up evil thoughts into the mind.

Distracted thoughts in hearing proceed from an evil habit. We inure ourselves to vain thoughts at other times, and therefore we cannot hinder them on a Sabbath. Habit is a second nature. 'Can the Ethiopian change his skin, or the leopard his spots? then may ye also do good that are accustomed to do evil?' Jer 13: 23. He that is used to bad company, knows not how to leave it; so such as have vain thoughts to keep them company all the week, know not how to get rid of them on the Sabbath. Let me show you how evil these vain distracting thoughts in hearing are: -

[1] To have the heart distracted in hearing, is a disrespect to God's omniscience. God is an all-seeing Spirit; and thoughts speak louder in his ears than words do in ours. 'He declareth unto man what is his thought.' Amos 4: 13. To make no conscience of wandering thoughts in hearing, is an affront to God's omniscience, as if he knew not our heart, or did not hear the language of our thoughts.

[2] To give way to wandering thoughts in hearing is hypocrisy. We pretend to hear what God says, and our minds are quite upon another thing. We present God with our bodies, but do not give him our hearts. Hos 7: 11. This hypocrisy God complains of. 'This people draw near me with their mouth, and with their lips do honour me, but have removed their hearts far from me.' Isa 29: 13. This is to prevaricate and deal falsely with God.

[3] Vain thoughts in hearing discover much want of love to God. Did we love him we should

listen to his words as oracles, and write them upon the table of our heart. Prov 3: 3. When a friend whom we love speaks to us, and gives us advice, we attend with seriousness, and suck in every word. Giving our thoughts leave to ramble in holy duties, shows a great defect in our love to God.

[4] Vain impertinent thoughts in hearing defile an ordinance. They are as dead flies in the box of ointment. When a string of a lute is out of tune, it spoils the music; so distraction of thought puts the mind out of tune, and makes our services sound harsh and unpleasant. Wandering thoughts poison a duty, and turn it into sin. 'Let his prayer become sin.' Psa 109: 7. What can be worse than to have a man's praying and hearing of the word become sin? Would it not be sad, if the meat we eat should increase bad humours? How much more when hearing the word, which is the food of the soul, is turned into sin!

[5] Vain thoughts in hearing offend God. If the king were speaking to one of his subjects, and he should not give heed to what the king says, but be thinking on another business, or playing with a feather, would not the king be provoked? So, when we are in God's presence, and he is speaking to us in his word, and we mind not much what he says, but our hearts go after covetousness, will it not offend God to be thus slighted? Ezek 33: 31. He has pronounced a curse upon such. 'Cursed be the deceiver, which has in his flock a male, and sacrificeth unto the Lord a corrupt thing.' Mal 1: 14. To have strong lively affections is to have a male in the flock; but to hear the word with distraction, is to give God duties fly-blown with vain thoughts, and to offer to the Lord a corrupt thing, which brings a curse. 'Cursed be the deceiver.'

[6] Vain thoughts in hearing, when allowed and not resisted, make way for hardening the heart. A stone in the heart is worse than in the kidneys. Distracted thoughts in hearing do not better the heart, but harden it. Vain thoughts take away the holy awe of God which should be upon the heart; they make conscience less tender, and hinder the efficacy the word should have upon the heart.

[7] Vain and distracting thoughts rob us of the comfort of an ordinance. A gracious soul often meets with God in the sanctuary, and can say, 'I found him whom my soul loveth.' Cant 3: 4. He is like Jonathan, who, when he had tasted the honey on the rod, had his eyes enlightened. But vain thoughts hinder the comfort of an ordinance, as a black cloud hides the warm comfortable beams of the sun. Will God speak peace to us when our minds are wandering and our thoughts are travelling to the ends of the earth? Prov 17: 24. If ever you would hear the word with attention, do as Abraham when he drove away the fowls from the sacrifice. Gen 15: 2. When you find these excursions and sinful wanderings in hearing, labour to drive away the fowls; get rid of these vain thoughts; they are vagrants, and must not be entertained.

How shall we get rid of these vagabond thoughts?

(1) Pray and watch against them. (2) Let the sense of God's omniscient eye overawe your hearts.

The servant will not sport in his master's presence. (3) Labour for a holy frame of heart. Were the heart more spiritual, the mind would be less feathery. (4) Bring more love to the word. We fix our minds upon that which we love. He that loves his pleasures and recreations, fixes his mind upon them, and can follow them without distraction. Were our love more set upon the preached word, our minds would be more fixed upon it; and surely there is enough to make us love the word preached; for it is the word of life, the inlet to knowledge, the antidote against sin, the quickener of all holy affections. It is the true manna, which has all sorts of sweet tastes in it; the pool of Bethesda, in which the rivers of life spring forth to heal the broken in heart; and a sovereign elixir or cordial to revive the sorrowful spirit. Get love to the word preached, and you will not be so distracted in hearing. What the heart delights in, the thoughts dwell upon.

[2] Take heed of drowsiness in hearing. Drowsiness shows much irreverence. How lively are many when they are about the world, but in the worship of God how drowsy, as if the devil had given them opium to make them sleep! A drowsy feeling here is very sinful. Are you not in prayer asking pardon of sin? Will the prisoner fall asleep when he is begging pardon? In the preaching of the word, is not the bread of life broken to you? and will a man fall asleep over his food? Which is worse, to stay from a sermon, or sleep at a sermon? While you slept, perhaps the truth was delivered which might have converted your souls. Besides, sleeping is very offensive in a holy assembly; it not only grieves the Spirit of God, but makes the hearts of the righteous sad. Ezek 13: 22. It troubles them to see any show such contempt of God and his worship; to see them busy in the shop, but drowsy in the temple. Therefore, as Christ said, 'Could ye not watch one hour?' so, can ye not wake one hour? Matt 26: 40. I deny not but a child of God may sometimes, through weakness and indisposition of body, drop asleep at a sermon, but not voluntarily or ordinarily. The sun may be in an eclipse, but not often. If sleeping be customary and allowed, it is a very bad sign, and a profanation of the ordinance. A good remedy against drowsiness is to use a spare diet upon the Sabbath. Such as indulge their appetite too much on a Sabbath, are fitter to sleep on a couch than pray in the temple. That you may throw off distracting thoughts and drowsiness on the Lord's-day, and may hear the word with reverend attention, consider -

(1) It is God that speaks to us in his word; therefore the preaching of the word is called the 'breath of his lips.' Isa 11: 4. Christ is said now to speak to us 'from heaven,' as a king speaks in his ambassador. Heb 12: 25. Ministers are but pipes and organs, it is the Spirit of the living God that breathes in them. When we come to the word, we should think within ourselves, God is speaking in this preacher. The Thessalonians heard the word Paul preached, as if God himself had spoken unto them. 'When ye received the word of God, which ye heard of us, ye received it not as the word of men, but (as it is in truth) the word of God.' 1 Thess 2: 13. When Samuel knew it was the Lord that spake to him, he lent his ear. 1 Sam 3: 10. If we do not regard God when he speaks to us, he will not regard us when we pray to him.

(2) Consider how serious and weighty the matters delivered to us are. Moses said, 'I call heaven

and earth to record this day, that I have set before you life and death.' Deut 30: 19. Can men be regardless of the word, or drowsy when the weighty matters of eternity are set before them? We preach faith, and holiness of life, and the day of judgement and eternal retribution. Here life and death are set before you; and does not all this call for serious attention? If a letter were read to one of special business, wherein his life and estate were concerned, would he not be very serious in listening to it? In the preaching of the word your salvation is concerned; and if ever you would attend, it should be now. 'It is not a vain thing for you; because it is your life.' Deut 32: 47.

(3) To give way to vain thoughts and drowsiness in hearing, gratifies Satan. He knows that not to mind a duty, is all one in religion as not to do it. 'What the heart does not do, is not done.' Therefore Christ says of some, 'Hearing, they hear not.' Matt 13: 13. How could that be? Because, though the word sounded in their ear, yet they minded not what was said to them, their thoughts were upon other things; therefore, it was all as one as if they did not hear. Does it not please Satan to see men come to the word, and as good stay away? They are haunted with vain thoughts; they are taken off from the duty while they are in it; their body is in the assembly, their heart in their shop. 'Hearing, they hear not.'

(4) Each Sabbath may be the last we shall ever keep; we may go from the place of hearing to the place of judging; and shall not we give reverend attention to the word? Did we think when we come into God's house 'Perhaps this will be the last time that ever God will counsel us about our souls, and before another sermon death's alarm will sound in our ears; with what attention and devotion should we feel, and our affections would be all on fire in hearing!

(5) You must give an account for every sermon you hear. Redde rationem: 'Give an account of thy stewardship.' Luke 16: 2. So will God say, 'Give an account of thy hearing. Hast thou been affected with the word? Hast thou profited by it?' How can we give a good account, if we have been distracted in hearing, and have not taken notice of what has been said to us? The judge to whom we must give an account is God. Were we to give account to man, we might falsify accounts; but we must give an account to God. Nec donis corrumpitur, nec blanditiis fallitur. Bernard. 'He is so just a God that he cannot be bribed, and so wise that he cannot be deceived.' Therefore, having to give an account to such an impartial Judge, how should we observe every word preached, remembering the account! Let all this make us shake off distraction and drowsiness in hearing, and have our ears chained to the word.

VI. IN order to hear the word aright, let the following things be attended to: -

[1] Lay aside those dispositions which may render the preached word ineffectual. As,

(1) Curiosity. Some go to hear the word preached, not so much to get grace, as to enrich themselves with notions: having 'itching ears.' 2 Tim 4: 3. Augustine confesses that, before his conversion, he went to hear Ambrose for his eloquence rather than for the spirituality of the matter. 'Thou art unto them as a very lovely song of one that has a pleasant voice, and can play

well on an instrument.' Ezek 33: 32. Many go to the word to feast their ears only; they like the melody of the voice, the mellifluous sweetness of the expression, and the novelty of the opinions. Acts 17: 21. This is to love the garnishing of the dish more than the food; it is to desire to be pleased rather than edified. Like a woman that paints her face, but neglects her health - they paint and adorn themselves with curious speculations, but neglect their soul's health. This hearing neither sanctifies the heart nor the Sabbath.

(2) Lay aside prejudice. Prejudice is sometimes against the truths preached. The Sadducees were prejudiced against the doctrine of the resurrection. Luke 20: 27. Sometimes prejudice is against the person preaching. 'There is one Micaiah, by whom we may inquire of the Lord, but I hate him.' 1 Kings 22: 8. This hinders the power of the word. If a patient has an ill opinion of his physician, he will not take any of his medicines, however good they may be. Prejudice in the mind is like an obstruction in the stomach, which hinders the nutritive virtue of the meat. It poisons the word, and causes it to lose its efficacy.

(3) Lay aside covetousness. Covetousness is not only getting worlds gain unjustly, but loving it inordinately. This is a great hindrance to the preached word. The seed which fell among thorns was choked, Matt 13: 22; a fit emblem of the word when preached to a covetous hearer. The covetous man is thinking on the world when he is hearing; his heart is in his shop. 'They sit before thee as my people, and they hear thy words, but their heart goes after their covetousness.' Ezek 33: 31. A covetous hearer derides the word. 'The Pharisees, who were covetous, heard all these things, and they derided him.' Luke 16: 14.

(4) Lay aside partiality. Partiality in hearing is, when we like to hear some truths preached, but not all. We love to hear of heaven, but not of self-denial; of reigning with Christ, but not of suffering with him; of the more facile duties of religion, but not those which are more knotty and difficult; as mortification, laying the axe to the root, and hewing down our beloved sin. 'Speak smooth things' (Isa 30: 10), such as may not grate upon the conscience. Many like to hear of the love of Christ, but not of loving their enemies; they like the comforts of the word, but not its reproofs. Herod heard John the Baptist gladly; he liked many truths, but not when he spake against his incest.

(5) Lay aside censoriousness. Some, instead of judging themselves for sin, sit as judges upon the preacher; his sermon had either too much gall in it, or it was too long. They would sooner censure a sermon than practice it. God will judge the judger. Matt 7: 1.

(6) Lay aside disobedience. 'All day long I have stretched forth my hands unto a disobedient people.' Rom 10: 21. It is said of the Jews that God stretched out his hands in the preaching of the word, but they rejected Christ. Let there be none among you that wilfully refuse the counsels of the word. It is sad to have an adder's ear and an adamant heart. Zech 7: 11, 12. If, when God speaks to us in his word, we are deaf, when we speak to him in prayer, he will be dumb.

[2] If you would hear the word aright, have good ends in hearing. 'Come to the word to be made better.' Some have no other end in hearing but because it is in fashion, or to gain repute, or stop the mouth of conscience; but come to the word to be made more holy. There is a great difference between one who goes to a garden for flowers to wear in her bosom, and another that goes for flowers to make syrups and medicines. We should go to the word for medicine to cure us; as Naaman the Syrian went to Jordan to be healed of his leprosy. 'Desire the sincere milk of the word, that ye may grow thereby.' 1 Pet 2: 2. Go to the word to be changed into its similitude. As the seal leaves its print upon the wax, so labour that the word preached may leave the print of its own holiness upon your heart.

Labour that the 'word' may have such a virtue in you, as the water of jealousy, to kill and make fruitful; that it may kill your sins, and make your souls fruitful in grace. Numb 5: 27.

[3] If you would hear the word aright, go to it with delight. The word preached is a feast of fat things. With what delight do men go to a feast! The word preached anoints the blind eye; mollifies the rocky heart; it beats off our fetters, and turns us from the 'power of Satan unto God.' Acts 26: 18. The word is the seed of regeneration, and the engine of salvation. James 1: 18. Hear the word with delight and complacency. 'Thy words were found, and I did eat them; and thy word was the joy and rejoicing of mine heart.' Jer 15: 16. 'How sweet are thy words unto my taste! yea, sweeter than honey to my mouth.' Psa 119: 103. Love the word that comes most home to the conscience; bless God when your corruptions have been met with, when the sword of the Spirit has divided between you and your sins. Who cares for the physic which will not work?

[4] If you would hear the word aright, mix it with faith. Believe the truth of the word preached, that it is the word by which you must be judged. Not only give credence to the word preached, but apply it to your own souls. Faith digests the word, and turns it into spiritual nourishment. Many hear the word, but it may be said of them, as in Psa 106: 24 'They believed not his word.' As Melanchthon once said to some Italians 'Ye Italians worship God in the bread, when ye do not believe him to be in heaven;' so, many hear God's words, but do not believe that God is; they question the truth of his oracles. If we do not mix faith with the word, it is like leaving out the chief ingredient in a medicine, which makes it ineffectual. Unbelief hardens men's hearts against the word. 'Divers were hardened, and believed not.' Acts 19: 9. Men hear many truths delivered concerning the preciousness of Christ, the beauty of holiness, and the felicity of a glorified estate; but, if through unbelief and atheism, they question these truths, we may as well speak to stones and pillars of the church as to them. That word which is not believed, can never be practised. Ubi male creditur, ibi nec bene vivitur [When belief is unstable, conduct also wavers]. Jerome. Unbelief makes the word preached of no effect. 'The word preached did not profit, not being mixed with faith in them that heard it.' Heb 4: 2. The word to an unbeliever is like a cordial put into a dead man's mouth, which loses all its virtue. If there be any unbelievers in our congregations, what shall ministers say of them to God at the last day? Lord, we have preached to the people thou sentest us to, we have showed them our commission, we have declared unto

them thy whole counsel, but they have not believed a word we spake. We told them what would be the fruit of sin, but they would not heed. They would drink their sugared draught, though there was death in the cup. Lord, we are free from their blood. God forbid that ministers should ever have to make this report to him of their people. But this they will be forced to do if their hearers live and die in unbelief. Would you sanctify a Sabbath by hearing the word aright? Hear it with faith. The apostle puts the two together, 'belief and salvation.' 'We are of them that believe to the saving of the soul.' Heb 10: 39.

[5] If you would hear the word aright, hear it with meek spirits. James 1: 21. Receive the word in mansuetudine, 'with meekness'. Meekness is a submissive frame of heart to the word. Contrary to this meekness is fierceness of spirit, when men rise up in rage against the word; as if the patient should be angry with the physician when he gives him a medicine to purge out his bad humours. 'When they heard these things, they were cut to the heart, and gnashed on him [Stephen] with their teeth.' Acts 7: 54. 'Asa was wroth with the seer, and put him in a prison house.' 2 Chron 16: 10. Pride and guilt make men fret at the word. What made Asa enraged but pride? He was a king, and thought he was too good to be told of his sin. What made Cain angry when God said to him, 'Where is Abel, thy brother?' He replied, 'Am I my brother's keeper?' What made him so touchy but guilt? He had imbrued his hands in his brother's blood. If you would hear the word aright, lay aside your passions. 'Receive the word with meekness;' get humble hearts to submit to the truths delivered. God takes the meek person for his scholar. 'The meek will he teach his way.' Psa 25: 9. Meekness makes the word preached to be an 'ingrafted word.' James 1: 21. A good scion grafted in a bad stock changes the nature of it, and makes it bear good and generous fruit; so, when the word preached is grafted into men's hearts, it sanctifies them and makes them bring forth the sweet fruits of righteousness. By meekness it becomes an ingrafted word.

[6] If you would hear the word aright, be not only attentive, but retentive. Lay it up in your memories and hearts. The seed 'on the good ground are they, which, having heard the word, keep it.' Luke 8: 15. The Greek word for 'to keep,' signifies to hold the word fast, that it does not run from us. If the seed be not kept in the ground, but is presently washed away, it is sown to little purpose; so if the word preached be not kept in your memories and hearts, it is preached in vain. Many persons have memories like leaky vessels. If the word goes out as fast as it comes in, how can it profit? If a treasure be put in a chest and the chest be not locked, it may easily be taken out; so a bad memory is a chest without a lock, out of which the devil can easily take all the treasure. 'Then comes the devil and taketh away the word out of their hearts.' Luke 8: 12. Labour to keep in memory the truths you hear. The things we esteem are not easily forgotten. 'Can a maid forget her ornaments or a bride her attire?' Jer 2: 32. Did we prize the word more, we should not forget it so soon. If meat does not stay in the stomach, but rises up as fast as we eat it, it cannot nourish; so, if the word stays not in the memory, but is presently gone, it can do the soul but little good.

[7] If you would hear aright, practice what you hear. Practice is the life of all. 'Blessed are they

that do his commandments, that they may have right to the tree of life.' Rev 22: 14. Hearing only will be no plea at the day of judgement - merely to say, 'Lord, I have heard many sermons.' God will say, 'What fruits of obedience have ye brought forth?' The word preached is not only to inform you but reform you; not only to mend your sight, but to mend your pace in the way to heaven. A good hearer opens and shuts to God as the heliotrope to the sun.

(1) If you do not hear the word to practice it, you lose all your labour. How many a weary step have you taken, your body has been crowded, and your spirit faint, if you are not bettered by hearing! If you are as proud, as vain, and as earthly as ever, all your hearing is lost. You would be loath to trade in vain, and why not to hear sermons in vain? 'Why then labour I in vain?' Job 9: 29. Put this question to your own soul: Why labour I in vain? Why do I take all these pains to hear, and yet have not grace to practice it? I am as bad as ever! Why then do I labour in vain?

(2) If you hear the word, and are not bettered by it, you are like the salamander, no hotter in the fire; and your hearing will increase your condemnation. 'That servant which knew his lord's will, neither did according to his will, shall be beaten with many stripes.' Luke 12: 47. We pity such as know not where to hear; it will be worse with such as care not how they hear. To graceless disobedient hearers, every sermon will be a faggot to heat hell. It is sad to go loaded to hell with ordinances. Oh, beg the Spirit to make the word preached effectual! Ministers can but speak to the ear, the Spirit speaks to the heart. 'While Peter spake, the Holy Ghost fell on all them which heard the word.' Acts 10: 44.

[8] Having heard the word in a holy and spiritual manner, for the further sanctification of the Sabbath, confer with the word. We are forbidden on this day to speak our own words, but we must speak of God's word. Isa 58: 13. Speak of the sermons as you sit together; which is one part of sanctifying the Sabbath. Good discourse brings holy truths into our memories, and fastens them upon our hearts. 'Then they that feared the Lord, spake often one to another.' Mal 3: 16. There is great power and efficacy in good discourse. 'How forcible are right words!' Job 6: 25. By holy conference on a Sabbath, one Christian helps to warm another when he is frozen, and to strengthen another when he is weak. Latimer confessed he was much furthered in religion by having conference with Mr. Bilney the martyr. 'My tongue shall speak of thy word.' Psa 119: 172. One reason why preaching the word on a Sabbath does no more good is because there is so little good conference. Few speak of the word they have heard, as if sermons were such secrets that they must not be spoken of again, or as if it were a shame to speak of that which will save us.

[9] Close the Sabbath evening with repetition, reading, singing Psalms, and prayer. Ask that God would bless the word you have heard. Could we but thus spend a Sabbath, we might be 'in the Spirit on the Lord's-day,' our souls would be nourished and comforted; and the Sabbaths we now keep, would be earnests of the everlasting Sabbaths which we shall celebrate in heaven.

Use one. See here the Christian's duty, 'to keep the Sabbath-day holy.'

(1) The whole Sabbath is to be dedicated to God. It is not said, Keep a part of the Sabbath holy, but the whole day must be religiously observed. If God has given us six days, and taken but one to himself, shall we grudge him any part of that day? It were sacrilege. The Jews kept a whole day to the Lord; and we are not to abridge or curtail the Sabbath, as Augustine says, more than the Jews did. The very heathen, by the light of nature, set apart a whole day in honour of false gods; and Scaevola, a high-priest of theirs, affirms that the wilful transgression of that day could have no expiation or pardon. If any one robs any part of the Christian Sabbath for servile work or recreation, Scaevola, the high priest of the heathenish gods, shall rise up in judgement to condemn him. Let those who say, that to keep a whole Sabbath is too Judaical, show where God has made any abatement of the time of worship; where he has said, you shall keep but a part of the Sabbath; and if they cannot show that, it robs God of his due. That a whole day be designed and set apart for his special worship, is a perpetual statute, while the church remains upon the earth, as Peter Martyr says. Of this opinion also were Theodore, Augustine, Irenaeus, and the chief of the fathers.

(2) As the whole Sabbath is to be dedicated to God, so it must be kept holy. You have seen the manner of sanctifying the Lord's-day by reading, meditation, prayer, hearing the word, and by singing of psalms to make melody to the Lord. Now, besides what I have said upon keeping this day holy, let me make a short comment or paraphrase on that Scripture. 'If thou turn away thy foot from the Sabbath, from doing thy pleasure on my holy day; and call the Sabbath a delight, the holy of the Lord, honourable: and shalt honour him, not doing thine own ways, nor finding thine own pleasure, nor speaking thine own words.' Isa 58: 13. Here is a description of rightly sanctifying a Sabbath.

'If thou turn away thy foot from the Sabbath.' This may be understood either literally or spiritually. Literally, that is, if thou withdrawest thy foot from taking long walks or journeys on the Sabbath-day. So the Jewish doctors expound it. Or, spiritually, if thou turn away thy affections (the feet of thy soul) from inclining to any worldly business.

'From doing thy pleasure on my holy day.' That is, thou must not do that which may please the carnal part, as in sports and pastimes. This is to do the devil's work on God's day.

'And call the Sabbath a delight.' Call it a delight, that is, esteem it so. Though the Sabbath be not a day for carnal pleasure, yet holy pleasure is not forbidden. The soul must take pleasure in the duties of a Sabbath. The saints of old counted the Sabbath a delight: the Jews called the Sabbath dies lucis, a day of light. The Lord's day, on which the Sun of Righteousness shines, is both a day of light and delight. This is the day of sweet intercourse between God and the soul. On this day a Christian makes his sallies out to heaven; his soul is lifted above the earth; and can this be without delight? The higher the bird flies, the sweeter it sings. On the Sabbath the soul fixes its love on God; and where love is, there is delight. On this day the believer's heart is melted, quickened, and enlarged in holy duties; and how can all this be, and not a secret delight go along with it? On a Sabbath a gracious soul can say, 'I sat down under his shadow with great delight, and his fruit was sweet to my taste.' Cant 2: 3. How can a spiritual heart choose but call the Sabbath a delight? Is it not delightful to a queen to be putting on her wedding robes in which she shall meet the king her bridegroom? When we are about Sabbath exercises, we are dressing ourselves, and putting on our wedding robes in which we are to meet our heavenly bridegroom the Lord Jesus; and is not this delightful? On the Sabbath God makes a feast of fat things; he feasts the ear with his word, and the heart with his grace. Well then may we call the Sabbath a delight. To find this holy delight, is to 'be in the Spirit on the Lord's-day.'

'The holy of the Lord, honourable.' In the Hebrew, it is glorious. To call the Sabbath honourable, is not to be understood so much of an outward honour given to it, by wearing richer apparel, or having better diet on this day, as the Jewish doctors corruptly gloss. This is the chief honour that some give to this day; but by calling the Sabbath honourable, is meant that honour of the heart which we give to the day, reverencing it, and esteeming it as the queen of days. We are to count the Sabbath honourable, because God has honoured it. All the persons in the Trinity have honoured it. God the Father blessed it, God the Son rose upon it, God the Holy Ghost descended on it. Acts 2: 1: This day is to be honoured by all good Christians, and had in high veneration. It is a day of renown, on which a golden sceptre of mercy is held forth. The Christian Sabbath is the very crepusculum and dawning of the heavenly Sabbath. It is honourable, because on this day 'God comes down to us and visits us.' To have the King of heaven present in a special manner in our assemblies, makes the Sabbath-day honourable. Besides, the work done on this day makes it honourable. The six days are filled up with servile work, which makes them lose much of their glory; but on this day sacred work is done. The soul is employed wholly about the worship of God; it is praying, hearing, meditating; it is doing angels' work, praising, and blessing God. Again, the day is honourable by virtue of a divine institution. Silver is of itself valuable; but when the royal stamp is put upon it, it is honourable; so God has put a sacred stamp upon this day, the stamp of divine authority, and the stamp of divine benediction. This makes it honourable; and this is sanctifying the Sabbath, to call it a delight, and honourable.

'Not doing thine own ways.' That is, thou shalt not defile the day by doing any servile work.

'Nor finding thine own pleasure.' That is, not gratifying the fleshly part by walks, visits, or pastimes.

'Nor speaking thine own Words.' That is, words heterogeneous and unsuitable for a Sabbath; vain, impertinent words; discourses of worldly affairs.

Use two. If the Sabbath-day is to be kept holy, they are reproved who, instead of sanctifying the Sabbath, profane it. They take the time which should be dedicated wholly to God, and spend it in the service of the devil and their lusts. The Lord has set apart this day for his own worship, and they make it common. He has set a hedge about this commandment, saying, 'Remember;' and they break this hedge; but he who breaks this hedge, a serpent shall bite him. Eccl 10: 8. The

Sabbath day in England lies bleeding; and oh! that our parliament would pour some balm into the wounds which it has received! How is this day profaned, by sitting idle at home, by selling meat, by vain discourse, by sinful visits, by walking in the fields, and by sports! The people of Israel might not gather manna on the Sabbath, and may we use sports and dancings on this day? Truly it should be matter of grief to us to see so much Sabbath-profanation. When one of Darius's eunuchs saw Alexander setting his feet on a rich table of Darius's, he wept. Alexander asked him why he wept? He said it was to see the table which his master so highly esteemed now made a footstool. So may we weep to see the Sabbath-day, which God highly esteems, and has honoured and blessed, made a footstool, and trampled upon by the feet of sinners. To profane the Sabbath is a great sin; it is a wilful contempt of God; it is not only casting his law behind our back, but trampling it under foot. He says, 'Keep the Sabbath holy;' but men pollute it. This is to despise God, to hang out the flag of defiance, to throw down the gauntlet, and challenge God himself. Now, how can God endure to be thus saucily confronted by proud dust? Surely he will not suffer this high impudence to go unpunished. God's curse will come upon the Sabbath-breaker; and it will blast where it comes. The law of the land lets Sabbath-breakers alone, but God will not. No sooner did Christ curse the fig-tree, but it withered. God will take the matter into his own hand; he will see after the punishing of Sabbath violation. And how does he punish it?

(1) With spiritual plagues. He gives up Sabbath profaners to hardness of heart, and a seared conscience. Spiritual judgements are sorest. 'So I gave them up unto their own hearts' lust.' Psa 81: 12. A sear in the conscience is a brand-mark of reprobation.

(2) God punishes this sin by giving men up to commit other sins. To revenge the breaking of his Sabbath, he suffers them to break open houses, and so come to be punished by the magistrate. How many such confessions have we heard from thieves going to be executed! They never regarded the Sabbath, and God suffered them to commit those sins for which they are to die.

(3) God punishes Sabbath-breaking by sudden visible judgements on men for this sin. He punishes them in their estates and in their persons. While a certain man was carrying corn into his barn on the Lord's-day, both house and corn were consumed with fire from heaven. In Wiltshire there was a dancing match appointed upon the Lord's-day; and while one of the company was dancing, he suddenly fell down dead. The 'Theatre of God's Judgements' relates of one, who used every Lord's-day to hunt in sermon-time, who had a child by his wife with a head like a dog, and it cried like a hound. His sin was monstrous, and it was punished with a monstrous birth. The Lord threatened the Jews, that if they would not hallow the Sabbath-day, he would kindle a fire in their gates. Jer 17: 27. The dreadful fire which broke out in London began on the Sabbath-day; as if God would tell us from heaven he was then punishing us for our Sabbath profanation. Nor does he punish it only in this life with death, but hereafter with damnation. Let such as break God's Sabbath see if they can break those chains of darkness in which they and the devils shall be held.

Use three. It exhorts us to Sabbath holiness.

Make conscience of keeping this day holy. The other commandments have an affirmative in them only, or a negative; this fourth commandment has both an affirmative in it and a negative. 'Thou shalt keep the Sabbath day holy,' and, 'thou shalt not do any manner of work in it,' shows how carefully God would have us observe this day. Not only must you keep this day yourselves, but have a care that all under your charge keep it; 'Thou, and thy son, and thy daughter, and thy man-servant, and thy maidservant;' that is, thou who art a superior, a parent or a master, thou must have a care that not only thou thyself, but those who are under thy trust and tuition, sanctify the day. Those masters of families are to blame who are careful that their servants serve them, but have no care that they serve God; who care not though their servants should serve the devil, so long as their bodies do them service. That which Paul says to Timothy, Serva depositum, 'That good thing, which was committed unto thee, keep,' is of large meaning. 1 Tim 1: 11. Not only have a care of thy own soul, but have a care of the souls thou art entrusted with. See that they who are under thy charge sanctify the Sabbath. God's law provided, that if a man met with an ox or an ass going astray, he should bring him back again; much more, when thou sees the soul of thy child or servant going astray from God, and breaking his Sabbath, thou shouldest bring him back again to a religious observation of this day.

That I may press you to Sabbath-sanctification, consider what great blessings God has promised to the strict observers of this day. Isa 58: 14. (1) A promise of joy. 'Then shalt thou delight thyself in the Lord.' Delighting in God is both a duty and a reward. In this text it is a reward, 'Then shalt thou delight thyself in the Lord;' as if God had said, If thou keep the Sabbath conscientiously, I will give thee that which will fill thee with delight; if thou keep the Sabbath willingly, I will make thee keep it joyfully. I will give thee those enlargements in duty, and that inward comfort, which shall abundantly satisfy thee; thy soul shall overflow with such a stream of joy, that thou shalt say, 'Lord, in keeping thy Sabbath there is great reward. (2) Of honour. And 'I will cause thee to ride upon the high places of the earth.' That is, I will advance thee to honour, ascendere faciam; so Munster interprets it. Some, by the high places of the earth, understand Judea; so Grotius. I will bring thee into the land of Judea, which is situated higher than the other countries adjacent. (3) Of earth and heaven. 'And I will feed thee with the heritage of Jacob;' that is, I will feed thee with all the delicious things of Canaan, and afterwards I will translate thee to heaven, whereof Canaan was but a type. Another promise is, 'Blessed is the man that does this, that keepeth the Sabbath from polluting it.' Isa 56: 2. 'Blessed is the man;' in the Hebrew it is, 'blessednesses.' To him that keeps the Sabbath holy, here is blessedness upon blessedness belonging to him; he shall be blessed with the upper and nether springs; he shall be blessed in his name, estate, soul, progeny. Who would not keep the Sabbath from polluting it that shall have so many blessings entailed upon him and his posterity after him? Again, a conscientious keeping of the Sabbath seasons the heart for God's service all the week after. Christian the more holy thou art on a Sabbath, the more holy thou wilt be on the week following.

2.5 The Fifth Commandment

'Honour thy father and thy mother: that thy days may be long upon the land which the Lord thy God giveth thee.' Exod 20: 12.

Having done with the first table, I am next to speak of the duties of the second table. The commandments may be likened to Jacob's ladder: the first table respects God, and is the top of the ladder that reaches to heaven; the second respects superiors and inferiors, and is the foot of the ladder that rests on the earth. By the first table, we walk religiously towards God; by the second, we walk religiously towards man. He cannot be good in the first table that is bad in the second. 'Honour thy father and thy mother.' In this we have a command, 'honour thy father and thy mother;' and, second, a reason for it, 'That thy days may be long in the land.' The command will chiefly be considered here, 'Honour thy father.'

I. Father is of different kinds; as the political, the ancient, the spiritual, the domestic, and the natural.

[1] The political father, the magistrate. He is the father of his country; he is to be an encourager of virtue, a punisher of vice, and a father to the widow and orphan. Such a father was Job. 'I was a father to the poor, and the cause which I knew not, I searched out.' Job 29: 16. As magistrates are fathers, so especially the king, who is the head of magistrates, is a political father; he is placed as the sun among the lesser stars. The Scripture calls kings, 'fathers.' 'Kings shall be thy nursing fathers.' Isa 49: 23. They are to train up their subjects in piety, by good edicts and examples; and nurse them up in peace and plenty. Such nursing fathers were David, Hezekiah, Josiah, Constantine, and Theodosius. It is well for a people to have such nursing fathers, whose breasts milk comfort to their children. These fathers are to be honoured, for -

(1) Their place deserves honour. God has set these political fathers to preserve order and harmony in a nation, and to prevent those state convulsions which otherwise might ensue. When 'there was no king in Israel, every man did that which was right in his own eyes.' Judges 17: 6. It is a wonder that locusts have no king, yet they go forth by bands.

(2) God has promoted kings, that they may promote justice. As they have a sword in their hand, to signify their power; so they have a sceptre, an emblem of justice. It is said of the Emperor Marcus Aurelius, that he allotted one hour of the day to hear the complaints of those who were oppressed. Kings place judges as cherubim about the throne, for distribution of justice. These political fathers are to be honoured. 'Honour the king.' 1 Pet 2: 17. This honour is to be shown by a civil respect to their persons, and a cheerful submission to their laws; so far as they agree and run parallel with God's law. Kings are to be prayed for, which is a part of the honour we give them. 'I exhort that supplications, prayers, intercessions, be made for kings, that we may lead a

quiet, peaceable life, in all godliness and honesty.' 1 Tim 2: 1. We are to pray for kings, that God would honour them to be blessings; that under them we may enjoy the gospel of peace, and the peace of the gospel. How happy was the reign of Numa Pompilius, when swords were beaten into ploughshares, and bees made hives of the soldiers' helmets!

[2] There is the grave ancient father, who is venerable for old age; whose grey hairs are resembled to the white flowers of the almond-tree. Eccl 12: 5. There are fathers for seniority, on whose wrinkled brows, and in the furrows of whose cheeks is pictured the map of old age. These fathers are to be honoured. 'Thou shalt rise up before the hoary head, and honour the face of the old man. Lev 19: 32. Especially those are to be honoured who are fathers not only for their seniority, but for their piety; whose souls are flourishing when their bodies are decaying. It is a blessed sight to see springs of grace in the autumn of old age; to see men stooping towards the grave, yet going up the hill of God; to see them lose their colour, yet keep their savour. They whose silver hairs are crowned with righteousness, are worthy of double honour; they are to be honoured, not only as pieces of antiquity, but as patterns of virtue. If you see an old man fearing God, whose grace shines brightest when the sun of his life is setting, O honour him as a father, by reverencing and imitating him.

[3] There are spiritual fathers, as pastors and ministers. These are instruments of the new birth. 'Though ye have ten thousand instructors, yet have ye not many fathers; for in Christ Jesus I have begotten you through the gospel.' 1 Cor 4: 15. The spiritual fathers are to be honoured in respect of their office. Whatever their persons are, their office is honourable; they are the messengers of the Lord of Hosts. Mal 2: 7. They represent no less than God himself. 'Now then we are ambassadors for Christ.' 2 Cor 5: 20. Jesus Christ was of this calling; he had his mission and sanction from heaven, and this crowns the ministerial calling with honour. John 8: 18.

These spiritual fathers are to be honoured 'for their work's sake.' They come, like the dove, with an olive branch in the mouth; they preach glad tidings of peace; their work is 'to save souls.' Other callings have only to do with men's bodies or estates, but the minister's calling is employed about the souls of men. Their work is to redeem spiritual captives, and turn men 'from the power of Satan unto God.' Acts 26: 18. Their work is 'to enlighten them who sit in the region of darkness,' and make them 'shine as stars in the kingdom of heaven.' These spiritual fathers are to be 'honoured for their work's sake;' and this honour is to be shown three ways: -

(1) By giving them respect. 'Know them which labour among you and are over you in the Lord, and esteem them very highly in love for their work's sake.' 1 Thess 5: 12, 13. I confess the scandalous lives of some ministers have been a great reproach, and have made the 'offering of the Lord to be abhorred' in some places of the land. The leper in the law was to have his lip covered; so such as are angels by office, but lepers in their lives, ought to have their lips covered, and to be silenced. But though some deserve 'no honour', yet such as are faithful, and make it their work to bring souls to Christ, are to be reverenced as spiritual fathers. Obadiah honoured

the prophet Elijah. 1 Kings 18: 7. Why did God reckon the tribe of Levi for the first-born, Num 3: 13; why did he appoint that the prince should ask counsel of God by the priest, Num 27: 21; why did the Lord show, by that miracle of Aaron's rod flourishing, that he had chosen the tribe of 'Levi to minister before him,' Num 17; why does Christ call his apostles 'the lights of the world'; why does he say to all his ministers, 'Lo, I am with you to the end of the world;' but because he would have these spiritual fathers reverenced? In ancient times the Egyptians chose their kings out of their priests. They are far from showing this respect and honour to their spiritual fathers who have slight thoughts of such as have the charge of the sanctuary, and do minister before the Lord. 'Know them,' says the apostle, 'which labour among you.' Many can be content to know their ministers in their infirmities, and are glad when they have anything against them, but do not know them in the apostle's sense, so as to give them 'double honour.' Surely, were it not for the ministry, you would not be a vineyard but a desert. Were it not for the ministry, you would be destitute of the two seals of the covenant, baptism and the Lord's Supper; you would be infidels; 'for faith comes by hearing; and how shall they hear without a preacher?' Rom 10:14

(2) Honour these spiritual fathers, by becoming advocates for them, and wiping off those slanders and calumnies which are unjustly cast upon them. 1 Tim 5: 19. Constantine was a great honourer of the ministry; he vindicated them; he would not read the envious accusations brought against them, but burnt them. Do the ministers open their mouths to God for you in prayer, and will not you open your mouths in their behalf? Surely, if they labour to preserve you from hell, you should preserve them from slander; if they labour to save your souls, you ought to save their credit.

(3) Honour them by conforming to their doctrine. The greatest honour you can put upon your spiritual fathers, is to believe and obey their doctrine. He is an honourer of the ministry who is not only a hearer, but a follower of the word. As disobedience reproaches the ministry, so obedience honours it. The apostle calls the Thessalonians his crown. 'What is our crown of rejoicing? are not ye?' 1 Thess 2: 19. A thriving people are a minister's crown. When there is a metamorphosis, a change wrought; when people come to the word proud, but go away humble; when they come earthly, but they go away heavenly; when they come, as Naaman to Jordan, lepers, but they go away healed; then the ministry is honoured. 'Need we, as some others, epistles of commendation?' 2 Cor 3: 1. Though other ministers might need letters of commendation, yet Paul needed none; for, when men heard of the obedience wrought in these Corinthians by Paul's preaching, it would be a sufficient certificate that God had blessed his labours. The Corinthians were a sufficient honour to him; they were his letters-testimonial. You cannot honour your spiritual fathers more, than by thriving under their ministry, and living upon the sermons which they preach.

[4] There is the domestic father, that is, the master. He is paterfamilias, 'the father of the family'; therefore Naaman's servants called their master, father. 2 Kings 5: 13. The centurion calls his servant, son. Matt 8: 6. (Greek.) The servant is to honour his master, as the father of the family.

Though the master be not so qualified as he should be, yet the servant must not neglect his duty, but show some kind of honour to him.

(1) In obeying his master in licitis et honestis, 'in things that are lawful and honest.' 'Servants, be subject to your masters; not only to the good and gentle, but also to the froward.' 1 Pet 2: 18. God has nowhere given a charter of exemption to free you from your duty. You cannot disobey your earthly master but you disobey your master in heaven. Think not that birth, or high parts, no, nor even grace, will exempt you from obedience to your master. To obey him is an ordinance of God; and an apostle says, 'They that resist the ordinance, shall receive to themselves damnation.' Rom 13: 2.

(2) The servant's honouring his master, is seen in being diligent in his service. Apelles painted a servant with his hands full of tools, as an emblem of diligence. The loitering servant is a kind of thief, who, though he does not steal his master's goods, steals the time which he should have employed in his master's service. The slothful servant is called a 'wicked servant.' Matt 25: 26.

(3) The servant is to honour his master by being faithful. 'Who then is a faithful and wise servant?' Matt 24: 45. Faithfulness is the chief thing in a servant. Faithfulness in a servant is seen in six things: [1] In tenaciousness; in concealing the secrets the master has intrusted you with. If those secrets are not sins, you ought not to betray them. What is whispered in your ear you are not to publish on the house-top. Servants who do this are spies. Who would keep a glass that is cracked? Who would keep a servant that has a crack in his brain, and cannot keep a secret? [2] Faithfulness in a servant is seen in designing the master's advantage. A faithful servant esteems his master's goods as his own. Such a servant had Abraham; who, when his master sent him to transact business for him, was as careful about it, as if it had been his own. 'O Lord God of my master Abraham, I pray thee send me good speed this day, and show kindness unto my master Abraham.' Gen 24: 12. Doubtless Abraham's servant was as glad he had got a wife for his master's son, as if he had got a wife for himself. [3] Faithfulness in a servant is seen in standing up for the honour of his master. When he hears him spoken against, he vindicates him. As the master is careful of the servant's body, so the servant should be careful of the master's name. When the master is unjustly reproached the servant cannot be excused if he be possessed with a dumb devil. [4] Faithfulness is, when a servant is true to his word. He dares not tell a lie, but will speak the truth, though it be against himself. A lie doubles the sin. 'He that telleth lies, shall not tarry in my sight.' Psa 101: 7. A liar is near akin to the devil. John 8: 44. And who would let any of the devil's kindred live with him? The lie that Gehazi told his master Elisha, entailed leprosy on Gehazi and his seed for ever. 2 Kings 5: 27. In a faithful servant, the tongue is the true index of the heart. [5] Faithfulness is, when a servant is against impropriation. He dares not convert his master's goods to his own use. 'Not purloining.' Tit 2: 10. What a servant filches from his master, is damnable gain. He who enriches himself by stealing from his master, stuffs his pillow with thorns, on which his head will lie very uneasy when he comes to die. [6] Faithfulness consists in preserving the master's person, if unjustly in danger. Banister betrayed his master the Duke of

Buckingham, in King Richard the Third's reign; and the judgements of God fell upon the traitorous servant. His eldest son became mad; his daughter, of a singular beauty, was suddenly struck with leprosy; his younger son was drowned, and he himself was arraigned, and would have been executed, had he not been saved by his clergy. That servant who is not true to his master, will never be true to God or his own soul.

(4) The servant is to honour his master, by serving him, as with love, so with silence, that is, without repining, and without replying. 'Exhort servants to be obedient unto their own masters, not answering again.' Tit 2: 9. In the Greek, 'not giving cross answers.' Some servants who are slow at work, are quick at speech; and instead of being sorry for a fault, provoke by unbecoming language. Were the heart more humble, the tongue would be more silent. The apostle's words are, 'not answering again.' To those servants who honour their masters, or family-fathers, by submission, diligence, faithfulness, love, and humble silence, great encouragement is given. 'Servants, obey in all things your masters according to the flesh, not with eye-service, knowing that of the Lord ye shall receive the reward of the inheritance, for ye serve the Lord Christ.' Col 3: 22, 24. In serving your masters, you serve Christ, and he will not let you lose your labour; ye shall receive the 'reward of the inheritance.' From serving on earth, you shall be taken up to reign in heaven, and shall sit with Christ upon his throne. Rev 3: 21.

Having shown how servants are to honour their masters, I shall next show how masters are to conduct themselves towards their servants, so as to be honoured by them.

In general, masters must remember that they have a master in heaven, who will call them to account. 'Knowing that your Master also is in heaven.' Eph 6: 9. More particularly: -

(1) Masters must take care to provide for their servants. As they appoint them work, so they must give them their meat in due season. Luke 17: 7. They should see that the food be wholesome and sufficient. It is most unworthy of some governors of families, to lay out so much upon their own back, as to pinch their servants' bellies.

(2) Masters should encourage their servants in their work, by commending them when they do well. Though a master is to tell a servant of his faults, yet he is not always to beat on one string, but sometimes to take notice of that which is praiseworthy. This makes a servant more cheerful in his work, and gains the master the love from his servant.

(3) Masters must not overburden their servants, but proportion their work to their strength. They must not lay too much load on their servants, to make them faint under it. Christianity teaches compassion.

(4) Masters must seek the spiritual good of their servants. They must be seraphim to kindle their love to religion; they must be monitors to put them in mind of their souls; they must bring them to the pool of the sanctuary, to wait till the angel stir the waters. John 5: 4. They must seek God

for them, that their servants may be his servants; and must allow them time convenient for secret devotion. Some are cruel to the souls of their servants; they expect them to do the work about the house, but abridge them of the time they should employ in working out their salvation.

(5) Masters should be mild and gentle in their behaviour towards servants. 'Forbearing threatening.' Eph. 6: 9. 'Thou shalt not rule over him with rigour, but shalt fear thy God.' Lev 25: 43. It requires wisdom in a master to know how to keep up his authority, and yet avoid austerity. We have a good copy to write after our Master in heaven, who is 'slow to anger, and of great mercy.' Psa 145: 8. Some masters are so harsh and implacable that they are enough to spoil a good servant.

(6) Be very exact and punctual in the agreements you make with your servants. Do not prevaricate; keep not back any of their wages; nor deal deceitfully with them, as Laban did with Jacob, changing his wages. Gen 31: 7. Falseness in promise is as bad as false weights.

(7) Be careful of your servants, not only in health, but in sickness. If they have become sick while in your service, use what means you can for their recovery; and be not like the Amalekite, who forsook his servant when he was sick; but be as the good centurion, who kept his sick servant, and sought to Christ for a cure. 1 Sam 30: 13; Matt 8: 6. If you have a beast that falls sick, you will not turn it off, but have it looked to, and pay for its cure; and will you be kinder to your horses than to your servants? Thus should masters carry themselves prudently and piously, that they may gain honour from their servants, and may give up their accounts to God with joy.

[8] The natural father, the father of the flesh. Heb 12: 9. Honour thy natural father. This is so necessary a duty, that Philo the Jew placed the fifth commandment in the first table, as though we had not performed our whole duty to God till we had paid this debt of honour to our natural parents. Children are the vineyard of the parent's planting, and honour done to the parent is some of the fruit of the vineyard.

II. Children are to show honour to their parents,

{I] By a reverential esteem of their persons. They must 'give them a civil veneration.' Therefore, when the apostle speaks of fathers of our bodies, he speaks also of 'giving them reverence.' Heb 12: 9. This veneration or reverence must be shown: -

(1) Inwardly, by fear mixed with love. 'Ye shall fear every man his mother and his father.' Lev 19: 3. In the commandment the father is named first, but here the mother is first named. Partly to put honour upon the mother, because, by reason of many weaknesses incident to her sex, she is apt to be more slighted by children. And partly because the mother endures more for the child.

(2) Reverence must be shown to parents outwardly, both in word and gesture.

In word: and that either in speaking to parents, or speaking of them. In speaking of parents, children must speak respectfully. 'Ask on, my mother,' said king Solomon to his mother Bathsheba. 1 Kings 2: 20. In speaking of parents, children must speak honourably. They ought to speak well of them, if they deserve well. 'Her children arise up, and call her blessed' (Prov 31: 28); and, in case a parent betrays weakness and indiscretion, the child should make the best of it, and, by wise apologies, cover his parent's nakedness.

In gesture. Children are to show reverence to their parents by submissive behaviour, by uncovering the head, and bending the knee. Joseph, though a great prince, and his father had grown poor, bowed to him, and behaved himself as humbly as if his father had been the prince, and he the poor man. Gen 46: 29. King Solomon, when his mother came to him, 'rose off his throne, and bowed himself unto her.' 1 Kings 2: 19. Among the Lacedemonians, if a child had carried himself arrogantly or saucily to his father, it was lawful for the father to appoint whom he would to be his heir. Oh, how many children are far from thus giving reverence to their parents! They despise their parents; they carry themselves with such pride and neglect towards them, that they are a shame to religion, and bring their parents' grey hairs with sorrow to the grave. 'Cursed be he that setteth light by his father or his mother.' Deut 27: 16. If all that set light by their parents are cursed, how many children in our age are under a curse! If such as are disrespectful to parents live to have children, their own children will be thorns in their sides, and God will make them read their sins in their punishment.

[2] The second way of showing honour to parents is by careful obedience. 'Children, obey your parents in all things.' Col 3: 20. Our Lord Christ herein set a pattern to children. He was subject to his parents. Luke 2: 51. He to whom angels were subject was subject to his parents. This obedience to parents is shown three ways: -

(1) In hearkening to their counsel, 'Hear the instruction of thy father, and forsake not the law of thy mother.' Prov 1: 8. Parents are, as it were, in the room of God; if they would teach you the fear of the Lord, you must listen to their words as oracles, and not be as the deaf adder to stop your ears. Eli's sons hearkened not to the voice of their father, but were called 'sons of Belial.' 1 Sam 2: 12, 25. And as children must hearken to the counsel of their parents in spiritual matters, so in affairs which relate to this life as in the choice of a calling, and in case of entering into marriage. Jacob would not dispose of himself in marriage, though he was forty years old, without the advice and consent of his parents. Gen 28: 1,2. Children are, as it were, the parents' proper goods and possession, and it is great injustice in a child to give herself away without the parents' leave. If parents should indeed counsel a child to match with one that is irreligious or Popish, I think the case is plain, and many of the learned are of opinion that here the child may have a negative voice, and is not obliged to be ruled by the parent. Children are to 'marry in the Lord;' not, therefore, with persons irreligious, for that is not to marry in the Lord. 1 Cor 7: 39.

(2) Obedience to parents is shown in complying with their commands. A child should be the parents' echo; when the father speaks, the child should echo back obedience. The Rechabites

were forbidden by their father to drink wine; and they obeyed him, and were commended for it. Jer 35: 14. Children must obey their parents in all things. Col 3: 20. In things against the grain, to which they have most reluctance, they must obey their parents. Esau would obey his father, when he commanded him to fetch him venison, because it is probable he took pleasure in hunting; but refused to obey him in a matter of greater concernment, in the choice of a wife. But though children must obey their parents 'in all things,' yet restringitur ad licita et honesta; 'it is with the limitation of things just and honest.' 'Obey in the Lord,' that is, so far as the commands of parents agree with God's commands. Eph 6: 1. If they command against God, they lose their right of being obeyed, and in this case we must unchild ourselves.

[3] Honour is to be shown to parents in relieving their wants. Joseph cherished his father in his old age. Gen 47: 12. It is but paying a just debt. Parents brought up children when they were young, and children ought to nourish their parents when they are old. The young storks, by an instinct of nature, bring meat to the old ones when, by reason of age, they are not able to fly. Pliny calls it Lex pelargica [a law of the storks]. The memory of Aeneas was honoured for carrying his aged father out of Troy when it was on fire. I have read of a daughter, whose father being condemned to be starved to death, who gave him in his prison suck with her own breasts; which, being known to the governors, procured his freedom. Such children, or monsters shall I say, are to blame who are ashamed of their parents when they are old and fallen into decay; and when they ask for bread give them a stone. When houses are shut up, we say the plague is there; when children's hearts are shut up against their parents, the plague is there. Our blessed Saviour took great care for his mother. When on the cross, he charged his disciple John to take her home to him as his mother, and see that she wanted nothing. John 19: 26, 27.

III. The reasons why children should honour their parents are: -

[1] It is a solemn command of God, 'Honour thy father,' &c. As God's word is the rule, so his will must be the reason of our obedience.

[2] They deserve honour in respect of the great love and affection which they bear to their children; and the evidence of that love both in their care and cost. Their care in bringing up their children is a sign their hearts are full of love to them. Parents often take more care of their children than for themselves. They take care of them when they are tender, lest, like wall fruit, they should be nipped in the bud. As children grow older, the care of parents grows greater. They are afraid of their children falling when young, and of worse than falls when they are older. Their love is evidenced by their cost. 2 Cor 12: 14. They lay up and they lay out for their children; and are not like the raven or ostrich, which are cruel to their young. Job 39: 16. Parents sometimes impoverish themselves to enrich their children. Children never can equal a parent's love, for parents are the instruments of life to their children, and children cannot be so to their parents.

[3] To honour parents is well pleasing to the Lord. Col 3: 20. As it is joyful to parents, so it is pleasing to the Lord. Children! is it not your duty to please God? In honouring and obeying your

parents, you please God as well as when you repent and believe. And that you may see how well it pleases God, he bestows a reward upon it. 'That thy days may be long in the land which the Lord thy God giveth thee.' Jacob would not let the angel go till he had blessed him; and God would not part with this commandment till he had blessed it. Paul calls this the first commandment with promise. Eph 6: 2. The second commandment has a general promise to mercy; but this is the first commandment that has a particular promise made to it. Long life is mentioned as a blessing. 'Thou shalt see thy children's children.' Psa 128: 6. It was a great favour of God to Moses that, though he was a hundred and twenty years old, he needed no spectacles: 'His eye was not dim, nor his natural force abated.' Deut 34: 7. God threatened it as a curse to Eli, that there should not be an old man in his family. 1 Sam 2: 31. Since the flood, life is much abbreviated and cut short: to some the womb is their tomb; others exchange their cradle for their grave; others die in the flower of their age; death serves its warrant every day upon one or other. Now, when death lies in ambush continually for us, if God satisfies us with long life, saying (as in Psa 91: 16), 'With long life will I satisfy him;' it is to be esteemed a blessing. It is a blessing when God gives a long time to repent, and a long time to do service, and a long time to enjoy the comforts of relations. Upon whom is this blessing of long life entailed, but obedient children? 'Honour thy father, that thy days may be long.' Nothing sooner shortens life than disobedience to parents. Absalom was a disobedient son, who sought to deprive his father of his life and crown; and he did not live out half his days. The mule he rode upon, being weary of such a burden, left him hanging in the oak betwixt heaven and earth, so as not fit to tread upon the one, or to enter into the other. Obedience to parents spins out the life. Nor does obedience to parents lengthen life only, but sweetens it. To live long, and not to have a foot of land, is a misery; but obedience to parents settles land of inheritance upon the child. 'Hast thou but one blessing, O my father,' said Esau. Behold, God has more blessings for an obedient child than one; not only shall he have a long life, but a fruitful land: and not only shall he have land, but land given in love, 'the land which the Lord thy God giveth thee.' Thou shalt have thy land not only with God's leave, but with his love. All these are powerful arguments to make children honour and obey their parents.

Use one. If we are to honour our fathers on earth, much more our Father in heaven. 'If then I be a father, where is mine honour?' Mal 1: 6. A father is but the instrument of conveying life, but God is the original cause of our being. 'For it is he that has made us, and not we ourselves.' Psa 100: 3. Honour and adoration is a pearl which belongs to the crown of heaven only.

(1) We show honour to our heavenly Father by obeying him. Thus Christ honoured his Father. 'I came down from heaven, not to do mine own will, but the will of him that sent me.' John 6: 38. This he calls honouring God. 'I do always those things which please him.' 'I honour my Father.' John 8: 29, 49. The wise men not only bowed the knee to Christ, but presented him with 'gold and myrrh.' Matt 2: 11. So we must not only bow the knee, give God adoration, but bring him presents, give him golden obedience.

(2) We show honour to our heavenly Father by advocating his cause, and standing up for his

truth in an adulterous generation. That son honours his father who stands up in his defence, and vindicates him when he is calumniated and reproached. Do they honour God who are ashamed of him? 'Many believed on him, but did not confess him.' John 12: 42. They are bastard-sons who are ashamed to own their heavenly Father. Such as are born of God, are steeled with courage for his truth; they are like the rock, which no waves can break; like the adamant, which no sword can cut. Basil was a champion for truth in the time of the emperor Valens; and Athanasius, when the world was Arian, appeared for God.

(3) We show honour to our heavenly Father by ascribing the honour of all we do to him. 'I laboured more abundantly than they all, yet not I, but the grace of God which was with me.' 1 Cor 15: 10. If a Christian has any assistance in duty, any strength against corruption, he rears up a pillar and writes upon it, 'Hitherto has the Lord helped me.' As when Joab had fought against Rabbah, and had like to have taken it, sent for king David, that he might carry away the honour of the victory; so when a child of God has any conquest over Satan, he give all the honour to God. 2 Sam 12: 27, 28. Hypocrites, whose lamp is fed with the oil of vain glory, while they do any eminent service to God, seek to honour themselves; and so their very serving him is dishonouring him.

(4) We show honour to our heavenly Father by celebrating his praise. 'Let my mouth be filled with thy praise, and with thy honour all the day.' Psa 71: 8. 'Blessing and honour and glory and power, be unto him that sitteth upon the throne.' Rev 5: 13. Blessing God is honouring God. It lifts him up in the eyes of others, and spreads his fame and renown in the world. In this manner the angels, the choristers of heaven, are now honouring God; they trumpet forth his praise. In prayer, we act like saints, in praise like angels.

(5) We show honour to our heavenly Father, by suffering dishonour, yea, death for his sake. Paul did bear in his body the 'marks of the Lord Jesus.' Gal 6: 17. As they were the marks of honour to him, so they were trophies of honour to the gospel. The honour which comes to God, is not by bringing the outward pomp and glory to him, which we do to kings; but it comes in another way, by the suffering of his people, by which they let the world see what a good God they serve, and how they love him, and will fight under his banner to the death.

God is 'worthy of honour.' 'Thou art clothed with honour and majesty.' Psa 104: 1: What are all his attributes but glorious beams shining from this sun? He deserves more honour than men or angels can give him. 'I will call on the Lord who is worthy to be praised.' 2 Sam 22: 4. He is worthy of honour. We often confer honour upon those that do not deserve it. To many noble persons, who are sordid and vicious, we give titles of honour: they do not deserve honour; but God is worthy of honour. 'Blessed be thy glorious name, which is exalted above all blessing and praise.' Neh 9: 5. He is above all the acclamations and triumphs of the archangels. O then, let every true child of God honour his heavenly Father! Though the wicked dishonour him by their flagitous lives, let not his own children dishonour him. Sins in them are worse than in others. A fault in a stranger is not so much taken notice of as in a child. A spot in black cloth is not so much observed, but a spot in scarlet attracts every one's eye; so a sin in the wicked is not so much wondered at, it is a spot in black; but a sin in a child of God is a spot in scarlet, which is more visible, and brings odium and dishonour upon the gospel. The sins of God's own children go nearer to his heart. 'When the Lord saw it, he abhorred them, because of the provoking of his sons and of his daughters.' Deut 32: 19. O forbear doing anything that may reflect dishonour upon God. Will you disgrace your heavenly Father? Let not God complain of the provocations of his sons and daughters; let him not cry out, 'I have nourished and brought up children, and they have rebelled against me.' Isa 1: 2.

Use two. Does God command us to honour father and mother? Then let children put this great duty in practice; be living commentaries upon this commandment. Honour and reverence your parents; not only obey their commands, but submit to their rebukes. You cannot honour your Father in heaven unless you honour your earthly parents. To deny obedience to parents, entails God's judgements upon children. 'The eye that mocketh at his father, and despiseth to obey his mother, the ravens of the valley shall pick it out, and the young eagle shall eat it.' Prov 30: 17. Eli's two disobedient sons were slain. 1 Sam 4: 2: God made a law that the 'rebellious son should be stoned;' the same death the blasphemer had. Lev 24: 14. 'If a man have a stubborn and rebellious son, which will not obey the voice of his father, or the voice of his mother; then shall his father and his mother lay hold on him, and bring him out unto the elders of his city, and all the men of his city shall stone him with stones, that he die.' Deut 21: 18, 19, 21. A father having once complained, 'Never had a father a worse son than I have;' 'Yes,' said the son, 'my grandfather had.' This was a prodigy of impudence hardly to be paralleled. Manlius, when grown old and poor, had a son very rich, of whom he desired some food, but the son denied him relief, yea, disowned him from being his father, and sent him away with reproachful language. The poor old father let fall tears in grief, But God, to revenge the disobedience, struck the unnatural son with madness, of which he could never be cured. Disobedient children stand in a place where all God's arrows fly.

Use three. Let parents so act that they may gain honour from their children.

How should parents so act towards their children as to be honoured and reverenced by them?

(1) Be careful to bring them up in the fear and nurture of the Lord. 'Bring them up in the admonition of the Lord.' Eph 6: 4. You conveyed the plague of sin to them, therefore endeavour to get them healed and sanctified. Augustine says that his mother, Monica, travailed more for his spiritual birth than his natural. Timothy's mother instructed him from a child. 2 Tim 3: 15. She not only gave him her breast-milk, but 'the sincere milk of the word.' Season your children with good principles betides, that they may, with Obadiah, fear the Lord from their youth. 1 Kings 18: 12. When parents instruct not their children, they seldom prove blessings. God often punishes the carelessness of parents with undutifulness in their children. It is not enough that in baptism your

child is dedicated to God, but it must be educated for him. Children are young plants which you must be continually watering with good instruction. 'Train up a child in the way he should go: and when he is old, he will not depart from it.' Prov 22: 6. The more your children fear God, the more they will honour you.

(2) If you would have your children honour you, keep up parental authority: be kind, but do not spoil them. If you let them get too much ahead, they will condemn you instead of honouring you. The rod of discipline must not be withheld. 'Thou shalt beat him with the rod, and deliver his soul from hell.' Prov 23: 14. A child indulged and humoured in wickedness, will be a thorn in the parent's eye. David spoiled Adonijah. 'His father had not displeased him at any time, in saying, Why hast thou done so?' 1 Kings 1: 6, 7, 9. Afterwards he became a grief of heart to his father, and was false to the crown. Keep up your authority, and you keep up your honour.

(3) Provide for your children what is fitting, both in their minority and when they come to maturity. 'The children ought not to lay up for the parents, but the parents for the children.' 2 Cor 12: 14. They are your own flesh and, as the apostle says, 'No man ever yet hated his own flesh.' Eph 5: 29. The parents' bountifulness will cause dutifulness in the child. If you pour water into a pump, the pump will send water again out freely; so, if parents pour in something of their estate to their children, children worthy of the name will pour out obedience again to their parents.

(4) When your children are grown up, put them to some lawful calling, wherein they may serve their generation. It is good to consult the natural genius and inclination of a child, for forced callings do as ill, sometimes, as forced matches. To let a child be out of a calling, is to expose him to temptation. Melanchthon says, Odium balneum diaboli [Idleness is the devil's pleasure resort]. A child out of a calling is like fallow ground; and what can you expect should grow up but weeds of disobedience.

(5) Act lovingly to your children. In all your counsels and commands let them read love. Love will command honour; and how can a parent but love the child who is his living picture, nay, part of himself. The child is the father in the second edition.

(6) Act prudently towards your children. It is a great point of prudence in a parent not to provoke his children to wrath. 'Fathers, provoke not your children to anger, lest they be discouraged.' Col 3: 21.

How may a parent provoke his children to wrath?

(1) By giving them opprobrious terms. 'Thou son of the perverse rebellious woman,' said Saul to his son Jonathan. 1 Sam 20: 30. Some parents use imprecations and curses to their children, which provoke them to wrath. Would you have God bless your children, and do you curse them?

(2) Parents provoke children to wrath when they strike them without a cause, or when the

correction exceeds the fault. This is to be a tyrant rather than a father. Saul cast a javelin at his son to smite him, and his son was provoked to anger. 'So Jonathan arose from the table in fierce anger.' I Sam 20: 33, 34. In filium pater obtinet non tyrannicum imperium, set basilicum [A father exercises a kingly power over his son, not that of a tyrant]. Davenant.

(3) When parents deny their children what is absolutely needful. Some have thus provoked their children: they have stinted them, and kept them so short, that they have forced them upon indirect courses, and made them put forth their hands to iniquity.

(4) When parents act partially towards their children, showing more kindness to one than to another. Though a parent may have a greater love to one child, yet discretion should lead him not to show more love to one than to another. Jacob showed more love to Joseph than to all his other children, which provoked the envy of his brethren. 'Now Israel loved Joseph more than all his children, and when his brethren saw that, they hated him, and could not speak peaceably to him.' Gen 37: 3, 4.

(5) When a parent does anything which is sordid and unworthy, which casts disgrace upon himself and his family, as to defraud or take a false oath, it provokes the child to wrath. As the child should honour his father, so the father should not dishonour the child.

(6) When parents lay commands upon their children which they cannot perform without wronging their consciences. Saul commanded his son Jonathan to bring David to him. 'Fetch him to me, for he shall surely die.' I Sam 20: 31. Jonathan could not do this with a good conscience; but was provoked to anger. 'Jonathan arose from the table in fierce anger.' I Sam 20: 34. The reason why parents should show their prudence in not provoking their children to wrath, is this: 'Lest they be discouraged.' Col 3: 21. This word 'discouraged' implies three things. Grief. The parent's provoking the child, the child so takes it to heart, that it causes premature death. Despondency. The parents' austerity dispirits the child, and makes it unfit for service; like members of the body stupefied, which are unfit for work. Contumacy and refractoriness. The child being provoked by the cruel and unnatural carriage of the parent, grows desperate, and often studies to irritate and vex his parents; which, though it be evil in the child, yet the parent is accessory to it, as being the occasion of it.

(7) If you would have honour from your children, pray much for them. Not only lay up a portion for them, but lay up a stock of prayer for them. Monica prayed much for her son Augustine; and it was said, it was impossible that a son of so many prayers and tears should perish. Pray that your children may be preserved from the contagion of the times; pray that as your children bear your images in their faces, they may bear God's image in their hearts; pray that they may be instruments and vessels of glory. One fruit of prayer may be, that the child will honour a praying parent.

(8) Encourage that which you see good and commendable in your children. Virtus laudata crescit

[Goodness increases when praised]. Commending that which is good in your children makes them more in love with virtuous actions; and is like the watering of plants, which makes them grow more. Some parents discourage the good they see in their children, and so nip virtue in the bud, and help to damn their children's souls. They have their children's curses.

(9) If you would have honour from your children, set them a good example. It makes children despise parents, when the parents live in contradiction to their own precepts; when they bid their children be sober, and yet they themselves get drunk; or bid their children fear God, and are themselves loose in their lives. Oh if you would have your children honour you, teach them by a holy example. A father is a looking-glass, which the child often dresses himself by; let the glass be clear and not spotted. Parents should observe great decorum in their whole conduct, lest they give occasion to their children to say to them, as Plato's servant, 'My master has made a book against rash anger, but he himself is passionate;' or, as a son once said to his father, 'If I have done evil, I have learned it of you.'

2.6 The Sixth Commandment

'Thou shalt not kill.' Exod 20: 13.

In this commandment is a sin forbidden, which is murder, 'Thou shalt not kill,' and a duty implied, which is, to preserve our own life, and the life of others.

The sin forbidden is murder: 'Thou shalt not kill.' Here two things are to be understood, the not injuring another, nor ourselves.

I. The not injuring another.

[1] We must not injure another in his name. 'A good name is a precious balsam.' It is a great cruelty to murder a man in his name. We injure others in their name, when we calumniate and slander them. David complains, 'They laid to my charge things that I knew not.' Psa 35: 11. The primitive Christians were traduced for incest, and killing their children, as Tertullian says, Dicimur infanaticidii incestus rei [They charge us with infanticide and label us incestuous]. This is to behead others in their good name; it is an irreparable injury. No physician can heal the wounds of the tongue.

[2] We must not injure another in his body. Life is the most precious thing; and God has set this commandment as a fence about it, to preserve it. He made a statute which has never to this day been repealed. 'Whose sheddeth man's blood, by man shall his blood be shed.' Gen 9: 6. In the old law, if a man killed another unawares, he might take sanctuary; but if he killed him willingly, though he fled to the sanctuary, the holiness of the place would not defend him. 'If a man come

presumptuously upon his neighbour, to slay him with guile, thou shalt take him from mine altar, that he may die.' Exod 21: 14. In the commandment, 'Thou shalt do no murder,' all sins are forbidden which lead to it, and are the occasions of it: As,

(1) Unadvised anger. Anger boils in the veins, and often produces murder. 'In their anger they slew a man.' Gen 49: 6.

(2) Envy. Satan envied our first parents the robe of innocence, and the glory of paradise, and could not rest till he had procured their death. Joseph's brethren, because his father loved him, and gave him a 'coat of divers colours,' envied him, and took counsel to slay him. Gen 37: 20. Envy and murder are near akin, therefore the apostle puts them together. 'Envyings, murders.' Gal 5: 21. Envy is a sin which breaks both tables at once; it begins in discontent against God, and ends in injury against man, as we see in Cain. Gen 4: 6, 8. Envious Cain was first discontented with God, by which he broke the first table; and then fell out with his brother and slew him, and thus broke the second table. Anger is sometimes 'soon over,' like fire kindled in straw, which is quickly out; but envy is deep rooted, and will not quench its thirst without blood. 'Who is able to stand before envy?' Prov 27: 4.

(3) Hatred. The Pharisees hated Christ because he excelled them in gifts, and had more honour among the people than they. They never left him till they had nailed him to the cross, and taken away his life. Hatred is a vermin which lives upon blood. 'Because thou hast had a perpetual hatred, and hast shed the blood of the children of Israel.' Ezek 35: 5. Haman hated Mordecai because he would not bow to him, and presently sought revenge, by getting a bloody warrant sealed for the destruction of the whole race and seed of the Jews. Esther 3: 9. Hatred is ever cruel. All these sins are forbidden in this commandment.

How many ways is murder committed?

We may be said to murder another twelve ways. (1) With the hand; as Joab killed Abner and Amass. 'He smote him in the fifth rib, and shed out his bowels.' 2 Sam 20: 10. (2) With the mind. Malice is mental murder. 'Whosoever hates his brother is a murderer.' 1 John 3: 15. To malign another, and wish evil against him in the heart, is murdering him. (3) With the tongue, by speaking to the prejudice of another, and causing him to be put to death. Thus the Jews killed the Lord of life, when they inveighed against him, and accused him falsely to Pilate. John 18: 30. (4) With the pen. Thus David killed Uriah by writing to Joab to 'set Uriah in the forefront of the battle.' 2 Sam 11:15. Though the Ammonites' sword cut off Uriah, yet David's pen was the cause of his death; and therefore the Lord tells David by the prophet Nathan, 'Thou hast killed Uriah.' 2 Sam 12: 9. (5) By plotting another's death. Thus, though Jezebel did not lay her own hands upon Naboth, yet because she contrived his death, and caused two false witnesses to swear against him, and bring him within the compass of treason, she was the murderer. 1 Kings 21: 9, 10. (6) By putting poison into cups. Thus the wife of Commodes the emperor killed her husband by poisoning the wine which he drank. So, many kill little children by medicines that cause their death. (7) By witchcraft and sorcery - which were forbidden under the law. 'There shall not be found among you an enchanter, or a witch, or a consulter with familiar spirits.' Deut 18: 10, 11. (8) By having an intention to kill another; as Herod, under a pretence of worshipping Christ, would have killed him. Matt 2: 8, 13. So, when Saul made David go against the Philistines, he designed that the Philistine should have killed him. 'Saul said, Let not mine hand be upon him, but let the hand of the Philistines be upon him.' I Sam 18: 17. Here was intentional murder, and it was in God's account as bad as actual murder. (g) By consenting to another's death; as Saul to the death of Stephen. 'I also was standing by and consenting unto his death.' Acts 22: 20. He that gives consent is accessory to the murder. (10) By not hindering the death of another when in our power. Pilate knew Christ was innocent. 'I find no fault in him,' he said, but did not hinder his death; therefore he was guilty. Washing his hands in water could not wash away the guilt of Christ's blood. (11) By unmercifullness. By taking away that which is necessary for the support of life; as to take away the tools or utensils by which a man gets his living. 'No man shall take the upper or the nether millstone to pledge, for he taketh a man's life.' Deut 24: 6. Or by not helping him when he is ready to perish. You may be the death of another, as well by not relieving him, as by offering him violence. If thou dost not feed him that is starving, thou killest him. How many are thus guilty of the breach of this commandment! (12) By not executing the law upon capital offenders. A felon having committed six murders, the judge may be said to be guilty of five of them, because he did not execute the felon for his first offence.

What are the aggravations of this sin of murder?

(1) To shed the blood of another ceaselessly; as to kill another in a humour or frolic. A bee will not sting unless provoked, but many when not provoked, will take away the life of another. This makes the sin of blood more bloody. The less provocation to a sin the greater sin.

(2) To shed the blood of another contrary to promise. Thus, after the princes of Israel had sworn to the Gibeonites that they should live, Saul slew them. Josh 9: 15. 2 Sam 21: 1. Here were two sins bound together, perjury and murder.

(3) To take away the life of any public person enhances the murder, and makes it greater, as to kill a judge upon the bench, because he represents the king's person. To murder a person whose office is sacred, and comes on the King of heaven's embassage; the murdering of whom may be the murdering of many. Herod added this sin above all, that he shut up John the Baptist in prison, much more to behead him in prison. Luke 3: 20. To stain one's hands with royal blood. David's heart smote him because he did but cut off the lap of king Saul's garment. I Sam 24: 5. How would David's heart have smitten him if he had cut off Saul's head?

(4) To shed the blood of a near relation aggravates the murder, and dyes it of a deeper crimson. For a son to kill his father is horrid. Parricides are monsters in nature. Qui occidit patrem, plurima committit peccata in uno. Cicero. 'He who takes away his father's life, commits many sins in one;' he is not guilty of murder only, but of disobedience, ingratitude, and diabolical

cruelty. 'He who striketh his father or mother, shall be surely put to death.' Exod 21: 15. Then how many deaths is he worthy of that destroys his father or mother! Such a monster was Nero, who caused his mother, Agrippina, to be slain.

(5) To shed the blood of any righteous person aggravates the sin. Hereby justice is perverted. Such a person being innocent, is unworthy of death. A saint being a public blessing, lies in the breach to turn away wrath; so that to destroy him is to pull down the pillars of a nation. He is precious to God. Psa 116: 15. He is a member of Christ's body; therefore what injury is offered to him is done to God himself. Acts 9: 4.

Though, however, this commandment forbids private persons to shed the blood of another, unless in their own defence, yet, such as are in office must punish public offenders, even with death. To kill an offender is not murder, but justice. A private person sins if he draws the sword; a public person sins if he puts up the sword. A magistrate ought not to let the sword of justice rust in the scabbard. As he should not let the sword be too sharp by severity, so neither should the edge of it be blunted by too much levity.

Neither does this commandment prohibit a just war. When men's sins grow ripe, and long plenty has bred surfeit, God says, 'Sword, go through the land.' Ezek 14: 17. He encouraged the war between the tribes of Israel and Benjamin. When the iniquity of the Amorites was full, he sent Israel to war against them. Judges 11: 21.

Use one. It should be for a lamentation that this land is defiled with blood. Numb 35: 33. How common is this sin in this boasting age! England's sins are written in letters of blood. Some make no more of killing men than sheep. 'In thy skirts is found the blood of the poor innocents.' Jer 2: 34. Junius reads it, in alis; and so in Hebrew, 'in thy wings' is found the blood of innocents. It alludes to the birds of prey, which stain their wings with the blood of other birds. May not the Lord justly take up a controversy with the inhabitants of the land, because 'blood toucheth blood'? Hos 4: 2. There are wholesale murders. And that which should increase our lamentation is, that not only man's blood is shed among us, but Christ's blood. Profane flagitious sinners are said to 'crucify the son of God afresh.' Heb 6: 6. (1) They swear by his blood, and so, as it were, make his wounds bleed afresh. (2) They crucify Christ in his members. 'Why persecutes thou me?' Acts 9: 4. The foot being trodden on, the head cries out. (3) If it lay in their power, were Christ alive on earth, they would nail him again to the cross. Thus men crucify Christ afresh; and, if man's blood so cries, how loud will Christ's blood cry against sinners?

Use two. Beware of having your hands imbrued in the blood of others.

But such a one has wronged me by defamation, or otherwise; and if I spill his blood, I shall but revenge my own quarrel!

If he has done you wrong, the law is open; but take heed of shedding blood. What! Because he has wronged you, will you therefore wrong God? Is it not doing wrong to God to take his work out of his hand? He has said 'Vengeance is mine; I will repay.' Rom 12: 19. You would undertake to revenge yourself; would be plaintiff, and judge, and executioner, in yourself. This is a great wrong done to God, and he will not hold you guiltless.

To deter all from having their hands defiled with blood, consider what a sin murder is. It is (1) A God-affronting sin. It is a breach of his command, and trampling upon his royal edict. It is a wrong offered to God's image. 'In the image of God made he man.' Gen 9: 6. It is tearing God's picture, and breaking in pieces the King of heaven's broad seal. Man is the temple of God. 'Know ye not that your body is the temple of the Holy Ghost?' I Cor 6: 19. The man-slayer destroys God's temple; and will God endure to be thus confronted by proud dust?

(2) It is a crying sin. Clamitat in coelum vox sanguinis [The voice of blood cries to Heaven]. There are three sins in Scripture which are said to cry. Oppression. Psa 12: 5. Sodomy. Gen 18: 21. Bloodshed. This cries so loud, that it drowns all the other cries. 'The voice of thy brother's blood crieth unto me from the ground.' Gen 4: 10. Abel's blood had as many tongues as drops, to cry aloud for vengeance. This sin of blood lay heavy on David's conscience; though he had sinned by adultery, yet, what he cried out for most was, this crimson sin of blood. 'Deliver me from blood-guiltiness, O God.' Psa 51: 14. Though the Lord visits for every sin, yet he will in a special manner make 'inquisition for blood.' Psa 9: 12. If a beast killed a man it was to be stoned, and its flesh was not to be eaten. Exod 21: 28. If God would have a beast stoned that killed a man, which had not the use of reason to restrain it, much more will he be incensed against those who, against both reason and conscience, take away the life of a man.

(3) Murder is a diabolical sin. It makes a man the devil's first born, for he was a murderer from the beginning. John 8: 44. By saying to our first parents, 'Ye shall not die,' he brought death into the world.

(4) It is a cursed sin. If there be a curse for him that smites his neighbour secretly, he is doubly cursed that kills him. Deut 27: 24. The first man that was born was a murderer. 'And now art thou cursed from the earth.' Gen 4: 11. He was an excommunicated person, banished from the place of God's public worship. God set a mark upon bloody Cain. Gen 4: 15. Some think that mark was horror of mind, which, above all sins, accompanies the sin of blood. Others think it was a continual shaking and trembling in his flesh. He carried a curse along with him.

(5) It is a wrath-procuring sin. 2 Kings 24: 4.

It procures temporal judgements. Phocas, to get the empire, put to death all the sons of Mauritius the emperor, and then slew the emperor himself; but he was pursued by Priscus, his son-in-law, who cut off his ears and feet, and then killed him. Charles IX, who caused the massacre of so many Christians at Paris, died from blood issuing out of several parts of his body. Albania killed a man and made of his skull a cup to drink in. His own wife, soon afterwards, caused him to be murdered in his bed. Vengeance as a bloodhound pursues the murderer. 'Bloody men shall not live out half their days.' Psa 55: 23. It brings eternal judgements. It binds men over to hell. The Papists make nothing of massacres, because theirs is a bloody religion; they give a dispensation for murder, if it be to propagate the Catholic cause. If a cardinal puts his red hat upon the head of a murderer going to execution, he saves him from death. Let all impenitent murderers read their doom in Rev 21: 8: 'Murderers shall have their part in the lake which burneth with fire and brimstone, which is the second death.' We read of 'fire mingled with blood.' Rev 8: 7. Such as have their hands full of blood must undergo the wrath of God. Here is fire mingled with blood, and this fire is inextinguishable. Mark 9: 44. Time will not finish it, tears will not quench it.

[3] We must not injure another in his soul. This is the greatest murder of all, because there is more of God's image in the soul than in the body. Though the soul cannot be annihilated, it is said to be murdered when it is deprived of its happiness, and is for ever in torment. How many are soul murderers!

(1) Such as corrupt others by bad example. The world is led by example; especially by the examples of great ones, which are very pernicious. We are apt to do as we see others before us, especially those above us. Such as are placed in high power, are like the pillar of cloud; where that went, Israel went. When great ones move, others will follow them, though it be to hell. Evil magistrates, like the tail of the dragon, draw the 'third part of the stars after them.'

(2) Such as entice others to sin. The harlot by curling her hair, rolling her eyes, laying open her breasts, does what in her lies to be both a tempter and a murderer. Such a one was Messalina, wife to Claudius the emperor. 'I discerned a young man, and there met him a woman with the attire of a harlot; so she caught him and kissed him.' Prov 7, 10, 13. Better are the reproofs of a friend, than the kisses of a harlot.

(3) Ministers are murderers, who either starve, or poison, or infect souls. [1] That starve souls. 'Feed the flock of God which is among you.' 1 Pet 5: 2. These feed themselves and starve the flock; either through non-residing, they do not preach, or through insufficiency, they cannot. There are many in the ministry so ignorant that they had need to be taught the 'first principles of the oracles of God.' Heb 5: 12. Was he fit to be a preacher in Israel, think ye, who being asked something concerning the decalogue, answered he never saw any such book? [2] That poison souls. Such are heterodox ministers, who poison people with error. The basilisk poisons herbs and flowers by breathing on them; so the breath of heretical ministers poisons souls. The Socinian, who would rob Christ of his Godhead; the Armenian, who by advancing the power of the will, would take off the crown from the head of free-grace; the Antinomian, who denies the use of the moral law to a believer, as if it were antiquated and out of date - poison men's souls. Error is as damnable as vice. 'There shall be false teachers among you, who privily shall bring in damnable heresies, denying the Lord that bought them.' 2 Pet 2: 1. [3] That infect souls by their scandalous lives. 'Let the priests which come near to the Lord sanctify themselves.' Exod 19: 22.

Ministers who by their places are nearer to God, should be holier than others. The higher the elements are, the purer they are; air is purer than water; fire is purer than air. The higher men are in office, the holier they should be. John the Baptist was a shining lamp. But there are many who infect their people with their bad life; they preach one thing, and live another. Qui Curios simulant et bacchanalia vivunt [They make a show of goodness, but live a life of riot]. Like Eli's sons, they are in white linen, but have scarlet sins. Some say, that Prester John, the lord of Africa, caused to be carried before him a golden cup full of dirt; a fit emblem of such ministers as have a golden office, but are dirty and polluted in their lives. They are murderers, and the blood of souls will cry against them at the last day.

(4) Such as destroy others by getting them into bad company, and so make them proselytes to the devil. Vitia in proximum quamque transiliunt [Our vices leap on to the man next to us]. Seneca. A man cannot live in the Ethiopian climate but he will be discoloured with the sun, nor can he be in bad company but he will partake of their evil. One drunkard makes another; as the prophet speaks in another sense. 'I set before them pots full of wine, and cups, and said unto them, Drink ye wine;' so the wicked set pots of wine before others, and made them drink till reason be stupefied, and lust inflamed. Jer 35: 5. Such are guilty of the breach of this commandment. How sad will it be with those who have not only their own sins, but the blood of others to answer for! So much for the first thing forbidden in the commandment, the injuring of others.

II. THE second thing forbidden in this commandment is, injuring ourselves. 'Thou shalt not kill:' thou shalt do no hurt to thyself.

Thou shalt not hurt thy own body. One may be guilty of self-murder, either 1. Indirectly or occasionally. Or, 2. Directly and absolutely.

[1] Indirectly and occasionally; as

(1) When a man thrusts himself into danger which he might prevent. If a company of archers were shooting, and one should put himself in the place where the arrows fly, so that an arrow kills him, he is accessory to his own death. In the law, God would have the leper shut up, to keep others from being infected. Lev 13: 4. If any should be so presumptuous as to go to a leper, and get the plague of leprosy, he might thank himself for his own death. (2) A person may be guilty of his own death, in some sense, by neglecting the use of means for preserving life. If sick, and he uses no remedy; if he has received a wound, and will not apply a cure, he hastens his own death. God commanded Hezekiah to lay a 'lump of figs upon the boil.' Isa 38: 21. If he had not done so, he would have been the cause of his own death. (3) By immoderate grief. 'The sorrow of the world worketh death.' 2 Cor 7: 10. When God takes away a dear relation, and any one is swallowed up with sorrow, he endangers his life. How many weep themselves into their graves! Queen Mary grieved so excessively for the loss of Calais, that it broke her heart. (4) By intemperance or excess in diet. Surfeiting shortens life. Plures periere crapula, quam gladio [More perish by drink than by the sword]. Many dig their grave with their teeth. Too much oil

chokes the lamp. The cup kills more than the cannon. Excessive drinking causes untimely death.

[2] One may be guilty of self-murder, directly and absolutely.

(1) By envy. Envy is tristitia de bonis alienis, 'a secret repining at the welfare of another.' Invidus alterius rebus macrescit opimis. 'An envious man is more sorry at another's prosperity, than at his own adversity.' He never laughs but when another weeps. Envy is a self-murder, a fretting canker. Cyprian calls it vulnus occultum, 'a secret wound;' it hurts a man's self most. Envy corrodes the heart, dries up the blood, rots the bones. Envy is 'the rottenness of the bones.' Prov 14: 30. It is to the body what the moth is to the cloth, that eats it and makes its beauty consume. Envy drinks its own venom. The viper, which leaped on Paul's hand, thought to have hurt Paul, but fell into the fire itself. Acts 28: 3. So, while the envious man thinks to hurt another, he destroys himself.

(2) By laying violent hands on himself, and thus he commits felo de se; as Saul fell upon his own sword and killed himself. It is the most unnatural and barbarous kind of murder for a man to butcher himself and imbrue his hands in his own blood. A man's self is most near to him, therefore this sin of self-murder breaks both the law of God, and the bonds of nature. The Lord has placed the soul in the body, as in a prison; and it is a sin to break open this prison till God opens the door. Self-murderers are worse than the brute-creatures, which will tear and gore open one another, but not destroy themselves. Self-murder is occasioned usually by discontent, and a sullen melancholy. The bird that beats itself in the cage, and is ready to kill itself, is a true emblem of a discontented spirit.

Whence comes this discontent?

This discontent arises - (1) From pride. A man who swells with a high opinion of himself, and thinks he deserves better than others, when any great calamity befalls him, is discontented, and in a sudden passion will make away with himself. Ahithophel had high thoughts of himself, his words were esteemed oracles, and he could not bear to have his wise counsel rejected. 'He put his household in order, and hanged himself.' 2 Sam 17: 23. (2) From poverty. Poverty is a sore temptation. 'Give me not poverty.' Prov 30: 8. Many have brought themselves to poverty by their sin; and when a great estate is boiled away to nothing, they are discontented, and think it better to die quickly, than languish in misery, and the devil soon helps them to dispatch themselves. (3) From covetousness. Avarice is a dry drunkenness, a horse-leech that is never satisfied. The covetous man is like behemoth. 'Behold he drinketh up a river,' and yet his thirst is not allayed. Job 40: 33. The covetous miser hoards up corn; and if he hears the price of corn begins to fall, he is troubled, and there is no cure for his discontent but a halter. (4) From horror of mind. A man has sinned a great sin, has swallowed down some pills of temptation the devil has given him, and these pills begin to work in his conscience, and the horror becomes so great, that he chooses strangling. Judas having betrayed innocent blood, was in such an agony of conscience, that he hanged himself; as if, to avoid the stinging of a gnat, any one should endure the bite of a serpent.

I can see no ground of hope for such as make away with themselves; for they die in the very act of sin, and cannot have time to repent.

Hurting our own souls is forbidden in the command, 'Thou shalt not kill.' Many who are free from other murders, are guilty here. They murder their own souls. They wilfully damn themselves, and throw themselves into hell.

Who are they that murder their own souls?

(1) They wilfully murder their souls who have no sense of God, or the world to come, and are past feeling. Eph 4: 19. Tell them of God's holiness and justice, and they are not at all affected. 'They made their hearts as an adamant stone.' Zech 7: 12, 'The adamant,' says Pliny, 'is insuperable, the hammer cannot conquer it.' Sinners have adamantine hearts. When the prophet spake to the altar of stone, it rent asunder, but sinner's hearts are so hardened in sin (I Kings 13: 5), nothing will work upon them, neither ordinances nor judgements. They do not believe in a God; they laugh at hell. Thus they murder their own souls, and throw themselves into hell as fast as they can.

(2) They wilfully murder their own souls who resign themselves to their lusts, let what will come of it. The soul cries out in you, I am killing myself; I am murdering myself. They 'have given themselves over to work all uncleanness with greediness.' Eph 4: 19. Let ministers speak to them about their sins, let conscience speak, let affliction speak, they will have their lusts, even though they go to hell for them. Do not these murder their own souls? As Agrippina, mother of Nero, said, occidat modo imperet, let my son kill me, so he may reign; so many say in their hearts, let our sins damn us, so that they but please us. Herod will have his incestuous lusts, though it costs him his soul; and for a drop of pleasure men will drink a sea of wrath. Do not these massacre and damn their own souls?

(3) They murder their souls who avoid all means of saving them. They will go to plays, to drunken meetings, but will not set their foot in God's house, or come near the sound of the gospel-trumpet; as if one that is diseased should shun the bath for fear of being healed. These are self murderers as much as one who has the means of cure offered him, but chooses rather to die.

(4) They voluntarily murder their souls who take false prejudices against religion; as if it were so strict and severe that they must live a melancholy life, like hermits and anchorites, and drown all their joys in tears. It is a slander which the devil casts upon religion, for there is no true joy but in believing. Rom 15: 1, 3. No honey is so sweet as that which drops from a promise. Some men foolishly take up a prejudice against religion; they are resolved never to go to heaven, rather than go through the strait gate. I may say of prejudice, as Paul to Elymas, 'O prejudice, thou child of the devil, thou enemy of all righteousness,' how many souls hast thou damned? Acts 13: 10.

(5) They wilfully murder their own souls who will neither be good themselves, nor suffer others

to be so. 'Ye neither go [into the kingdom of heaven] yourselves, neither suffer ye them that are entering to go in.' Matt 23: 13. Such are they who persecute others for their religion. Drunken meetings may escape punishments from them, but if men meet to serve God, all severity will be used. They are resolved to shipwreck others, though they themselves are cast away in the storm. Oh! take heed of murdering your own souls. No creature but man willingly kills itself.

III. THE positive duty implied in the command is, that we should do all the good we can to ourselves and others.

[1] In reference to others. We should endeavour to preserve the lives and souls of others. [2] In reference to ourselves. We should preserve our own life and soul.

[1] In reference to others. We are to preserve the life of others. We should comfort them in their sorrows, relieve them in their wants, and like the good Samaritan, pour wine and oil into their wounds. 'I was a father to the poor.' Job 29: 16. 'The blessing of him that was ready to perish came upon me.' Ver 13. It is a great means of preserving the life of another to relieve him when he is ready to perish. When there was a great dearth in Rome, Pompey provided corn for its relief; and when the mariners were afraid to sail thither in a tempest, he said, 'It is not necessary that we should live, but it is necessary that Rome be relieved.' Grace makes the heart tender, it causes sympathy and charity. As it melts the heart in contrition towards God, so in compassion towards others. 'He has dispersed, he has given to the poor.' Psa 29: 9. This commandment implies that we should be so far from ruining others, that we should do all we can to preserve the lives of others. When you see the picture of death drawn in their faces, administer to their necessities; be temporal saviours to then; draw them out of the waters of affliction with a silver cord of charity. That I may persuade you to this, let me lay before you some arguments: -

(1) Works of charity evidence grace. As Faith. 'I will show thee my faith by my works.' James 2: 18. Works are faith's letters of credence. We judge of the health of the body by the pulse where the blood stirs and operates; so Christian, judge of the health of thy faith by the pulse of charity. The word of God is the rule of faith, and good works are the witnesses of faith. It evidences also Love. Love loves mercy; it is a noble bountiful grace. Mary loved Christ, and how liberal was her love! She bestowed on Christ her tears, kisses, and costly ointments. Love, like a full vessel, will have vent; it vents itself in acts of liberality.

(2) To communicate to the necessities of others is not left to our choice, but is an incumbent duty. 'Charge them that are rich in this world that they do good; that they be rich in good works.' I Tim 6: 17, 18. This is not only a counsel, but a charge. If God should lay a charge upon the inanimate creatures, they would obey; if he should charge the rocks, they would send forth water; if he should charge the clouds, they would melt into showers; if he should charge the stones, they would become bread. And shall we be harder than the stones, not to obey God when he charges us to 'be rich in good works?'

(3) God supplies our wants, and shall not we supply the wants of others? 'We could not live without mercy.' God makes every creature helpful to us: the sun to enrich us with its golden beams; the earth to yield us its increase, veins of gold, crops of corn, and store of flowers. God opens the treasury of his mercy; he feeds us every day out of the alms-basket of his providence. 'Thou openest thy hand, and satisfies the desire of every living thing.' Psa 145: 16. Does God supply our wants, and shall we not minister to the wants of others? Shall we be as a sponge to suck in mercy, and not as breasts to milk it out to others?

(4) Herein we resemble God, to be doing good to others. It is our excellence to be like God. 'Godliness is Godlikeness.' When are we more like him than in acts of bounty and munificence? 'Thou art good, and does good.' Psa 119: 68. 'Thou art good,' there is his essential goodness; and 'doest good,' there is his communicative goodness. The more helpful we are to others, the more like we are to God. We cannot be like God in omniscience, or in working miracles; but we may be like him in doing works of mercy.

(5) God remembers all our deeds of charity, and takes them kindly at our hands. 'God is not unrighteous to forget your labour of love which ye have shewed towards his name, in that you have ministered to the saints.' Heb 6: 10. The chief butler may forget Joseph's kindness, but the Lord will not forget any kindness we show to his people. 'I was an hungred and ye gave me meat; thirsty, and ye gave me drink.' Matt 25: 35. Christ takes the kindness done to his saints as done to himself. God has a bottle for your tears, and a book to write down your alms. 'A book of remembrance was written before him.' Mal 3: 16. Tamerlane had a register to write down all the names and good services of his soldiers; so God has a book of remembrance to write down all your charitable works; and at the day of judgement there shall be an open and honourable mention made of them in the presence of the angels.

(6) Hardheartedness to others in misery reproaches the gospel. When men's hearts are like pieces of rock, or as the scales of the leviathan, 'shut up as with a close seal,' you may as well extract oil out of flint, as the golden oil of charity out of them. Job 41: 15. They unchristianize themselves. Unmercifullness is the sin of the heathen. 'Unmerciful.' Rom 1: 31. It eclipses the glory of the gospel. Does the gospel teach uncharitableness? Does it not bid us 'draw out thy soul to the hungry'? Isa 58: 10. 'These things I will that thou affirm, that they which have believed in God, might be careful to maintain good works.' Tit 3: 8. While you relieve not such as are in want, you walk in opposition to the gospel; you cause it to be evil spoken of, and lay it open to the lash and censure of others.

(7) There is nothing lost by relieving the necessitous. The Shunammite woman was kind to the prophet, she welcomed him to her house, and she received kindness from him another way; he restored her dead child to life. 2 Kings 4: 35. Such as are helpful to others, shall 'find grace to help in time of need.' Such as pour out the golden oil of compassion to others, shall have the golden oil of salvation by God poured out to them; for 'a cup of cold water' they shall have 'rivers

of pleasure.' God will make it up some way or other in this life. 'The liberal soul shall be made fat.' Prov 11: 25. It shall be as the loaves in breaking multiplied; or, as the widow's oil, increased in pouring out. I Kings 17: 16. An estate may be imparted without being impaired.

(8) To do good to others in necessity keeps up the credit of religion. Works of mercy adorn the gospel, as the fruit adorns the tree. When 'one light so shines that others see our good works,' it glorifies God, crowns religion, and silences the lips of gainsayers. Basil says nothing rendered the true religion more famous in the primitive times, and made more proselytes to it, than the bounty and charity of Christians.

(9) The evil that accrues by not preserving the lives of others, and helping them in their necessities. God often sends a secret moth into their estate. 'There is that withholdeth more than is meet, but it tendeth to poverty.' Prov 11: 24. 'Whose stoppeth his ears at the cry of the poor, he also shall cry himself, but shall not be heard.' Prov 21: 13. 'He shall have judgement without mercy, that has shewed no mercy.' James 2: 13. Dives denied Lazarus a crumb of bread, and Dives was denied a drop of water. 'Depart from me, ye cursed; for I was an hungred, and ye gave me no meat.' Matt 15: 41. Christ says not, 'Ye took away my meat;' but 'Ye gave me no meat;' ye did not feed my members, therefore 'depart from me.' By all this, be ready to distribute to the necessities of others. This is included in the commandment, 'Thou shalt not kill.' Not only thou shalt not destroy another's life, but thou shalt preserve it by ministering to his necessities.

It is implied that we should endeavour to preserve the souls of others: counsel them about their souls; set life and death before them; help them to heaven. In the law, if one met his neighbour's ox or ass going astray, he must bring him back again. Exod 23: 4. Much more, if we see our neighbour's soul going astray, we should use all means to bring him back to God by repentance.

[2] In reference to ourselves. The commandment, 'Thou shalt not kill,' requires that we should preserve our own life and soul. It is engraven upon every creature that he should preserve his own natural life. We must be so far from self-murder, that we must do all we can to preserve natural life. We must use all means of diet, exercise, and lawful recreation, which, like oil, preserves the lamp of life from going out. Some have been tempted by Satan to believe they are such sinners that they do not deserve a bit of bread, and so they have been ready to starve themselves. This is contrary to the commandment, 'Thou shalt do no murder,' which implies that we are to use all proper means for the preservation of life. 'Drink no longer water, but use a little wine for thy stomach's sake.' 1 Tim 5: 23. Timothy was not, by drinking too much water, to overcool his stomach, and weaken nature, but to use means for self-preservation - to drink 'a little wine,' &c.

This commandment requires that we should also endeavour to preserve our own souls. Omnia si perdas animam servare memento [Though you lose all else, remember to save your soul]. It is engraven upon every creature, as with the point of a diamond, to look to its own preservation. If the life of the body must be preserved, much more the life of the soul. If he who does not provide for his own house is worse than an infidel, much more he who does not provide for his own soul. 1 Tim 5: 8. A main thing implied in the commandment is a special care for preserving our souls. The soul is a jewel, a diamond set in a ring of clay; Christ puts the soul in balance with the world, and it outweighs all. Matt 16: 26. The soul is a glass, in which some rays of divine glory shine; it has in it some faint idea and resemblance of a Deity; it is a celestial spark lighted by the breath of God. The body was made of the dust, but the soul is of a more noble origin. God breathed into man a living soul. Gen 2: 7.

(1) The soul is excellent in its nature. It is a spiritual being, 'it is a kind of angelical thing.' The mind sparkles with knowledge, the will is crowned with liberty, and all the affections are as stars shining in their orb. The soul being spiritual, it is of quick operation. How quick are the motions of a spark! How swift the wing of a cherubim! So quick and agile is the motion of the soul! What is quicker than thought? How many miles can the soul travel in an instant! The soul, being spiritual, moves upwards, it contemplates God and glory. 'Whom have I in heaven but thee?' Psa 73: 25. The motion of the soul is upward; but sin has put a wrong bias upon it, and made it move downward. The soul, being spiritual, has a self-moving power; it can subsist and move when the body is dead, as the mariner can subsist when the ship is broken. The soul, being spiritual, is immortal (Scaliger), aeternitatis gemma, 'a bud of eternity.'

(2) As the soul is excellent in its nature, so in its capacities. It is capable of grace, it is fit to be an associate and companion of angels. It is capable of communion with God, of being Christ's spouse. 'I have espoused you to one husband that I may present you as a chaste virgin to Christ.' 2 Cor 11: 2. It is capable of being crowned with glory for ever. Oh! then, carrying such precious souls about you, created with the breath of God, redeemed with the blood of God, what endeavours should you use for the saving of these souls! Let not the devil have your souls. Heliogabalus fed his lions with pheasants: the devil is called a roaring lion: feed him not with your souls. Besides the excellence of the soul, which may make you labour to get it saved, consider how sad it will be not to have the soul saved; it is such a loss as there is none like it; because in losing the soul, you lose many things with it. A merchant in losing his ship, loses many things with it: he loses money, jewels, spices, &c.; so he that loses his soul, loses Christ and the company of angels in heaven. It is an infinite loss - an irreparable loss; it can never be made up again. 'Two eyes and one soul.' Chrysostom. Oh! what care should be taken of the immortal soul! I would request but this of you, that you take as much care for the saving of your souls as you do for getting an estate. Nay, do but take as much care for saving your souls as the devil does for destroying them. Oh! how industrious is Satan to damn souls! How does he play the serpent in his subtle laying of snares to catch souls! How does he shoot the fiery darts! He is never idle; he is a busy bishop in his diocese; he 'walketh about seeking whom he may devour.' 1 Pet 5: 8. Now, is it not a reasonable request to take as much care for saving your souls as the devil does for destroying them?

How can we have our souls saved?

By having them sanctified. Only the 'pure in heart shall see God.' Get your souls inlaid and enamelled with holiness. I Pet 1: 16. It is not enough that 'we cease to do evil;' which is all the evidence some have to show, and lose heaven by short shooting; but we must be inwardly sanctified. Not only the 'unclean spirit' must go out, but we must be filled with the Holy Ghost. Eph 5: 19. This holiness must needs be, if you consider God is to dwell with you here, and you are to dwell with him hereafter.

God is to dwell with you here. He takes up the soul for his own lodging. 'That Christ may dwell in your hearts.' Eph 3: 17. Therefore the soul must be consecrated. A king's palace must be kept clean, especially his presence chamber. The body is the temple of the Holy Ghost. I Cor 6: 19. The soul is the sanctum sanctorum; how holy should it be!

You are to dwell with God. Heaven is a holy place. 'An inheritance undefiled.' I Pet 1: 4. And how can you dwell with God till you are sanctified? We do not put wine into a musty vessel; and God will not put the new wine of glory into a sinful heart. Oh, then, as you love your souls, and would have them saved eternally, endeavour after holiness! By this means you will have a fitness for the kingdom of heaven, and your souls will be saved in the day of the Lord Jesus.

2.7 The Seventh Commandment

'Thou shalt not commit adultery.' Exod 20: 14.

God is a pure, holy spirit, and has an infinite antipathy against all uncleanness. In this commandment he has entered his caution against it; non moechaberis, 'Thou shalt not commit adultery.' The sum of this commandment is, The preservations of corporal purity. We must take heed of running on the rock of uncleanness, and so making shipwreck of our chastity. In this commandment there is something tacitly implied, and something expressly forbidden.

1. The thing implied is that the ordinance of marriage should be observed. 'Let every man have his own wife, and let every woman have her own husband.' 1 Cor 7: 2. 'Marriage is honourable and the bed undefiled.' Heb 13: 4. God instituted marriage in paradise; he brought the woman to the man. Gen 2: 22. He gave them to each other in marriage. Jesus Christ honoured marriage with his presence. John 2: 2. The first miracle he wrought was at a marriage, when he turned the 'water into wine.' Marriage is a type and resemblance of the mystical union between Christ and his church. Eph 5: 32.

In marriage there are general and special duties. The general duty of the husband is to rule. 'The husband is the head of the wife.' Eph 5: 23. The head is the seat of rule and judgement; but he must rule with discretion. He is head, therefore must not rule without reason. The general duty on the wife's part is submission. 'Wives, submit yourselves unto your own husbands, as unto the

Lord.' Eph 5: 22. It is observable that the Holy Ghost passed by Sarah's failings, not mentioning her unbelief; but he takes notice of that which was good in her, as her reverence and obedience to her husband. 'Sarah obeyed Abraham, calling him lord.' I Pet 3: 6.

The special duties belonging to marriage, are love and fidelity. Love is the marriage of the affections. Eph 5: 25. There is, as it were, but one heart in two bodies. Love lines the yoke and makes it easy; it perfumes the marriage relation; and without it there is not conjugium but conjurgium [not harmony but constant wrangling]. Like two poisons in one stomach, one is ever sick of the other. In marriage there is mutual promise of living together faithfully according to God's holy ordinance. Among the Romans, on the day of marriage, the woman presented to her husband fire and water: signifying that as fire refines, and water cleanses, she would live with her husband in chastity and sincerity.

II. The thing forbidden in the commandment is infecting ourselves with bodily pollution and uncleanness. 'Thou shalt not commit adultery.' The fountain of this sin is lust. Since the fall, holy love has degenerated to lust. Lust is the fever of the soul.

There is a twofold adultery.

[1] Mental. 'Whosoever looketh on a woman to lust after her has committed adultery with her already in his heart.' Matt 5: 28. As a man may die of an inward bleeding, so he may be damned for the inward boilings of lust, if it be not mortified.

{2] Corporal; as when sin has conceived, and brought forth in the act. This is expressly forbidden under a sub poena. 'Thou shalt not commit adultery.' This commandment is set as a hedge to keep out uncleanness; and they that break this hedge a serpent shall bite them. Job calls adultery a 'heinous crime.' Job 31: 2: Every failing is not a crime; and every crime is not a heinous crime; but adultery is flagitium, 'a heinous crime.' The Lord calls it villany. 'They have committed villany in Israel, and have committed adultery with their neighbours' wives.' Jer 29: 23.

Wherein appears the greatness of this sin?

(1) It is a breach of the marriage-oath. When persons come together in a matrimonial way, they bind themselves by covenant to each other, in the presence of God, to be true and faithful in the conjugal relation. Unchastity falsifies this solemn oath; and herein adultery is worse than fornication, because it is a breach of the conjugal bond.

(2) The greatness of the sin lies in this: that it is a great dishonour done to God. God says, 'Thou shalt not commit adultery.' The adulterer sets his will above God's law, tramples upon his command, affronts him to his face; as if a subject should tear his prince's proclamation. The adulterer is highly injurious to all the Persons in the Trinity. To God the Father. Sinner, God has given thee thy life, and thou dost waste the lamp of life, the flower of thine age in lewdness. He

has bestowed on thee many mercies, health, and estate, and thou spendest all on harlots. Did God give thee wages to serve the devil? It is injurious to God the Son, in two ways. As he has purchased thee with his blood. 'Ye are bought with a price.' 1 Cor 6: 20. Now he who is bought is not his own; it is a sin for him to go to another, without consent, from Christ, who has bought him with a price. As by virtue of baptism thou art a Christian, and professes that Christ is thy head, and thou art a member of Christ; therefore, what an injury is it to Christ, to 'take the members of Christ, and make them the members of a harlot'? I Cor 6: 15. It is injurious to God the Holy Ghost; for the body is his temple. 'Know ye not that your body is the temple of the Holy Ghost which is in you?' I Cor 6: 19. And how great a sin is it to defile his temple!

(3) The sin of adultery lies in this: that it is committed with mature deliberation. There is contriving the sin in the mind, then consent in the will, and then the sin is put forth into act. To sin against the light of nature, and to sin deliberately, is like the dye to the wool, it gives sin a tincture, and dyes it of a crimson colour.

(4) That which makes adultery so sinful is, that it is needless. God has provided a remedy to prevent it. 'To avoid fornication, let every man have his own wife.' I Cor 7: 2. Therefore, after this remedy prescribed, to be guilty of fornication or adultery, is inexcusable; it is like a rich thief, that steals when he has no need. This increases the sin.

Use one. The church of Rome is here condemned, which allows the sin of fortification and adultery. It suffers not its priests to marry, but they may have their courtesans. The worst kind of uncleanness, incest with the nearest of kin, is dispensed with for money. It was once said of Rome, Urbs est jam tota lupanar, Rome was become a common stew. And no wonder, when the Pope, for a sum of money, could give a license and patent to commit uncleanness; and, if the patent were not enough, he would give them a pardon. Many of the Papists judge fornication to be venial. God condemns the very lusting. Matt 5: 28. If God condemns the thought, how dare they allow the fact of fornication? You see what a cage of unclean birds the church of Rome is. They call themselves the Holy Catholic Church; but how can they be holy who are so steeped and parboiled in fornication, incest, sodomy, and all manner of uncleanness?

Use two. It is a matter for lamentation to see this commandment so slighted and violated among us. Adultery is the reigning sin of the times. 'They are all adulterers, as an oven heated by the baker.' Hos 7: 4. The time of King Henry VIII was called the golden age, but this may be called the unclean age, wherein whore-hunting is common. 'In thy filthiness is lewdness.' Ezek 24: 13. Luther tells us of one who said, 'If he might but satisfy his lust, and be carried from one whore-house to another, he would desire no other heaven'; and who afterwards breathed out his soul betwixt two notorious strumpets. This is to love forbidden fruit, to love to drink of stolen waters. 'Son of man, dig in the wall; and when I had digged, behold a door; and he said, Go in and behold the wicked abominations that they do here.' Ezek 8: 8, 9. Could we, as the prophet, dig in the walls of many houses, what vile abominations should we see there! In some chambers we might see fornication; dig further, and we may see adultery; dig further, and we may see incest, &c. And may not the Lord go from his sanctuary? 'Sees thou the great abominations that the house of Israel committeth, that I should go far off from my sanctuary?' Ezek 8: 6. God might remove his gospel, and then we might write Ichabod on this nation, 'The glory is departed.' Let us mourn for what we cannot reform.

Use three. For exhortation, to keep ourselves from the sin of adultery. 'Let every man have his own wife,' says Paul, not his concubine, nor his courtesan. 1 Cor 7: 2. That I may deter you from adultery, let me show you the great evil of it.

(1) It is a thievish sin. It is the highest sort of theft. The adulterer steals from his neighbour that which is more than his goods and estate; he steals away his wife from him, who is flesh of his flesh.

(2) Adultery debases a person; it makes him resemble the beasts; therefore the adulterer is described like a horse neighing. 'Every one neighed after his neighbour's wife.' Jer 5: 8. Nay, it is worse than brutish; for some creatures that are void of reason, yet by the instinct of nature, observe some decorum and chastity. The turtle dove is a chaste creature, and keeps to its mate; and the stork, wherever he flies, comes into no nest but his own. Naturalists write that if a stork, leaving his own mate, joins with any other, all the rest of the storks fall upon it, and pull its feathers from it. Adultery is worse than brutish, it degrades a person of his honour.

(3) Adultery pollutes. The devil is called an unclean spirit. Luke 11: 24. The adulterer is the devil's first-born; he is unclean; he is a moving quagmire; he is all over ulcerated with sin; his eyes sparkle with lust; his mouth foams out filth; his heart burns like mount Etna, in unclean desires; and he is so filthy, that if he die in this sin, all the flames of hell will never purge away his uncleanness. And, as for the adulteress, who can paint her black enough? The Scriptures calls her a deep ditch. Prov 23: 27. She is a common drain; whereas a believer's body is a living temple, and his soul a little heaven, be spangled with the graces, as so many stars. The body of a harlot is a walking dung hill, and her soul a lesser hell.

(4) Adultery is destructive to the body. 'And thou mourn at the last, when thy flesh and thy body are consumed.' Prov 5: 11. It brings into a consumption. Uncleanness turns the body into a hospital, it wastes the radical moisture, rots the skull, and eats the beauty of the face. As the flame wastes the candle, so the fire of lust consumes the bones. The adulterer hastens his own death. 'Till a dart strike through his liver.' Prov 7: 23. The Romans had their funerals at the gate of Venus's temple, to signify that lust brings death. Venus is lust.

(5.) Adultery is a drain upon the purse; it wastes not the body only, but the estate. 'By means of a whorish woman, a man is brought to a piece of bread.' Prov 6: 26. Whores are the devil's horse-leeches, sponges that suck in money. The prodigal son spent his portion when he fell among harlots. Luke 15: 30. The concubine of King Edward III, when he was dying, got all she could from him, and even plucked the rings off his fingers, and so left him. He that lives in luxury, dies in beggary.

(6) Adultery destroys reputation. 'Whoso committeth adultery with a woman, a wound and dishonour shall he get, and his reproach shall not be wiped away.' Prov 6: 32, 33. Some, when they get wounds, get honour. The soldier's wounds are full of honour; the martyr's wounds for Christ are full of honour; but the adulterer gets wounds, but no honour to his name. 'His reproach shall not be wiped away.' Wounds of reputation no physician can heal. When the adulterer dies, his shame lives. When his body rots underground, his name rots above ground. His base-born children are living monuments of his shame.

(7) This sin impairs the mind; it steals away the understanding; it stupefies the heart. 'Whoredom and wine take away the heart.' Hos 4: 11. It eats out all heart for good. Solomon besotted himself with women, and they enticed him to idolatry.

(8) This sin incurs temporal judgements. The Mosaic law made adultery death. 'The adulterer and adulteress shall surely be put to death;' and the usual death was stoning. Lev 20: 10; Deut 22: 24. The Salons commanded persons taken in this sin to be burnt. The Romans caused their heads to be stricken off. Like a scorpion, this sin carries a sting in its tail. The adultery of Paris and Helen was the death of both, and the ruin of Troy. 'Jealousy is the rage of a man.' Prov 6: 34. The adulterer is often killed in the act of his sin. Adultery cost Otho the emperor, and Pope Sixtus IV their lives. Laeta venire Venus, tristis abire solet [Lust's practice is to make a joyful entrance, but she leaves in misery]. I have read of two citizens in London, in 1583, who, having defiled themselves with adultery on the Lord's-day, were immediately struck dead with fire from heaven. If all who are now guilty of this sin were to be punished in this manner, it would rain fire again, as on Sodom.

(9) Adultery, without repentance, damns the soul. 'Neither fornicators, nor adulterers, nor effeminate, shall enter into the kingdom of God.' I Cor 6: 9. The fire of lust brings to the fire of hell. 'Whoremongers and adulterers God will judge.' Heb 13: 4. Though men may neglect to judge them, yet God will judge them. But will not God judge all other sinners? Yes. Why then does the apostle say, 'Whoremongers and adulterers God will judge'? The meaning is, he will judge them assuredly; they shall not escape the hand of justice; and he will punish them severely. 'The Lord knoweth how to reserve the unjust to the day of judgement to be punished, but chiefly them that walk in the lust of uncleanness.' 2 Pet 2: 9, 10. The harlot's breast keeps from Abraham's bosom. Momentaneum est quod delectat, auternum quod cruciat [The delight lasts a moment, the torment an eternity]. Who for a cup of pleasure would drink a sea of wrath? 'Her guests are in the depths of hell.' Prov 9: 18. A wise traveller, though many pleasant dishes are set before him at the inn, forbears to taste, because of the reckoning. We are all travellers to Jerusalem above; and when many baits of temptation are set before us, we should refrain, and think of the reckoning which will be brought in at death. With what stomach could Dionysius eat

his dainties, when he imagined there was a naked sword hung over his head as he sat at meat? While the adulterer feeds on strange flesh, the sword of God's justice hangs over his head. Causinus speaks of a tree growing in Spain, that is of a sweet smell, and pleasant to the taste, but the juice of it is poisonous. This is an emblem of a harlot; who is perfumed with powders, and fair to look on, but poisonous and damnable to the soul. 'She has cast down many wounded, yea, many strong men have been slain by her.' Prov 7: 26.

(10) The adulterer not only wrongs his own soul, but does what in him lies to destroy the soul of another, and so kills two at once. He is worse than the thief; for, suppose a thief robs a man, yea, takes away his life, the man's soul may be happy; he may go to heaven as well as if he had died in his bed. But he who commits adultery, endangers the soul of another, and deprives her of salvation so far as in him lies. Now, what a fearful thing is it to be an instrument to draw another to hell!

(11) The adulterer is abhorred of God. 'The mouth of strange women is a deep pit: he that is abhorred of the Lord shall fall therein.' Prov 22: 14. What can be worse than to be abhorred of God? God may be angry with his own children; but for God to abhor a man, is the highest degree of hatred.

How does the Lord show his abhorrence of the adulterer?

In giving him up to a reprobate mind, and a seared conscience. Rom 1: 28. He is then in such a condition that he cannot repent. He is abhorred of God. He stands upon the threshold of hell; and when death gives him a push, he tumbles in. All this should sound a retreat in our ears, and call us off from the pursuit of so damnable a sin as uncleanness. Hear what the Scriptures say: 'Come not nigh the door of her house.' Prov 5: 8. 'Her house is the way to hell.' Prov 7: 27.

(12) Adultery sows discord. It destroys peace and love, the two best flowers that grow in a family. It sets husband against wife, and wife against husband; and so causes the 'joints of the same body to smite one against another.' This division in a family works confusion; for 'A house divided against a house falleth.' Luke 11: 17. Omne divisibile est corruptibile.

Use four. I shall give some directions, by way of antidote, to keep from the infection of this sin.

(1) Come not into the company of a whorish woman; avoid her house, as a seaman does a rock. 'Come not nigh the door of her house.' Prov 5: 8. He who would not have the plague, must not come near infected houses; every whore-house has the plague in it. Not to beware of the occasion of sin, and yet pray, 'Lead us not into temptation,' is, as if one should put his finger into the candle, and yet pray that it may not be burnt.

(2) Look to your eyes. Much sin comes in by the eye. 'Having eyes full of adultery.' 2 Pet 2: 14. The eye tempts the fancy, and the fancy works upon the heart. A wanton amorous eye may usher

in sin. Eve first saw the tree of knowledge, and then she took. Gen 3: 6. First she looked and then she loved. The eye often sets the heart on fire; therefore Job laid a law upon his eyes. 'I made a covenant with my eyes, why then should I think upon a maid?' Job 31: 1. Democritus the philosopher plucked out his eyes, because he would not be tempted with vain objects; the Scripture does not bid us do this, but to set a watch before our eyes.

(3) Look to your lips. Take heed of any unseemly word that may enkindle unclean thoughts in yourselves or others. 'Evil communications corrupt good manners.' I Cor 15: 33. Impure discourse is the bellows to blow up the fire of lust. Much evil is conveyed to the heart by the tongue. 'Set a watch, O Lord, before my mouth.' Psa 141: 3.

(4) Look in a special manner to your heart. 'Keep thy heart with all diligence.' Prov 4: 23. Every one has a tempter in his own bosom. 'Out of the heart proceed evil thoughts.' Matt 15: 19. Thinking of sin makes way for the act of sin. Suppress the first risings of sin in your heart. As the serpent, when danger is near, keeps his head, so keep your heart, which is the spring from whence all lustful motions proceed.

(5) Look to your attire. We read of the attire of a harlot. Prov 7: 10. A wanton dress is a provocation to lust. Cuttings and braidings of the hair, a painted face, naked breasts, are allurements to vanity. Where the sign is hung out, people will go in and taste the liquor. Jerome says, they who by their lascivious attire endeavour to draw others to lust, though no evil follows, are tempters, and shall be punished, because they offered the poison to others, though they would not drink.

(6) Take heed of evil company. Serpunt vitia et in proximum quemque transiliunt [Vices spread abroad and spring on to any standing by]. Seneca. Sin is a very catching disease; one tempts another to sin, and hardens him in it. There are three cords that draw men to adultery: the inclination of the heart, the persuasion of evil company, and the embraces of the harlot; and this threefold cord is not easily broken. 'A fire was kindled in their company.' Psa 106: 18. The fire of lust is kindled in bad company.

(7) Beware of going to plays. A play-house is often a preface to a whorehouse. Ludi praebent semina nequitiae [Plays furnish the seeds of wickedness]. We are bid to avoid all appearance of evil: and are not plays the appearance of evil? Such sights are there that are not fit to be beheld with chaste eyes. Both Fathers and Councils have shown their dislike to going to plays. A learned divine observes, that many have on their death-beds confessed, with tears, that the pollution of their bodies has been occasioned by going to plays.

(8) Take heed of mixed dancing. Instrumenta luxuriae tripudia [Dances are instruments of wantonness]. From dancing, people come to dalliance with another, and from dalliance to uncleanness. 'There is,' says Calvin, 'for the most part, some unchaste behaviour in dancing.' Dances draw the heart to folly by wanton gestures, by unchaste touches, and by lustful looks.

Chrysostom inveighed against mixed dancing in his time. 'We read,' he says, 'of a marriage feast, and of virgins going before with lamps, but of dancing there we read not.' Matt 25: 7. Many have been ensnared by dancing; as the duke of Normandy, and others. Saltatio adadulteras non ad pudicas pertinet [Dancing is the province not of the chaste woman, but of the adulteress]. Ambrose. Chrysostom says, where dancing is, there the devil is. I speak chiefly of mixed dancing. We read of dances in Scripture, but they were sober and modest. Exod 15: 20. They were not mixed dances, but pious and religious, being usually accompanied with singing praises to God.

(9) Take heed of lascivious books, and pictures that provoke to lust. As the reading of the Scripture stirs up love to God, so reading bad books stirs up the mind to wickedness. I could name one who published a book to the world full of effeminate, amorous, and wanton expressions, who, before he died, was much troubled for it, and burned the book which made so many burn in lust. To lascivious books I may add lascivious pictures, which bewitch the eye, and are incendiaries to lust. They secretly convey poison to the heart. Qui aspicit innocens aspectu fit nocens. Popish pictures are not more prone to stir up idolatry than unclean pictures are to stir up to concupiscence.

(10) Take heed of excess in diet. When gluttony and drunkenness lead the van, chambering and wantonness bring up the rear. Vinum fomentum libidinis; 'any wine inflames lust;' and fulness of bread is made the cause of Sodom's uncleanness. Ezek 16: 49. The rankest weeds grow out of the fattest soil. Uncleanness proceeds from excess. 'When I had fed them to the full, every one neighed after his neighbour's wife.' Jer 5: 8. Get the 'golden bridle of temperance.' God allows recruits of nature, and what may fit us the better for his service; but beware of surfeit. Excess in the creature clouds the mind, chokes good affections, and provokes lust. Paul did 'keep under his body.' I Cor 9: 27. The flesh pampered is apt to rebel. Corpus impinguatum recalcitrat.

(11) Take heed of idleness. When a man is out of a calling, he is ready to receive any temptation. We do not sow seed in fallow-ground; but the devil sows most seed of temptation in such as lie fallow. Idleness is the cause of sodomy and uncleanness. Ezek 16:49. When David was idle on the top of his house, he espied Bathsheba, and took her to him. 2 Sam 11: 4. Jerome gave his friend counsel to be always well employed in God's vineyard, that when the devil came, he might have no leisure to listen to temptation.

(12) To avoid fornication and adultery, let every man have a chaste, entire love to his own wife. Ezekiel's wife was the desire of his eyes. Chap 24: 16. When Solomon had dissuaded from strange women, he prescribed a remedy against it. 'Rejoice with the wife of thy youth.' Prov 5: 18. It is not having a wife, but loving a wife, that makes a man live chastely. He who loves his wife, whom Solomon calls his fountain, will not go abroad to drink of muddy, poisoned waters. Pure conjugal love is a gift of God, and comes from heaven; but, like the vestal fire, it must be cherished, that it go not out. He who loves not his wife, is the likeliest person to embrace the

bosom of a stranger.

(13) Labour to get the fear of God into your hearts. 'By the fear of the Lord men depart from evil.' Prov 16: 6. As the embankment keeps out the water, so the fear of the Lord keeps out uncleanness. Such as want the fear of God, want the bridle that should check them from sin. How did Joseph keep from his mistress's temptation? The fear of God pulled him back. 'How can I do this great wickedness, and sin against God?' Gen. 39: 9. Bernard calls holy fear, janitor animae, 'the door-keeper of the soul.' As a nobleman's porter stands at the door, and keeps out vagrants, so the fear of God stands and keeps out all sinful temptations from entering.

(14) Take delight in the word of God. 'How sweet are thy words unto my taste.' Psa 119: 103. Chrysostom compares God's word to a garden. If we walk in this garden, and suck sweetness from the flowers of the promises, we shall never care to pluck the 'forbidden fruit.' Sint castae deliciae meae scripturae [Let the Scriptures be my pure pleasure]. Augustine. The reason why persons seek after unchaste, sinful pleasures, is because they have no better. Caesar riding through a city, and seeing the women play with dogs and parrots, said, 'Sure they have no children.' So they that sport with harlots have no better pleasures. He that has once tasted Christ in a promise, is ravished with delight; and how would he scorn a motion to sin! Job said, the word was his 'appointed food.' Job 23: 12. No wonder then he made a 'covenant with his eyes.'

(15) If you would abstain from adultery, use serious consideration. Consider, [1] God sees thee in the act of sin. He sees all thy curtain wickedness. He is totus oculus, 'all eye.' The clouds are no canopy, the night is no curtain to hide thee from God's eye. Thou canst not sin, but thy Judge looks on. 'I have seen thy adulteries and thy neighings.' Jer 13: 27. 'They have committed adultery with their neighbours' wives; even I know, and am a witness, saith the Lord.' Jer 29: 23. [2] Few that are entangled in the sin of adultery, recover from the snare. 'None that go to her return again.' Prov 2: 19. This made some of the ancients conclude that adultery was an unpardonable sin; but it is not so. David repented. Mary Magdalene was a weeping penitent; upon her amorous eyes that sparkled with lose, she sought to be revenged, by washing Christ's feet with her tears. Some, therefore have recovered from the snare. 'None that go to her return,' that is, 'very few;' it is rare to hear of any who are enchanted and bewitched with this sin of adultery, that recover from it. Her 'heart is snares and nets, and her hands are bands.' Eccl 7: 26. Her 'heart is snares,' that is, she is subtle to deceive those who come to her; and 'her hands are bands,' that is her embraces are powerful to hold and entangle her lovers. Plutarch said of the Persian kings, 'They were captives to their concubines,' they were so inflamed, that they had no power to leave their company. This consideration should make all fearful of this sin. Soft pleasures harden the heart. [3] Consider what Scripture says, which may ponere obicem, 'lay a bar in the way' to this sin. 'I will be a swift witness against the adulterers.' Mal 3: 5. It is good when God is a witness 'for us', when he witnesses to our sincerity, as he did to Job's; but it is sad to have God a 'witness against us.' 'I,' says God, 'will be a witness against the adulterer.' And who shall disprove his witness? He is both witness and judge. 'Whoremongers and adulterers God will

judge.' Heb 13: 4. [4] Consider the sad farewell the sin of adultery leaves. It leaves a hell in the conscience. 'The lips of a strange woman drop as a honeycomb, but her end is bitter as wormwood.' Prov 5: 4. The goddess Diana was so artificially drawn, that she seemed to smile upon those that came into her temple, but frown on those that went out. So the harlot smiles on her lovers as they come to her, but at last come the frown and the sting. 'Till a dart strike through his liver.' Prov 7: 23. 'Her end is bitter.' When a man has been virtuous, the labour is gone, but the comfort remains; but when he has been vicious and unclean, the pleasure is gone, but the sting remains. Delectat in momentum, cruciat in aeternum [He gains momentary pleasure and then eternal torment]. Jerome. When the senses have been feasted with unchaste pleasures, the soul is left to pay the reckoning. Stolen waters are sweet; but, as poison, though sweet in the mouth, it torments the bowels. Sin always ends in a tragedy. Memorable is that which Fincelius reports of a priest in Flanders, who enticed a maid to uncleanness. She objected how vile a sin it was, he told her that by authority from the Pope he could commit any sin; so at last he drew her to his wicked purpose. But when they had been together a while, in came the devil, and took away the harlot from the priest's side, and, notwithstanding all her crying out, carried her away. If the devil should come and carry away all that are guilty of bodily uncleanness in this nation, I fear more would be carried away than would be left behind.

(16) Pray against this sin. Luther gave a lady this advice, that when any lust began to rise in her heart, she should go to prayer. Prayer is the best armour of proof; it quenches the wild fire of lust. If prayer will 'cast out the devil,' why may it not cast out those lusts that come from the devil?

Use five. If the body must be kept pure from defilement, much more the 'soul of a Christian must be kept pure.' The meaning of the commandment is not only that we should not stain our bodies with adultery, but that we should keep our souls pure. To have a chaste body, but an unclean soul, is like a fair face with bad lungs; or a gilt chimney-piece, that is all soot within. 'Be ye holy, for I am holy.' I Pet 1: 16. The soul cannot be lovely to God till it has Christ's image stamped upon it, which consists in righteousness and true holiness. Eph 4: 24. The soul must especially be kept pure, because it is the chief place of God's residence. Eph 3: 17. A king's palace must be kept clean, especially his presence-chamber. If the body is the temple, the soul is the 'Holy of holies,' and must be consecrated. We must not only keep our bodies from carnal pollution, but our souls from envy and malice.

How shall we know our souls are pure?

(1) If our souls are pure, we flee from the appearance of evil. 1 Thess 5: 22. We shall not do that which looks like sin. When Joseph's mistress courted and tempted him, he 'left his garment in her hand, and fled.' Gen 39: 12 He was suspicious to be near her. Polycarp would not be seen in company with Marcion the heretic, because it would not be good report.

(2) If our souls are pure, the light of purity will shine forth. Aaron had 'Holiness to the Lord'

written upon his golden plate. Where there is sanctity in the soul, there 'Holiness to the Lord' is engraven upon the life. We are adorned with patience, humility, good works, and shine as 'Lights in the world.' Phil 2: 15. Carry Christ's picture in your conversation. I John 2: 6. O let us labour for this soul purity! Without it there is no seeing God. Heb 12: 14. 'What communion has light with darkness?' 2 Cor 6:14. To keep the soul pure, have recourse to the blood of Christ: which is the 'fountain open for sin and uncleanness.' Zech 13: 1. A soul steeped in the briny tears of repentance, and bathed in the blood of Christ, is made pure. Pray much for a pureness of soul. 'Create in me a clean heart, O God.' Psa 51: 10. Some pray for children, others for riches; but pray thou for soul purity. Say, 'Lord, though my body is kept pure, yet my soul is defiled, I pollute all I touch. O purge me with hyssop, let Christ's blood sprinkle me, let the Holy Ghost come upon me and anoint me. O make me evangelically pure, that I may be translated to heaven, and placed among the cherubim, where I shall be as holy as thou wouldst have me to be, and as happy as I can desire to be.'

2.8 The Eighth Commandment

'Thou shalt not steal.' Exod 20: 15.

As the holiness of God sets him against uncleanness, in the command 'Thou shalt not commit adultery;' so the justice of God sets him against rapine and robbery, in the command, 'Thou shalt not steal.' The thing forbidden in this commandment, is meddling with another man's property. The civil lawyers define furtum, stealth or theft to be 'the laying hands unjustly on that which is another's;' the invading another's right.

I. The causes of theft.

[1] The internal causes are, (1) Unbelief. A man has a high distrust of God's providence. 'Can God furnish a table in the wilderness?' Psa 78:19. Can God spread a table for me? says the unbeliever. No, he cannot. Therefore he is resolved he will spread a table for himself, but it shall be at other men's cost, and both first and second course shall be served in with stolen goods. (2) Covetousness. The Greek word for covetousness signifies 'an immoderate desire of getting;' which is the root of theft. A man covets more than his own, and this itch of covetousness makes him scratch what he can from another. Achan's covetous humour made him steal the wedge of gold, a wedge which cleaved asunder his soul from God. Joshua 7: 21.

[2] The external cause of theft is Satan's solicitation. Judas was a thief. John 12: 6. How came he to be a thief? 'Satan entered into him'. John 13: 27. The devil is the great master-thief, he robbed us of our coat of innocence, and he persuades men to take up his trade; he tells men how bravely they shall live by thieving, and how they may catch an estate. As Eve listened to the serpent's voice, so do they. As birds of prey, they live upon spoil and plunder.

II. The kinds of theft.

[1] There is stealing from God. They are thieves who rob God of any part of his day. 'Remember to keep holy the Sabbath day.' Not a part of the day only, but the whole day must be dedicated to God. And, lest any should forget this, the Lord has prefixed a memento, 'remember.' Therefore, after morning sacrifice, to spend the other part of the Sabbath in vanity and pleasure, is spiritual theft. It robs God of his due, and the very heathen will rise up in judgement against such Christians; for the heathen, as Macrobius notes, observed a whole day to their false gods.

[2] There is stealing from others. A stealing away souls, as heretics, by robbing men of the truth, rob them of their souls. Stealing money and goods. There is

(1) The highway thief, who takes a purse, contrary to the letter of the commandment. 'Thou shalt not rob thy neighbour.' Lev 19: 13. 'Do not steal.' Mark 10: 19. This is not the violence which takes the 'kingdom of heaven by force.' Matt 11: 12.

(2) The house-thief, who purloins and filches out of his master's cash, or steals his wares and drugs. The apostle says, 'Some have entertained angels unawares' (Heb 13: 2), but many masters have entertained thieves in their houses unawares. The house-thief is a hypocrite as well as a thief; for he has demure looks, and pretends to be helping his master, when he only helps himself.

(3) The thief that shrouds himself under law, as the unjust attorney or lawyer, who prevaricates and deals falsely with his client. This is to steal from the client. By deceit and prevarication, the lawyer robs the client of his land, and may be the means of ruining his family, and is no better than a thief in God's account.

(4) The church-thief or pluralist, who holds several benefices, but seldom or never preaches to the people. He gets the golden fleece, but lets the flock starve. 'Woe be to the shepherds of Israel.' Ezek 34: 2. They 'fed themselves, and fed not my flock;' ver. 8. These ministers will be indicted for thieves at God's bar.

(5) The shop-thief, who steals in selling. He who uses false weights and measures steals from others what is their due. 'Making the ephah small.' Amos 8: 5. The ephah was a measure the Jews used in selling. Some made the ephah small, and gave scant measure, which was plainly stealing. 'The balances of deceit are in his hand.' Hos 12: 7. By making their weights lighter, men make their accounts heavier. He steals in selling who puts excessive prices on his commodities. He takes thrice as much for an article as it cost him, or as it is worth. To overreach others in selling, is to steal money from them. 'Thou shalt not defraud thy neighbour, neither rob him.' Lev 19: 13. To defraud him is to rob him; to overreach others in selling is a cunning way of stealing, and is against both law and gospel. It is against the law of God. 'If thou sell ought to thy neighbour, ye shall not oppress one another.' Lev 25: 14. It is against the gospel. 'That no man go beyond, and

defraud his brother.' 1 Thess 4: 6.

(6) The usurer, who takes by extortion from others. He seems to help another by letting him have money in his necessity, but gets him into bonds, and sucks out his very blood and marrow. I read of a woman whom Satan had bound (Luke 13: 16), and truly he is almost in as bad a condition whom the usurer has bound. The usurer is a robber. A usurer once asked a prodigal when he would leave off spending? The prodigal replied, 'I will leave off spending what is my own, when thou leavest off stealing from others.' Zacchaeus was an extortioner who, after his conversion, made restitution. Luke 19: 8. He thought all he got by extortion was theft.

(7) The trustee, who has the orphan's estate committed to him, is deputed to be his guardian, and manages his estate for him; if he curtails the estate, and gets a fleece out of it for himself, and wrongs the orphan, he is a thief. This is worse than taking a purse by violence, because he betrays his trust, which is the highest piece of treachery and injustice.

(8) The borrower, who borrows money from others, with an intention never to pay them again. 'The wicked borroweth, and payeth not again.' Psa 37: 21. What is it but thievery to take money and goods from others, and not restore them again. The prophet Elisha bade the widow sell her oil, and pay her debts, and then live upon the rest. 2 Kings 4: 7.

(9) The last sort of theft is, the receiver of stolen goods. The receiver, if he be not the principal, yet is accessory to the theft, and the law makes him guilty. The thief steals the money, and the receiver holds the sack to put it in. The root would die if it were not watered, and thieving would cease if it were not encouraged by the receiver. I am apt to think that he who does not scruple to take stolen goods into his house, would as little scruple to have stolen them.

What are the aggravations of this sin?

(1) To steal when there is no need; to be a rich thief.

(2) To steal sacrilegiously; to devour things set apart to holy uses. 'It is a snare to the man who devoureth that which is holy.' Prov 20: 25. Such an one was Dionysius, who robbed the temple, and took away the silver vessels.

(3) To commit the sin of theft against checks of conscience, and examples of God's justice; which, like the dye to the wool, dyes the sin of a crimson colour.

(4) To rob the widow and orphan. 'Ye shall not afflict the widow or fatherless.' Peccatum clamans [This sin shrieks aloud]. 'If they cry unto me, I will surely hear them.' Exod 22: 23.

(5) To rob the poor. How angry was David that the rich man should take away the poor man's lamb! 'As the Lord lives, he shall surely die.' 2 Sam 12: 5. What is inclosing of commons but robbing the poor!

[3] There is a stealing from a man's self. A man may be a thief to himself.

How so?

(1) By niggardliness. The niggard is a thief; he steals from himself in not allowing himself what is needful. He thinks that lost which is bestowed upon himself; he robs himself of necessaries. 'A man to whom God has given riches, yet God giveth him not power to eat thereof' Eccl 6: 2. He gluts his chest and starves his belly; he is like the ass that is loaded with gold, but feeds upon thistles; he robs himself of what God allows him. This is to be punished with riches; to have an estate and want a heart to take the comfort of it.

(2) A man may rob himself by foolishly wasting his estate. The prodigal lavishes gold out of the bag; he is like Crates, the philosopher, who threw his gold into the sea. The prodigal boils a great estate to nothing. He is a thief to himself who spends away that estate which might conduce to the comfort of life.

(3) He is a thief to himself, by idleness, when he misspends his time. He who spends his hours in pleasure and vanity robs himself of that precious time which God has given him to work out salvation in. Time is a rich commodity, because on well spending present time a happy eternity depends. He that spends his time idly and vainly, is a thief to himself; he robs himself of golden seasons, and by consequence, of salvation.

(4) A man may be a thief to himself by suretiship. 'Be not thou one of them that are sureties for debts.' Prov 22: 26. The creditor comes upon the surety for debt, and so, by paying another's debt, he is a thief to himself. Let not any man say he would have been counted unkind if he had not entered into a bond for his friend. Better thy friend should count thee unkind than all men count thee unwise. Lend another what you can spare; nay, give him if he needs, but never be a surety. It is no wisdom for a man so to help another as to undo himself. It is to rob himself and his family.

Use one. For confutation of the doctrine of community, that all things are common, and one man has a right to another's estate. This is confuted by Scripture. 'When thou comest into the standing corn of thy neighbour, thou shalt not move a sickle unto thy neighbour's corn.' Deut 23: 25. Property must be respected; God has set this eighth commandment as a hedge about a man's estate, and this hedge cannot be broken without sin. If all things be common, there can be no theft, and so this commandment would be in vain.

Use two. For reproof of such as live by stealing. Instead of living by faith, they live by their shifts. The apostle exhorts that 'every man eat his own bread.' 2 Thess 3: 12. The thief does not eat his own bread, but another's. If there be any who are guilty of this sin, let them labour to recover out of the snare of the devil, by repentance, and let them show their repentance by restitution. Non remittitur peccatum nisi restituatur ablatum. Augustine. 'Without restitution, no remission.' 'If I have taken away any thing from any man by false accusation, I restore him fourfold.' Luke 19: 8. Ill-gotten things may be restored by one's own hand, or by proxy. Better a thousand times restore goods unlawfully gotten, than stuff your pillow with thorns, and have guilt trouble your conscience upon a death-bed.

Use three. For exhortation to all to take heed of the sin of thieving; which is against the light of nature. Some may endeavour to excuse this sin. It is a coarse wool that will take no dye, and a bad sin that has no excuse.

I am (says one) grown low in the world, and trading is bad, and I have no other way to a livelihood.

(1) This shows great distrust in God, as if he could not provide for thee without thy sin. (2) It shows sin to be at a great height, that, because a man is grown low in the world, therefore he will Acheronta movere [knock at Hell's door], go to the devil for a livelihood. Abraham would not have it said, that 'the king of Sodom had made him rich.' Gen 14: 22. O let it never be said, that the devil has made thee rich! (3) Thou oughtest not to undertake any action upon which thou canst not pray for a blessing; but thou canst not pray for a blessing upon stolen goods. Therefore take heed of this sin; lucrum in arca, damnum in conscientia [you gain materially, but your conscience suffers loss]. Augustine. Take heed of getting the world with the loss of heaven.

Use four. To dissuade all from this horrid sin, consider - (1) Thieves are the caterpillars of the earth, enemies to civil society. (2) God hates them. In the law, the cormorant was unclean, because a thievish, devouring creature, a bird of prey; by which God showed his hatred of this sin. Lev 11: 17. (3) The thief is a terror to himself, he is always in fear. 'There were they in great fear,' is true of the thief. Psa 53: 5. Guilt breeds fear: if he hears but the shaking of a tree, his heart shakes. It is said of Catiline, he was afraid of every noise. If a briar does but take hold of a thief's garment, he is afraid it is the officer to apprehend him; and fear has torment in it. I John 4: 18. (4) The judgements that follow this sin. Achan the thief was stoned to death. Josh 7: 25. 'What sees thou? And I answered, A flying roll.... This is the curse that goes forth over the face of the whole earth; I will bring it forth, saith the Lord, and it shall enter into the house of the thief' Zech 5: 2, 3, 4. Fabius, a Roman censor, condemned his own son to die for theft. Thieves die with ignominy, the ladder is their preferment: and there is a worse thing than death; for while they rob others of money, they rob themselves of salvation.

What is to be done to avoid stealing?

(1) Live in a calling. 'Let him that stole steal no more, but rather let him labour, working with his hands.' Eph 4: 28, &c. The devil hires such as stand idle, and puts them to the pilfering trade. An idle person tempts the devil to tempt him.

(2) Be content with the estate that God has given you. 'Be content with such things as ye have.'

Heb 13: 5. Theft is the daughter of avarice. Study contentment. Believe that condition best which God has carved out to you. He can bless the little meal in the barrel. We shall not need these things long: we shall carry nothing out of the world with us but our winding sheet. If we have but enough to bear out our charges to heaven, it is sufficient.

2.9 The Ninth Commandment

'Thou shalt not bear false witness against thy neighbour.' Exod 20: 16.

THE tongue which at first was made to be an organ of God's praise, is now become an instrument of unrighteousness. This commandment binds the tongue to its good behaviour. God has set two natural fences to keep in the tongue, the teeth and lips; and this commandment is a third fence set about it, that it should not break forth into evil. It has a prohibitory and a mandatory part: the first is set down in plain words, the other is clearly implied.

I. The prohibitory part of the commandment, or, what it forbids in general. It forbids anything which may tend to the disparagement or prejudice of our neighbour. More particularly, two things are forbidden in this commandment.

[1] Slandering our neighbour. This is a sin against the ninth commandment. The scorpion carries his poison in his tail, the slanderer carries his poison in his tongue. Slandering 'is to report things of others unjustly.' They laid to my charge things that I knew not.' Psa 35: 11. It is usual to bring in a Christian beheaded of his good name. They raised for a slander of Paul, that he preached 'Men might do evil that good might come of it.' 'We be slanderously reported; and some affirm that we say, "Let us do evil, that good may come".' Rom 3: 8. Eminence is commonly blasted by slander. Holiness itself is no shield from slander. The lamb's innocence will not preserve it from the wolf. Christ, the most innocent upon earth, was reported to be a friend of sinners. John the Baptist was a man of a holy and austere life, and yet they said of him, 'He has a devil.' Matt 11: 18. The Scripture calls slandering, smiting with the tongue. 'Come, and let us smite him with the tongue.' Jer 18: 18. You may smite another and never touch him. Majora sunt linguae vulnera quam gladii [The tongue inflicts greater wounds than the sword]. Augustine. The wounds of the tongue no physician can heal; and to pretend friendship to a man, and slander him, is most odious. Jerome says: 'The Arian faction made a show of kindness; they kissed my hands, but slandered me, and sought my life.' As it is a sin against this commandment to raise a false report of another, so it is to receive a false report before we have examined it. 'Lord, who shall dwell in thy holy hill?' Psa 15: 1. Quis ad coelum? 'He that backbiteth not, nor taketh up a reproach against his neighbour;' ver. 3. We must not only not raise a false report, but not take it up. He that raises a slander, carries the devil in his tongue; and he that receives it, carries the devil in his ear. [2] The second thing forbidden in this commandment is false witness. Here three sins are condemned: (1) Speaking. (2) Witnessing. (3) Swearing that which is false, contra proximum

[against your neighbour].

(1) Speaking that which is false. 'Lying lips are abomination to the Lord.' Prov 12: 22. To lie is to speak that which one knows to be an untruth. There is nothing more contrary to God than a lie. The Holy Ghost is called the 'Spirit of Truth.' I John 4: 6. Lying is a sin that does not go alone; it ushers in other sins. Absalom told his father a lie, when he said that he was going to pay his vow at Hebron, and this was a preface to his treason. 2 Sam 15: 7. Where there is a lie in the tongue, the devil is in the heart. 'Why has Satan filled thine heart to lie?' Acts 5: 3. Lying is a sin that unfits men for civil society. How can you converse or bargain with a man when you cannot trust a word he says? This sin highly provokes God. Ananias and Sapphire were struck dead for telling a lie. Acts 5: 5. The furnace of hell is heated for liars. 'Without are sorcerers, and whosoever loveth and maketh a lie.' Rev 22: 15. O abhor this sin! Quicquid dixeris jura tum putes [Consider your every word an oath]. Jerome. When thou speakest, let thy word be as authentic as thy oath. Imitate God, who is the pattern of truth. Pythagoras being asked what made men like God, answered, cum vera loquuntur, 'when they speak the truth.' The character of a man that shall go to heaven, is that 'He speaketh the truth in his heart.' Psa 15: 2.

(2) That which is condemned in the commandment is, witnessing that which is false. 'Thou shalt not bear false witness.' There is a twofold bearing false witness: 1. There is bearing false witness for another. 2. Bearing false witness against another.

Bearing false witness for another; as when we give our testimony for a person who is criminal and guilty, and we justify him as if he were innocent. 'Which justify the wicked for reward.' Isa 5: 23. He that seeks to make a wicked man just, makes himself unjust.

It is bearing false witness against another, when we accuse him in open court falsely. This is to imitate the devil, who is the 'accuser of the brethren.' Though the devil is no adulterer, yet he is a false witness. Solomon says, 'A man that beareth false witness against his neighbour, is a maul and a sword.' Prov 25: 18. In his face he is hardened like a hammer: he cannot blush, he cares not what lie he witnesses to; and he is a sword: his tongue is a sword to wound the person he witnesses against in his goods or life. 'There came in two men, children of Belial, and witnessed against Naboth, saying, Naboth did blaspheme God and the king:' and their witness took away his life. I Kings 21: 13. The queen of Persia being sick, the magicians accused two godly virgins of having by charms procured the queen's sickness; whereupon she caused those virgins to be sawn asunder. A false witness perverts the place of judicature; he corrupts the judge by making him pronounce a wrong sentence, and causes the innocent to suffer. Vengeance will find out the false witness. 'A false witness shall not be unpunished.' Prov 19: 5. 'If the witness be a false witness, and has testified falsely against his brother; then shall ye do unto him, as he had thought to have done unto his brother;' if, for instance, he had thought to have taken away his life, his own life shall go for it. Deut 19: 18, 19.

(3) That which is condemned in the commandment is, swearing to what is false; as when men

take a false oath, and by that take away the life of another. 'Love no false oath.' Zech 8: 17. 'What seest thou? I said, a flying roll,' chap. 5: 2. 'This is the curse that goes forth, and it shall enter, saith the Lord, into the house of him that sweareth falsely by my name; and it shall consume it, with the timber and stones thereof;' ver 3, 4. The Scythians made a law that when a man bound together a lie with an oath, he was to lose his head; because these sins took away all truth and faith from among men. The devil has taken great possession of those who dare swear to a lie.

Use one. For reproof. (1) The church of Rome is reproved, which dispenses with a lie, or a false oath, if it promotes the Catholic cause. It approves of an officious lie; and holds some sins to be lawful. It may as well hold some lies to be lawful. God has no need of our lie. It is not lawful to tell a lie, propter Dei gloriam [for the glory of God], if we were sure to bring glory to God by it, as Augustine speaks.

(2) They are reproved who make no conscience of slandering others. 'Thou fittest and slenderest thine own mother's son.' Psa 50:20. 'Report, say they, and we will report.' Jer 20: 10. 'This city (i.e. Jerusalem) is a rebellious city, and hurtful to kings and provinces.' Ezra 4: 15. Paul was slandered as a mover of sedition, and the head of a faction. Acts 24: 5. The same word signifies both a slanderer and a devil. 1 Tim 3: 11. 'Not slanderers;' in the Greek, 'not devils.' Some think it is no great matter, to misrepresent and slander others; but it is to act the part of a devil. Clipping a man's credit, to make it weigh lighter, is worse than clipping coin. The slanderer wounds three at once: he wounds him that is slandered; he wounds him to whom he reports the slander, by causing uncharitable thoughts to arise up in his mind against the party slandered; and he wounds his own soul, by reporting of another what is false. This is a great sin; and I wish I could say it is not common. You may kill a man in his name as well as in his person. Some are loath to take away their neighbour's goods - conscience would fly in their face; but better take away their corn out of their field, their wares out of their shop, than take away their good name. This is a sin for which no reparation can be made; a blot in a man's name, being like a blot on white paper, which will never be got out. Surely God will visit for this sin. If idle words shall be accounted for, shall not unjust slanders? The Lord will make inquisition one day, as well for names as for blood. Oh therefore take heed of this sin! Was it not a sin under the law to defame a virgin? Deut 22: 19. And is it not a greater sin to defame a saint, who is a member of Christ? The heathen, by the light of nature, abhorred the sin of slandering. Diogenes used to say, 'Of all wild beasts, a slanderer is the worst.' Antonius made a law, that, if a person could not prove the crime he reported another to be guilty of, he should be put to death.

(3) They are reproved who are so wicked as to bear false witness against others. These are monsters in nature, unfit to live in a civil society. Eusebius relates of one Narcissus, a man famous for piety, who was accused by two false witnesses of unchastity. To prove their accusations, they endeavoured to confirm it with oaths and curses. One said, 'If I speak not true, I pray God I may perish by fire:' the other said, 'If I speak not true, I wish I may be deprived of my sight.' It pleased God that the first witness who forswore himself should be burned in the flames,

his house being set on fire: the other being troubled in conscience, confessed his perjury, and continued to weep so long that he wept himself blind. Jezebel, who suborned two false witnesses against Naboth, was thrown down from a window and 'the dogs licked her blood.' 2 Kings 9: 33. Oh, tremble at this sin! A perjured person is the devil's excrement. He is cursed in his name, and seared in his conscience. Hell gapes for such a windfall.

Use two. For exhortation. (1) Let all take heed of breaking this commandment, by lying, slandering, and bearing false witness. To avoid these sins get the fear of God. Why does David say, 'The fear of the Lord is clean'? Psa 19: 9. Because it cleanses the heart from malice, and the tongue from slander. 'The fear of the Lord is clean:' it is to the soul as lightning to the air, which cleanses it. Get love to your neighbour. Lev 19: 18. If we love a friend, we shall not speak or attest anything to his prejudice. Men's minds are cankered with envy and hatred; hence come slandering and false witnessing. Love is a lovely grace; love 'thinketh no evil.' I Cor 13: 5. It puts the best interpretation upon another's words. Love is a well-wisher, and it is rare to speak ill of him we wish well to. Love is that which cements Christians together; it is the healer of division, and the hinderer of slander.

(2) Let those whose lot it is to meet with slanderers and false accusers - [1] Labour to make a sanctified use of it. When Shimei railed on David, David made a sanctified use of it. 'The Lord has said unto him, Curse David.' 2 Sam 16: 10. So, if you are slandered, or falsely accused, make a good use of it. See if you have no sin unrepented of, for which God may suffer you to be calumniated and reproached. See if you have not at any time wronged others in their name, and said that of them which you cannot prove; then lay your hand on your mouth, and confess the Lord is righteous to let you fall under the scourge of the tongue. [2] If you are slandered, or falsely accused, but know your own innocence, be not too much troubled; let your rejoicing be the witness of your conscience. Murus aheneus esto nil conscire sibi [Let this be a bulwark, to know oneself guiltless]. A good conscience is a wall of brass, that will be able to stand against a false witness. As no flattery can heal a bad conscience, so no slander can hurt a good one. God will clear up the names of his people. 'He shall bring forth thy righteousness as the light.' Psa 37: 6. As he will wipe away tears from the eyes, so will he wipe off reproaches from the name. Believers shall come forth out of all their slanders and reproaches, as 'the wings of a dove, covered with silver, and her feathers with yellow gold.'

(3) Be very thankful to God, if he has preserved you from slander and false witness. Job calls it 'the scourge of the tongue;' chap 5: 21. As a rod scourges the back, so the slanderer's tongue scourges the name. It is a great mercy to be kept from the scourge of a tongue; a mercy that God stops malignant mouths from bearing false witness. What mischief might not a lying report or a false oath do! One destroys the name, the other the life. It is the Lord who muzzles the mouths of the wicked, and keeps those dogs, that snarl at us, from flying upon us. 'Thou shalt keep them secretly in a pavilion, from the strife of tongues.' Psa 31: 20. There is, I suppose, an allusion to kings, who being resolved to protect their favourites against the accusation of men, take them

into their bed-chamber, or bosom, where none may touch them. So God has a pavilion, or secret hiding-place for his favourites, where he preserves their credit and reputation untouched; he keeps them from the 'strife of tongues.' We ought to acknowledge this to be a great mercy before God.

II. The mandatory part of the commandment implied is that we stand up for others and vindicate them when they are injured by lying lips. This is the sense of the commandment, not only that we should not slander falsely or accuse others; but that we should witness for them, and stand up in their defence, when we know them to be traduced. A man may wrong another as well by silence as by slander, when he knows him to be wrongfully accused, yet does not speak in his behalf. If others cast false aspersions on any, we should wipe them off. When the apostles were filled with the wine of the Spirit, and were charged with drunkenness, Peter openly maintained their innocence. 'These are not drunken, as ye suppose.' Acts 2: 15. Jonathan knowing David to be a worthy man, and all those things Saul said of him to be slanders, vindicated him. 'David has not sinned against thee; his works have been to thee-ward very good. Wherefore then wilt thou sin against innocent blood, to slay David without a cause?' I Sam 19: 4, 5. When the primitive Christians were falsely accused for incest, and killing their children, Tertullian wrote a famous apology in their vindication. This is to act the part both of a friend and of a Christian, to be an advocate for another, when he is wronged in his good name.

2.10 The Tenth Commandment

'Thou shalt not covet thy neighbour's house, thou shalt not covet thy neighbour's wife, nor his man-servant, nor his maid-servant, nor his ox, nor his ass, nor any thing that is thy neighbour's.' Exod 20: 17.

This commandment forbids covetousness in general, 'Thou shalt not covet;' and in particular, 'Thy neighbour's house, thy neighbour's wife, &c.

I. It forbids covetousness in general. 'Thou shalt not covet.' It is lawful to use the world, yea, and to desire so much of it as may keep us from the temptation of poverty: 'Give me not poverty, lest I steal, and take the name of my God in vain' (Prov 30: 8, 9); and as may enable us to honour God with works of mercy. 'Honour the Lord with thy substance.' Prov 3: 9. But all the danger is, when the world gets into the heart. Water is useful for the sailing of the ship: all the danger is when the water gets into the ship; so the fear is, when the world gets into the heart. 'Thou shalt not covet.'

What is it to covet?

There are two words in the Greek which set forth the nature of covetousness. Pleonexia, which signifies an 'insatiable desire of getting the world.' Covetousness is a dry dropsy. Augustine defines covetousness Plus velle quam sat est; 'to desire more than enough;' to aim at a great estate; to be like the daughter of the horse-leech, crying, 'Give, give.' Prov 30: 15. Or like behemoth, 'He trusteth that he can draw up Jordan into his mouth.' Job 40: 23. The other word is Philarguria, which signifies an 'inordinate love of the world.' The world is the idol: it is so loved, that a man will not part with it for any good use. He may be said to be covetous not only who gets the world unrighteously, but who loves it inordinately.

[1] For a more full answer to the question, 'What is it to covet?' I shall show in six particulars, when a man may be said to be given to covetousness: -

(1) When his thoughts are wholly taken up with the world. A good man's thoughts are in heaven; he is thinking of Christ's love and eternal recompense. 'When I awake I am still with thee,' that is, in divine contemplation. Psa 139: 18. A covetous man's thoughts are in the world; his mind is wholly taken up with it; he can think of nothing but his shop or farm. The fancy is a mint-house, and most of the thoughts in a covetous man's mint are worldly. He is always plotting and projecting about the things of this life; like a virgin whose thoughts all centre upon her suitor.

(2) A man may be said to be given to covetousness, when he takes more pains for getting earth than for getting heaven. He will turn every stone, break his sleep, take many a weary step for the world; but will take no pains for Christ or heaven. After the Gauls, who were an ancient people of France, had tasted the sweet wine of the Italian grape, they inquired after the country, and never rested till they had arrived at it; so a covetous man, having had a relish of the world, pursues after it, and never ceases till he has got it; but he neglects the things of eternity. He would be content if salvation were to drop into his mouth, as a ripe fig into the mouth of the eater (Nahum 3: 12); but he is loath to put himself to too much sweat or trouble to obtain Christ or salvation. He hunts for the world, he wishes only for heaven.

(3) A man may be said to be given to covetousness, when all his discourse is about the world. 'He that is of the earth, speaketh of the earth.' John 3: 31. It is a sign of godliness to be speaking of heaven, to have the tongue turned to the language of Canaan. 'The words of a wise man's mouth are gracious;' he speaks as if he had been already in heaven. Eccl. 10: 12. So it is a sign of a man given to covetousness to speak always of secular things, of his wares and drugs. A covetous man's breath, like a dying man's, smells strong of the earth. As it was said to Peter, 'Thy speech bewrayeth thee;' so a covetous man's speech betrayeth him. Matt 26: 73. He is like the fish in the gospel, which had a piece of money in its mouth. Matt 17: 27. Verba sunt speculum mentis. Bernard. 'The words are the looking-glass of the heart,' they show what is within. Ex abundantia cordis [From the abundance of the heart].

(4) A man is given to covetousness when he so sets his heart upon worldly things, that for the love of them, he will part with heavenly; for the 'wedge of gold,' he will part with the 'pearl of price.' When Christ said to the young man in the gospel, 'Sell all, and come and follow me;' abiit

tristis, 'he went away sorrowful.' Matt 19: 22. He would rather part with Christ than with all his earthly possessions. Cardinal Bourbon said, he would forego his part in paradise, if he might keep his cardinalship in Paris. When it comes to the critical point that men must either relinquish their estate or Christ, and they will rather part with Christ and a good conscience than with their estate, it is a clear case that they are possessed with the demon of covetousness.

(5) A man is given to covetousness when he overloads himself with worldly business. He has many irons in the fire; he is in this sense a pluralist; he takes so much business upon him, that he cannot find time to serve God; he has scarce time to eat his meat, but no time to pray. When a man overcharges himself with the world, and as Martha, cumbers himself about many things, that he cannot have time for his soul, he is under the power of covetousness.

(6) He is given to covetousness whose heart is so set upon the world, that, to get it, he cares not what unlawful means he uses. He will have the world per fas et nefas [by fair means or foul]; he will wrong and defraud, and raise his estate upon the ruins of another. 'The balances of deceit are in his hand, he loveth to oppress.... Ephraim said, 'Yet I am become rich.' Hos 12: 7, 8. Pope Sylvester II sold his soul to the devil for a popedom.

Use. 'Take heed and beware of covetousness.' Luke 12: 15. It is a direct breach of the tenth commandment. It is a moral vice, it infects and pollutes the whole soul.

(1) It is a subtle sin, a sin that many cannot so well discern in themselves; as some have the scurvy, but do not know it. This sin can dress itself in the attire of virtue. It is called the 'cloak of covetousness.' Thess 2: 5. It is a sin that wears a cloak, it cloaks itself under the name of frugality and good husbandry. It has many pleas and excuses for itself; more than any other sin: as providing for one's family. The more subtle the sin is, the less discernible it is.

(2) Covetousness is a dangerous sin, as it checks all that is good. It is an enemy to grace; it damps good affections, as the earth puts out the fire. The hedgehog, in the fable, came to the cony-burrows, in stormy weather, and desired harbour; but when once he had got entertainment, he set up his prickles, and never ceased till he had thrust the poor conies out of their burrows; so covetousness, by fair pretences, winds itself into the heart; but as soon as you have let it in, it will never leave till it has choked all good beginnings, and thrust all religion out of your hearts. 'Covetousness hinders the efficacy of the word preached.' In the parable, the thorns, which Christ expounded to be the care of this life, choked the good seed. Matt 13: 22. Many sermons lie dead and buried in earthly hearts. We preach to men to get their hearts in heaven; but where covetousness is predominant, it chains them to earth, and makes them like the woman which Satan had bowed together, that she could not lift up herself. Luke 13: 11. You may as well bid an elephant fly in the air, as a covetous man live by faith. We preach to men to give freely to Christ's poor; but covetousness makes them like the man in the gospel, who had 'a withered hand.' Mark 3: 1. They have a withered hand, and cannot stretch it out to the poor. It is impossible to be earthly-minded and charitably-minded. Covetousness obstructs the efficacy of

the word, and makes it prove abortive. They whose hearts are rooted in the earth, will be so far from profiting by the word, that they will be ready rather to deride it. The Pharisees, who were covetous, 'derided him.' Luke 16: 14.

(3) Covetousness is a mother sin, a radical vice. 'The love of money is the root of all evil.' I Tim 6: 10. Quid non mortalia pectora cogis, auri sacra fames! [O accursed lust for gold! what crimes do you not urge upon the human heart!] Virgil. He who has an earthly itch, a greedy desire of getting the world, has in him the root of all sin. Covetousness is a mother sin. I shall make it appear that covetousness is a breach of all the ten commandments. It breaks the first commandment; 'Thou shalt have no other gods but one.' The covetous man has more gods than one; Mammon is his god. He has a god of gold, therefore he is called an idolater. Col 3: 5. Covetousness breaks the second commandment: 'Thou shalt not make any graven image, thou shalt not bow thyself to them.' A covetous man bows down, though not to the graven image in the church, yet to the graven image in his coin. Covetousness is a breach of the third commandment; 'Thou shalt not take the name of the Lord thy God in vain.' Absalom's design was to get his father's crown, which was covetousness; but he talked of paying his 'vow to God,' which was to take God's name in vain. Covetousness is a breach of the fourth commandment; 'Remember the Sabbath-day to keep it holy.' A covetous man does not keep the Sabbath holy; he will ride to fairs on a Sabbath; instead of reading in the Bible, he will cast up his accounts. Covetousness is a breach of the fifth commandment; 'Honour thy father and thy mother.' A covetous person does not honour his father, if he does not feed him with money. Nay; he will get his father to make over his estate to him in his lifetime, so that the father may be at his son's command. Covetousness is a breach of the sixth commandment; 'Thou shalt not kill.' Covetous Ahab killed Naboth to get his vineyard. I Kings 21: 13. How many have swum to the crown in blood? Covetousness is a breach of the seventh commandment, 'Thou shalt not commit adultery.' It causes uncleanness; you read of the 'hire of a whore.' Deut 23: 18. An adulteress for money sets both conscience and chastity to sale. Covetousness is a breach of the eighth commandment 'Thou shalt not steal.' It is the root of theft: covetous Achan stole the wedge of gold. Thieves and covetous are put together. I Cor 6: 10. Covetousness is a breach of the ninth commandment; 'Thou shalt not bear false witness.' What makes the perjurer take a false oath but covetousness? He hopes for a reward. It is plainly a breach of the last commandment; 'Thou shalt not covet.' The mammonist covets his neighbour's house and goods, and endeavours to get them into his own hands. Thus you see how vile a sin covetousness is; it is a mother sin; it is a plain breach of every one of the ten commandments.

(4) Covetousness is a sin dishonourable to religion. For men to say their hopes are above, while their hearts are below; to profess to be above the stars, while they 'lick the dust' of the serpent; to be born of God, while they are buried in the earth; how dishonourable is this to religion! The lapwing, which wears a little coronet on its head, and yet feeds on dung, is an emblem of such as profess to be crowned kings and priests unto God, and yet feed immoderately on terrene dunghill comforts. 'And seekest thou great things for thyself? seek them not.' Jer 45: 5. What, thou

Baruch, who art ennobled by the new birth, and art illustrious by thy office, a Levite, dost thou seek earthly things, and seek them now? When the ship is sinking, art thou trimming thy cabin? O do not so degrade thyself, nor blot thy escutcheon! Seekest thou great things? seek them not. The higher grace is, the less earthly should Christians be; as the higher the sun is, the shorter is the shadow.

(5) Covetousness exposes us to God's abhorrence, 'The covetous, whom the Lord abhorreth.' Psa 10: 3. A king abhors to see his statue abused, so God abhors to see man, made in his image, having the heart of a beast. Who would live in such a sin as makes him abhorred of God? Whom God abhors he curses, and his curse blasts wherever it comes.

(6) Covetousness precipitates men to ruin, and shuts them out of heaven. 'This ye know, that no covetous man, who is an idolater, has any inheritance in the kingdom of Christ and of God.' Eph 5: 5. What could a covetous man do in heaven? God can no more converse with him than a king can converse with a swine. 'They that will be rich fall into a snare, and many hurtful lusts, which drown men in perdition.' I Tim 6: 9. A covetous man is like a bee that gets into a barrel of honey, and there drowns itself. As a ferry man takes in so many passengers to increase his fare, that he sinks his boat; so a covetous man takes in so much gold to increase his estate, that he drowns himself in perdition. I have read of some inhabitants near Athens, who, living in a very dry and barren island, took much pains to draw a river to the island to water it and make it fruitful; but when they had opened the passages, and brought the river to it, the water broke in with such force, that it drowned the land, and all the people in it. This is an emblem of a covetous man, who labours to draw riches to him, and at last they come in such abundance, that they drown him in perdition. How many, to build up an estate, pull down their souls! Oh, then, flee from covetousness! I shall next prescribe some remedies against covetousness.

[2] 1 AM, in the next place, to solve the question, What is the cure for this covetousness?'

(1) Faith. 'This is the victory that overcometh the world, even our faith.' I John 5: 4. The root of covetousness is distrust of God's providence. Faith believes that God will provide; that he who feeds the birds will feed his children; that he who clothes the lilies will clothe his lambs; and thus faith overcomes the world. Faith is the cure of care. It not only purifies the heart, but satisfies it; it makes God our portion, and in him we have enough. 'The lord is the portion of mine inheritance, the lines are fallen unto me in pleasant places; yea, I have a goodly heritage.' Psa 16: 5, 6. Faith, by a divine chemistry, extracts comfort out of God. A little with God is sweet. Thus faith is a remedy against covetousness; it overcomes, not only the fear of the world, but the love of the world.

(2) The second remedy is, judicious considerations. As what poor things these things below are that we should covet them! They are far below the worth of the soul, which carries in it an idea and resemblance of God. The world is but the workmanship of God, the soul is his image. We covet that which will not satisfy us. 'He that loveth silver, shall not be satisfied with silver.' Eccl

5: 10. Solomon had put all the creatures in a retort, and distilled out their essence, and behold, 'All was vanity.' Eccl 2: 11. Covetousness is a dry dropsy - the more a man has the more he thirsts. Quo plus sunt potae, plus sitiuntur aquae [The more water is drunk, the more is craved]. Ovid. Worldly things cannot remove trouble of mind. When King Saul was perplexed in conscience, his crown jewels could not comfort him. I Sam 28: 15. The things of the world can no more ease a troubled spirit than a gold cap can cure the headache. The things of the world cannot continue with you. The creature has a little honey in its mouth, but it has wings to fly away. These things either go from us, or we from them. What poor things are they to covet!

The second consideration is the frame and texture of the body. God has made the face look upward towards heaven. Os homini sublime dedit, coelumque tueri jussit [He gave man an uplifted face, with the order to gaze up to Heaven]. Ovid. Anatomists observe, that whereas other creatures have but four muscles to their eyes, man has a fifth muscle, by which he is able to look up to heaven; and as for the heart, it is made narrow and contracted downwards, but wide and broad upwards. As the frame and texture of the body teaches us to look to things above, so especially the soul is planted in the body, as a divine spark, to ascend upwards. Can it be imagined that God gave us intellectual and immortal souls to covet earthly things only? What wise man would fish for gudgeons with golden hooks? Did God give us glorious souls only to fish for the world? Sure our souls are made for a higher end; to aspire after the enjoyment of God in glory.

The third consideration is the examples of those who have been condemners and despisers of the world. The primitive Christians, as Clemens Alexandrinus observes, were sequestered from the world, and were wholly taken up in converse with God; they lived in the world above the world; like the birds of paradise, who soar above in the air, and seldom or never touch the earth with their feet. Luther says that he was never tempted to the sin of covetousness. Though the saints of old lived in the world they traded in heaven. 'Our conversation is in heaven.' Phil 3: 20. The Greek word signifies our commerce, or traffic, or citizenship, is in heaven. 'Enoch walked with God.' Gen 5: 24. His affections were sublimated, and took a turn in heaven every day. The righteous are compared to a palm-tree. Psa 92: 12. Philo observes, that whereas all other trees have their sap in their root, the sap of the palm-tree is towards the top; and thus is an emblem of saints, whose hearts are in heaven, where their treasure is.

(3) The third remedy for covetousness is to covet spiritual things more. Covet grace, for it is the best blessing, it is the seed of God. I John 3: 9. Covet heaven, which is the region of happiness - the most pleasant clime. If we covet heaven more, we shall covet earth less. To those who stand on the top of the Alps, the great cities of Campania seem but as small villages; so if our hearts were more fixed upon the Jerusalem above, all worldly things would disappear, would diminish, and be as nothing in our eyes. We read of an angel coming down from heaven, and setting his right foot on the sea, and his left foot on the earth. Rev 10: 2. Had we been in heaven, and viewed its superlative glory, how should we, with holy scorn, trample with one foot upon the

earth and with the other foot upon the sea! O covet after heavenly things! There is the tree of life, the mountains of spices, the rivers of pleasure, the honeycomb of God's love dropping, the delights of angels, and the flower of joyfully ripe and blown. There is the pure air to breathe in; no fogs or vapours of sin arise to infect that air, but the Sun of Righteousness enlightens the whole horizon continually with his glorious beams. O let your thoughts and delights be always taken up with the city of pearls, the paradise of God! It is reported of Lazarus that, after he was raised from the grave, he was never seen to smile or take delight in the world. Were our hearts raised by the power of the Holy Ghost up to heaven we should not be much taken with earthly things.

(4) The fourth remedy is to pray for a heavenly mind. Lord, let the loadstone of thy Spirit draw my heart upward. Lord, dig the earth out of my heart; teach me how to possess the world, and not love it; how to hold it in my hand, and not let it get into my heart.

II. Having spoken of the command in general, I proceed to speak of it more particularly. 'Thou shalt not covet thy neighbour's house, thou shalt not covet thy neighbour's wife,' &c. Observe the holiness and perfection of the law that forbids the motus primo primi, the first motions and risings of sin in the heart. 'Thou shalt not covet.' The laws of men take hold of actions, but the law of God goes further, it forbids not only actions, but desires. 'Thou shalt not covet thy neighbour's house.' It is not said, 'Thou shalt not take away his house;' but 'Thou shalt not covet it.' These lusts and desires after the forbidden fruit are sinful. The law has said, 'Thou shalt not covet.' Rom 7: 7. Though the tree bears no bad fruit, it may be faulty at the root; so though a man does not commit any gross sin, he cannot say his heart is pure. There may be faultiness at the root: there may be sinful covetings and lustings in the soul.

Use. Let us be humbled for the sin of our nature, the risings of evil thoughts coveting that which we ought not. Our nature is a seed-plot of iniquity; like charcoal that is ever sparkling, the sparks of pride, envy, covetousness, arise in the mind. How should this humble us! If there be not sinful acting, there are sinful covetings. Let us pray for mortifying grace, which like the water of jealousy, may make the thigh of sin to rot.

Why is the house here put before the wife? In Deuteronomy the wife is put first. 'Neither shalt thou desire thy neighbour's wife, neither shalt thou covet thy neighbour's house.' Deut 5: 21.

In Deuteronomy the wife is set down first, in respect of her value. She (if a good wife) is of far greater value and estimate than the house. 'Her price is far above rubies.' Prov 31: 10. She is the furniture of the house and this furniture is more worth than the house. When Alexander had overcome King Darius in battle, Darius seemed not to be much dismayed, but when he heard his wife was taken prisoner, his eyes, like spouts gushed forth water, for he valued his wife more than his life. But in Exodus the house is put before the wife, because the house is first in order, the house is erected before the wife can live in it; the nest is built before the bird is in it; the wife is first esteemed, but the house must be first provided.

[1] Then, 'Thou shalt not covet thy neighbour's house.' How depraved is man since the fall! He knows not how to keep within bounds, but covets more than his own. Ahab, one would think, had enough: he was a king; and we should suppose his crown-revenues would have contented him; but he was coveting more. Naboth's vineyard was in his eye, and stood near the smoke of his chimney, and he could not be quiet till he had it in possession. Were there not so much coveting, there would not be so much bribing. One man takes away another's house from him. It is only the prisoner who lives in such a tenement that he may be sure none will seek to take it from him.

[2] 'Thou shalt not covet thy neighbour's wife.' This is a bridle to check the inordinate and brutish lusts. It was the devil that sowed another man's ground. Matt 13: 25. But how is the hedge of this commandment trodden down in our times! There are many who do more than covet their neighbours' wives! they take them. 'Cursed be he that lieth with his father's wife; and all the people shall say, Amen.' Deut 27: 20. If it were to be proclaimed, 'Cursed be he that lieth with his neighbour's wife,' and all that were guilty should say, 'Amen,' how many would curse themselves!

[3] 'Thou shalt not covet thy neighbour's man-servant, nor his maidservant.' Servants, when faithful, are a treasure. What a true and trusty servant had Abraham! He was his right hand. How prudent and faithful he was in the matter entrusted with him, of getting a wife for his master's son! Gen 24: 9. It would surely have grieved Abraham if any one had enticed away his servant from him. But this sin of coveting servants is common. If one has a good servant, others will be laying snares for him, and endeavour to draw him away from his master. This is a sin against the tenth commandment. To steal away another's servant by enticement, is no better than direct thieving.

[4] 'Nor his ox, nor his ass, nor any thing that is thy neighbour's.' Were there no coveting ox and ass, there would not be so much stealing. First men break the tenth commandment by coveting, and then the eighth commandment by stealing. It was an excellent appeal that Samuel made to the people when he said, 'Witness against me before the Lord, whose ox have I taken, or whose ass, or whom have I defrauded?' I Sam 12: 3. It was a brave speech of Paul, when he said, 'I have coveted no man's silver, or gold, or apparel.' Acts 20: 33.

What means should we use to keep us from coveting that which is our neighbour's?

The best remedy is contentment. If we are content with our own, we shall not covet that which is another's. Paul could say, 'I have coveted no man's gold or silver.' Whence was this? It was from contentment. 'I have learned, in whatsoever state I am, therewith to be content.' Phil 4: 11. Content says, as Jacob did, 'I have enough. 'Gen 33: 11. I have a promise of heaven, and have sufficient to bear my charges thither; I have enough. He who has enough, will not covet that which is another's. Be content: and the best way to be contented, is, (1) Believe that condition to be best which God by his providence carves out to you. If he had seen fit for us to have more, we should have had it. Perhaps we could not manage a great estate; it is hard to carry a full cup without spilling, and a full estate without sinning. Great estates may be snares. A boat may be overturned by having too much sail. The believing that estate to be best which God appoints us, makes us content; and being contented, we shall not covet that which is another's. (2) The way to be content with such things as we have, and not to covet another's, is to consider the less we have, the less account we shall have to give at the last day. Every person is a steward, and must be accountable to God. They who have great estates have the greater reckoning. God will say, What good have you done with your estates? Have you honoured me with your substance? Where are the poor you have fed and clothed? If you cannot give a good account, it will be sad. It should make us contented with a less portion, to consider, the less riches, the less reckoning. This is the way to have contentment. There is no better antidote against coveting that which is another's than being content with that which is our own.

3.1 Man's Inability to keep the Moral Law

Is any man able perfectly to keep the commandments of God?

No mere man, since the fall, is able in this life perfectly to keep the commandments of God, but does daily break them, in thought, word, and deed.

'In many things we offend all.' James 3: 2. Man in his primitive state of innocence, was endowed with ability to keep the whole moral law. He had rectitude of mind, sanctity of will, and perfection of power. He had the copy of God's law written on his heart; no sooner did God command but he obeyed. As the key is suited to all the wards in the lock, and can open them, so Adam had a power suited to all God's commands, and could obey them. Adam's obedience ran parallel with the moral law, as a well made dial goes exactly with the sun. Man in innocence was like a well tuned organ, he was sweetly in tune to the will of God; he was adorned with holiness as the angels, but not confirmed in holiness as the angels. He was holy, but mutable; he fell from his purity, and we with him. Sin cut the lock of original righteousness where our strength lay; it brought a languor and faintness into our souls; and has so weakened us, that we shall never recover our full strength till we put on immortality. What I am now to demonstrate, is, that we cannot yield perfect obedience to the moral law.

I. The case of an unregenerate man is such, that he cannot perfectly obey all God's commands. He may as well touch the stars, or span the ocean, as yield exact obedience to the law. A person unregenerate cannot act spiritually, he cannot pray in the Holy Ghost, he cannot live by faith, he cannot do duty out of love to duty; and if he cannot do duty spiritually, much less perfectly. Now, that a natural man cannot yield perfect obedience to the moral law, is evident. (1) Because he is spiritually dead. Eph 2: 1. How can he, being dead, keep the commandments of God perfectly? A dead man is not fit for action. A sinner has the symptoms of death upon him. He has no sense; he has no sense of the evil of sin, of God's holiness and veracity; therefore he is said to be without feeling. Eph 4: 19. He has no strength. Rom 5: 6. What strength has a dead man? A natural man has no strength to deny himself, or to resist temptation; he is dead; and can a dead man fulfil the moral law? (2) A natural man cannot perfectly keep all God's commandments, because he is born in sin, and lives in sin. Psa 51: 5. 'He drinketh iniquity like water.' Job 15: 16. All the imaginations of his thoughts are evil, and only evil. Gen 6: 5. The least evil thought is a breach of the royal law; and if there be defection, there cannot be perfection. As a natural man has no power to keep the moral law, so he has no will. He is not only dead, but worse than dead. A dead man does no hurt, but there is a life of resistance against God that accompanies the death of sin. A natural man not only cannot keep the law through weakness, but he breaks it through wilfulness. 'We will do whatsoever goes out of our own mouth, to burn incense unto the queen of heaven.' Jer 44: 17.

II. As the unregenerate cannot keep the moral law perfectly, so neither can the regenerate. 'There is not a just man upon earth, that does good and sinneth not;' nay, that 'sins not in doing good.' Eccl 7: 20. There is that in the best actions of a righteous man that is damnable, if God should weigh him in the balance of justice. Alas! how are his duties fly-blown! He cannot pray without wandering, nor believe without doubting. 'To will is present with me, but how to perform I find not.' In the Greek it is, 'How to do it thoroughly I find not.' Rom 7: 18. Paul, though a saint of the first magnitude, was better at willing than at performing. Mary asked where they had laid Christ; for she had a mind to have carried him away, but she wanted strength: so the regenerate have a will to obey God's law perfectly, but they want strength; their obedience is weak and sickly. The mark they are to shoot at, is perfection of holiness; but though they take a right aim, yet do what they can, they come short of the mark. 'The good that I would, I do not.' Rom 7: 19. A Christian, while serving God, like a ferry man that plies the oar, and rows hard, is hindered, for a gust of wind carries him back again: so says Paul, 'The good I would, I do not,' I am driven back by temptation. Now, if there be any failure in a man's obedience, he cannot be a perfect commentary upon God's law. The Virgin Mary's obedience was not perfect; she needed Christ's blood to wash her tears. Aaron was to make atonement for the altar, to show that the most holy offering has defilement in it, and needs atonement to be made for it. Exod 29: 37.

If a man has no power to keep the whole moral law, why does God require it of him? Is this justice?

Though man has lost his power of obeying, God has not lost his right of commanding. If a master entrusts a servant with money to lay out, and the servant spends it dissolutely, may not the master justly demand it? God gave us power to keep the moral law, which by tampering with sin, we lost; but may not God still call for perfect obedience, or, in case of default, justly punish us?

Why does God permit such an inability in man to keep the law?

He does it: (1) To humble us. Man is a self-exalting creature; and if he has but anything of worth, he is ready to be puffed up; but when he comes to see his deficiencies and failings, and how far short he comes of the holiness and perfection which God's law requires, it pulls down the plumes of his pride, and lays them in the dust; he weeps over his inability; he blushes over his leprous spots; he says with Job, 'I abhor myself in dust and ashes.' (2) God lets this inability be upon us, that we may have recourse to Christ to obtain pardon for our defects, and to sprinkle our best duties with his blood. When a man sees that he owes perfect obedience to the law, but has nothing to pay, it makes him flee to Christ to be his friend, and answer for him all the demands of the law, and set him free in the court of justice.

Use one. Here is matter of humiliation for our fall in Adam. In the state of innocence we were perfectly holy; our minds were crowned with knowledge, and our wills, as a queen, swayed the sceptre of liberty; but now we may say, 'The crown is fallen from our head.' Lam 5: 16. We have lost that power which was inherent in us. When we look back to our primitive glory, when we shone as earthly angels, we may take up Job's words, 'Oh that I were as in months past!' chap 29: 2. 0 that it were with us as at first, when there was no stain upon our virgin nature, when there was a perfect harmony between God's law and man's will! But, alas! how is the scene altered, our strength is gone from us; we tread awry at every step: we come below every precept; our dwarfishness will not reach the sublimity of God's law; we fail in our obedience; and while we fail, we forfeit. This should put us in deep mourning, and spring a leak of sorrow in all our souls.

Use two. Of confutation. (1) It confutes the Armenians, who cry up the power of the will. They hold they have a will to save themselves. But by nature, we not only want strength, but we want will to that which is good. Rom 5: 6. The will is not only full of weakness, but obstinacy. 'Israel would none of me.' Psa 81: 11. The will hangs forth a flag of defiance against God. Such as speak of the sovereign power of the will, forget 'It is God that worketh in you both to will and to do.' Phil 2: 13. If the power be in the will of man, then what need is there for God to work in us to will? If the air can enlighten itself, what need is there for the sun to shine? Such as talk of the power of nature, and their ability to save themselves, disparage Christ's merits. I may say (as Gal 5: 4), 'Christ has become of no effect to them.' They who advance the power of their will in matters of salvation, without the medicinal grace of Christ, do absolutely put themselves under the covenant of works. I would ask, 'Can they perfectly keep the moral law?' Malum oritur ex quolibet defectu [Evil is manifested in any blemish at all]. If there be but the least defect in their obedience, they are lost. For one sinful thought the law of God curses them, and the justice of God condemns them. Confounded be their pride, who cry up the power of nature, as if, by their own inherent abilities, they could rear up a building, the top whereof should reach to heaven.

(2) It confutes that sort of people who brag of perfection; and who, according to that principle, can keep all God's commandments perfectly. I would ask such whether at no time a vain thought has come into their minds? If there has, then they are not perfect. The Virgin Mary was not perfect. Though her womb was pure (being overshadowed by the Holy Ghost), yet her soul was not perfect. Christ tacitly supposes a failing in her. Luke 2: 49. And are they more perfect than

the blessed Virgin was? Such as hold perfection, need not confess sin. David confessed sin, and Paul confessed sin. Psa 32: 5; Rom 7: 25. But they are got beyond David and Paul; they are perfect, they never transgress; and where there is no transgression, what need for confession? Again, if they are perfect, they need not ask pardon. They can pay God's justice what they owe; therefore, why pray, 'Forgive us our debts'? Oh, that the devil should rock men so fast asleep, as to make them dream of perfection! Do they plead, 'Let us therefore as many as be perfect be thus minded'? Phil 3: 15. Perfection there, is meant of sincerity. God is best able to interpret his own word. He calls sincerity perfection. 'A perfect and an upright man.' Job 1: 8. But who is exactly perfect? A man full of diseases may as well say he is healthful, as a man full of sins say he is perfect.

Use three. For encouragement to regenerate persons. Though you fail in your obedience, and cannot keep the moral law exactly, yet be not discouraged.

What comfort may be given to a regenerate person under the failures and imperfections of his obedience?

That a believer is not under the covenant of works, but under the covenant of grace. The covenant of works requires perfect, personal, perpetual obedience; but in the covenant of grace, God will make some abatements; he will accept less than he required in the covenant of works. (1) In the covenant of works God required perfection of degrees; in the covenant of grace he accepts perfection of parts. There he required perfect working, here he accepts sincere believing. In the covenant of works, God required us to live without sin; in the covenant of grace he accepts of our combat with sin. (2) Though a Christian cannot, in his own person, perform all God's commandments; yet Christ, as his Surety, and in his stead, has fulfilled the law for him: and God accepts of Christ's obedience, which is perfect, to satisfy for that obedience which is imperfect. Christ being made a curse for believers, all the curses of the law have their sting pulled out. (3) Though a Christian cannot keep the commands of God to satisfaction, yet he may to approbation.

How is that?

(1) He gives his full assent and consent to the law of God. 'The law is holy and just:' there was assent in the judgement. Rom 7: 12. 'I consent unto the law;' there was consent in the will. Rom 7: 16.

(2) A Christian mourns that he cannot keep the commandments fully. When he fails he weeps; he is not angry with the law because it is so strict but he is angry with himself because he is so deficient.

(3) He takes a sweet complacent delight in the law. 'I delight in the law of God after the inward man.' Rom 7: 22. Greek: 'I take pleasure in it.' 'O! how love I thy law.' Psa 119: 97. Though a Christian cannot keep God's law, yet he loves his law; though he cannot serve God perfectly, yet

he serves him willingly.

(4) It is his cordial desire to walk in all God's commands. 'O that my ways were directed to keep thy statutes.' Psa 119: 5. Though his strength fails, yet his pulse beats.

(5) He really endeavours to obey God's law perfectly; and wherein he comes short he runs to Christ's blood to supply his defects. This cordial desire, and real endeavour, God esteems as perfect obedience. 'If there be a willing mind, it is accepted.' 2 Cor 8: 12. 'Let me hear thy voice, for sweet is thy voice.' Cant 2: 14. Though the prayers of the righteous are mixed with sin, yet God sees they would pray better. He picks out the weeds from the flowers; he sees the faith and bears with the failing. The saints' obedience, though short of legal perfection, yet having sincerity in it, and Christ's merits mixed with it, finds gracious acceptance. When the Lord sees endeavours after perfect obedience, he takes it well at our hands; as a father who receives a letter from his child, though there be blots in it, and false spellings, takes all in good part. Oh! what blotting are there in our holy things; but God is pleased to take all in good part. He says, 'It is my child, and he would do better if he could; I will accept it.'

3.2 Degrees of Sin

Are all transgressions of the law equally heinous?

Some sins in themselves, and by reason of several aggravations, are more heinous in the sight of God than others.

'He that delivered me unto thee, has the greater sin.' John 19: 11. The Stoic philosophers held that all sins were equal; but this Scripture clearly holds forth that there is a gradual difference in sin; some are greater than others; some are 'mighty sins,' and crying sins.' Amos 5: 12; Gen 18: 21. Every sin has a voice to speak, but some sins cry. As some diseases are worse than others, and some poisons more venomous, so some sins are more heinous. 'Ye have done worse than your fathers, your sins have exceeded theirs.' Jer 16: 12; Ezek 16: 47. Some sins have a blacker aspect than others; to clip the king's coin is treason; but to strike his person is a higher degree of treason. A vain thought is a sin, but a blasphemous word is a greater sin. That some sins are greater than others appears, (1) Because there was difference in the offerings under the law; the sin offering was greater than the trespass offering. (2) Because some sins are not capable of pardon as others are, therefore they must needs be more heinous, as the blasphemy against the Holy Ghost. Matt 12: 31. (3) Because some sins have a greater degree of punishment than others. 'Ye shall receive the greater damnation.' Matt 23: 14. 'Shall not the Judge of all the earth do right?' God would not punish one more than another if his sin was not greater. It is true, 'all sins are equally heinous in respect of the object,' or the infinite God, against whom sin is committed, but, in another sense, all sins are not alike heinous; some sins have more bloody circumstances in them, which are like the dye to the wool, to give it a deeper colour.

[1] Such sins are more heinous as are committed without any occasion offered; as when a man swears or is angry, and has no provocation. The less the occasion of sin, the greater is the sin itself.

[2] Such sins are more heinous that are committed presumptuously. Under the law there was no sacrifice for presumptuous sins. Num 15: 30. What is the sin of presumption, which heightens and aggravates sin, and makes it more heinous?

To sin presumptuously, is to sin against convictions and illuminations, or an enlightened conscience. 'They are of those that rebel against the light.' Job 24: 13. Conscience, like the cherubim, stands with a flaming sword in its hand to deter the sinner; and yet he will sin. Did not Pilate sin against conviction, and with a high hand, in condemning Christ? He knew that for envy the Jews had delivered him. Matt 27: 18. He confessed he 'found no fault in him.' Luke 23: 14. His own wife sent to him saying, 'Have nothing to do with that just man.' Matt 27: 19. Yet for all this, he gave the sentence of death against Christ. He sinned presumptuously, against an enlightened conscience. To sin ignorantly does something to extenuate and pare off the guilt. 'If I had not come and spoken unto them, they had not had sin,' that is, their sin had been less. John 15: 22. But to sin against illuminations and convictions enhances men's sins. These sins make deep wounds in the soul; other sins fetch blood; they are a stab at the heart.

How many ways may a man sin against illuminations and convictions?

(1) When he lives in the total neglect of duty. He is not ignorant that it is a duty to read the Word, yet he lets the Bible lie by as rusty armour, seldom made us of. He is convinced that it is a duty to pray in his family, yet he can go days and months, and God never hears of him; he calls God Father, but never asks his blessing. Neglect of family-prayer, as it were, uncovers the roof of men's houses, and makes way for a curse to be rained down upon their table.

(2) When a man lives in the same sins he condemns in others. 'Thou that judges, does the same things.' Rom 2: 1. As Augustine says of Seneca, 'He wrote against superstition, yet he worshipped those images which he reproved.' One man condemns another for rash censuring, yet lives in the same sin himself; a master reproves his apprentice for swearing, yet he himself swears. The snuffers of the tabernacle were of pure gold: they who reprove and snuff the vices of others, had need themselves be free from those sins. The snuffers must be of gold.

(3) When a man sins after vows. 'Thy vows are upon me, O God.' Psa 56: 12. A vow is a religious promise made to God, to dedicate ourselves to him. A vow is not only a purpose, but a promise. Every votary makes himself a debtor; he binds himself to God in a solemn manner. Now, to sin after a vow, to vow himself to God, and give his soul to the devil, must needs be against the highest convictions.

(4) When a man sins after counsels, admonitions, warnings, he cannot plead ignorance. The trumpet of the gospel has been blown in his ears, and sounded a retreat to call him off from his sins, he has been told of his injustice, living in malice, keeping bad company, yet he would venture upon sin. This is to sin against conviction; it aggravates the sin, and is like a weight put into the scale, to make his sin weigh the heavier. If a sea-mark be set up to give warning that there are shelves and rocks in that place, yet if the mariner will sail there, and split his ship, it is presumption; and if he be cast away, who will pity him?

(5) When a man sins against express combinations and threatening. God has thundered out threatenings against such sins. 'God shall would the hairy scalp of such an one as goes on still in his trespasses.' Psa 68: 21. Though God set the point of his sword to the breast of a sinner, he will still commit sin. The pleasure of sin delights him more than the threatenings affright him. Like the leviathan, 'he laugheth at the shaking of a spear.' Job 41: 29. Nay, he derides God's threatenings. 'Let him make speed, and hasten his work, that we may see it:' we have heard much what God intends to do, and of judgement approaching, we would fain see it. Isa 5: 19. For men to see the flaming sword of God's threatening brandished, yet to strengthen themselves in sin, is in an aggravated manner to sin against illumination and conviction.

(6) When a man sins under affliction. God not only thunders by threatening, but lets his thunderbolt fall. He inflicts judgements on a person so that he may read his sins in his punishment, and yet he sins. His sin was uncleanness, by which he wasted his strength, as well as his estate. He has had a fit of apoplexy; and yet while feeling the smart of sin, he retains the love of sin. This is to sin against conviction. 'In his distress did he trespass yet more; this is that king Ahab' 2 Chron 28: 22. It makes the sin greater to sin against an enlightened conscience. It is full of obstinacy. Men give no reason, make no defence for their sins, and yet are resolved to hold fast iniquity. Voluntas est regula et mensura actionis [An action can be measured and judged by the will involved], the more of the will in a sin, the greater the sin. 'We will walk after our own devices.' Jer 18: 12. Though there be death and hell at every step, we will march on under Satan's colours. What made the sin of apostate angels so great was that it was wilful; they had no ignorance in their mind, no passion to stir them up; there was no tempter to deceive them, but they sinned obstinately and from choice. To sin against convictions and illuminations, is joined with rejection and contempt of God. It is bad for a sinner to forget God, but it is worse to condemn him. 'Wherefore does the wicked condemn God?' Psa 10: 13. An enlightened sinner knows that by his sin he disobliges and angers God; but he cares not whether God be pleased or not, he will have his sin; therefore such a one is said to reproach God. 'The soul that does ought presumptuously, the same reproacheth the Lord.' Numb 15: 30. Every sin displeases God, but sins against an enlightened conscience reproach the Lord. To condemn the authority of a prince, is a reproach done to him. It is accompanied with impudence. Fear and shame are banished, the veil of modesty is laid aside. 'The unjust knoweth no shame.' Zeph 3: 5. Judas knew Christ was the Messiah; he was convinced of it by an oracle from heaven, and by the miracles he wrought, and yet he impudently went on in his treason, even when Christ said, 'He that dips his hand with

me in the dish, he shall betray me:' and he knew Christ meant him. When he was going about his treason, and Christ pronounced a woe to him, yet, for all that, he proceeded in his treason. Luke 22: 22. Thus to sin presumptuously, against an enlightened conscience, dyes the sin of a crimson colour, and makes it greater than other sins.

[3] Such sins are more heinous than others, which are sins of continuance. The continuing of sin is the enhancing of sin. He who plots treason, makes himself a greater offender. Some men's heads are the devil's minthouse, they are a mint of mischief. 'Inventors of evil things.' Rom 1: 30. Some invent new oaths, others new snares. Such were those presidents that invented a decree against Daniel, and got the king to sign it. Dan 6: 9.

[4] Those sins are greater which proceed from a spirit of malignity. To malign holiness is diabolical. It is a sin to want grace, it is worse to hate it. In nature there are antipathies, as between the vine and laurel. Some have an antipathy against God because of his purity. 'Cause the Holy One of Israel to cease from before us.' Isa 30: 11. Sinners, if it lay in their power, would not only enthrone God, but annihilate him; if they could help it, God should no longer be God. Thus sin is boiled up to a greater height.

[5] Those sins are of greater magnitude, which are mixed with ingratitude. Of all things God cannot endure to have his kindness slighted. His mercy is seen in reprieving men so long, in wooing them by his Spirit and ministers to be reconciled, in crowning them with so many temporal blessings: and to abuse all this love - when God has been filling up the measure of his mercy, for men to fill up the measure of their sins - is high ingratitude, and makes their sins of a deeper crimson. Some are worse for mercy. 'The vulture,' says Aelian, 'draws sickness from perfumes.' So the sinner contracts evil from the sweet perfumes of God's mercy. The English chronicle reports of one Parry, who being condemned to die, Queen Elizabeth sent him her pardon; and after he was pardoned, he conspired and plotted the queen's death. Just so some deal with God, he bestows mercy, and they plot treason against him. 'I have nourished and brought up children, and they have rebelled against me.' Isa 1: 2. The Athenians, in lieu of the good service Themistocles had done them, banished him their city. The snake, in the fable, being frozen, stung him that gave it warmth. Certainly sins against mercy are more heinous.

[6] Those sins are more heinous than others which are committed with delectation. A child of God may sin through a surprisal, or against his will. 'The evil which I would not, that I do.' Rom 7: 19. He is like one that is carried down the stream involuntarily. But to sin with delight heightens and greatens the sin. It is a sign the heart is in the sin. 'They set their heart on their iniquity,' as a man follows his gain with delight. Hos 4: 8. 'Without are dogs, and whosoever loveth and maketh a lie.' Rev 22: 15. To tell a lie is a sin; but to love to tell a lie is a greater sin.

[7] Those sins are more heinous than others which are committed under a pretence of religion. To cheat and defraud is a sin, but to do it with a Bible in one's hand, is a double sin. To be unchaste is a sin; but to put on a mask of religion to play the whore makes the sin greater. 'I have

peace offerings with me; this day have I paid my vows; come let us take our fill of love.' Prov 7: 14, 15. She speaks as if she had been at church, and had been saying her prayers: who would ever have suspected her of dishonesty? But, behold her hypocrisy; she makes her devotion a preface to adultery. 'Which devour widows' houses, and for a show make long prayers.' Luke XX 47. The sin was not in making long prayers; for Christ was a whole night in prayer; but to make long prayers that they might do unrighteous actions, made their sin more horrid.

[8] Sins of apostasy are more heinous than others. Demas forsook the truth and afterwards became a priest in an idol temple, says Dorotheus. 2 Tim 4: 10. To fall is a sin; but to fall away is a greater sin. Apostates cast a disgrace upon religion. 'The apostate,' says Tertullian, 'seems to put God and Satan in the balance; and having weighed both their services, prefers the devil's, and proclaims him to be the best master.' In which respect the apostate is said to put Christ to 'open shame.' Heb 6: 6. This dyes a sin in grain, and makes it greater. It is a sin not to profess Christ, but it is a greater to deny him. Not to wear Christ's colours is a sin, but to run from his colours is a greater sin. A pagan sins less than a baptised renegade.

[9] To persecute religion makes sin greater. Acts 7: 52. To have no religion is a sin, but to endeavour to destroy religion is a greater. Antiochus Epiphanes took more tedious journeys and ran more hazards, to vex and oppose the Jews, than all his predecessors had done to obtain victories. Herod 'added this above all, that he shut up John in prison.' Luke 3: 20. He sinned before by incest; but by imprisoning the prophet he added to his sin and made it greater. Persecution fills up the measure of sin. 'Fill ye up the measure of your fathers.' Matt 23: 32. If you pour a porringer of water into a cistern it adds something to it, but if you pour in a bucketful or two it fills up the measure of the cistern; so persecution fills up the measure of sin, and makes it greater.

[10] To sin maliciously makes sin greater. Aquinas, and other of the schoolmen, place the sin against the Holy Ghost in malice. The sinner does all he can to vex God, and despite the Spirit of grace. Heb 10: 29. Thus Julia threw up his dagger in the air, as if he would have been revenged upon God. This swells sin to its full size, it cannot be greater. When a man is once come to this, blasphemously to despite the Spirit, there is but one step lower he can fall, and that is to hell.

[11] It aggravates sin, and makes it greater, when a man not only sins himself, but endeavours to make others sin. (1) Such as teach errors to the people, who decry Christ's deity, or deny his virtue, making him only a political head, not a head of influence: who preach against the morality of the Sabbath, or the immortality of the soul; these men's sins are greater than others. If the breakers of God's law sin, what do they that teach men to break them? Matt 5: 19. (2) Such as destroy others by their bad example. The swearing father teaches his son to swear, and damns him by his example. Such men's sins are greater than others, and they shall have a hotter place in hell.

Use. You see all sins are not equal; some are more grievous than others, and bring greater wrath;

therefore especially take heed of these sins. 'Keep back thy servant from presumptuous sins.' Psa 19: 13. The least sin is bad enough; you need not aggravate your sins, and make them more heinous. He that has a little wound will not make it deeper. Oh, beware of those circumstances which increase your sin and make it more heinous! The higher a man is in sinning, the lower he shall lie in torment.

3.3 The Wrath of God

What does every sin deserve?

God's wrath and curse, both in this life, and in that which is to come.

'Depart from me, ye cursed, into everlasting fire.' Matt 25: 4I. Man having sinned, is like a favourite turned out of the king's favour, and deserves the wrath and curse of God. He deserves God's curse. Gal 3: 10. As when Christ cursed the fig-tree, it withered; so, when God curses any, he withers in his soul. Matt 21: 19. God's curse blasts wherever it comes. He deserves also God's wrath, which is nothing else but the execution of his curse.

What is this wrath?

I. It is privative; that is, deprives of the smiles of God's face. It is hell enough to be excluded his presence: in whose 'presence is fulness of joy.' Psa 16: 11. His smiling face has that splendour and beauty in it that ravishes the angels with delight. This is the diamond in the ring of glory. If it were such a misery for Absalom, that he might not see the King's face, what will it be for the wicked to be shut out from beholding God's pleasant face! Privatio Divinae visionis omnium suppliciorum summum [To be deprived of the sight of God is the greatest of all punishments].

II. This wrath has something in it positive. It is 'wrath come upon them to the uttermost.' I Thess 2: 16.

[I] God's wrath is irresistible. 'Who knoweth the power of thine anger?' Psa 90: 2: Sinners may oppose God's ways, but not his wrath. Shall the briers contend with the fire? Shall finite contend with infinite? 'Hast thou an arm like God?' Job 40: 9.

[2] God's wrath is terrible. The Spanish proverb is, The lion is not so fierce as he is painted. We are apt to have slight thoughts of God's wrath; but it is very tremendous and dismal, as if scalding lead should be dropped into one's eyes. The Hebrew word for wrath signifies heat. To show that the wrath of God is hot, therefore it is compared to fire in the text. Fire, when in its rage, is dreadful. So the wrath of God is like fire, it is the terrible of terrible. Other fire is but painted to this. If when God's wrath is kindled but a little, and a spark of it flies into a wicked man's conscience in this life, it is so terrible, what will it be when God shall 'stir up all his

wrath'? Psa 78: 38. How sad is it with a soul in desertion! God then dips his pen in gall, and 'writes bitter things;' his poisoned arrows stick fast into the heart. 'While I suffer thy terrors, I am distracted; thy fierce wrath goes over me.' Psa 88: 15, 16. Luther, in desertion, was in such horror of mind, that nec calor, nec sanguis superesset [no warmth or blood remained]; he had no blood seen in his face, but he lay as one dead. Now, if God's wrath be such towards those whom he loves, what will it be towards those whom he hates? If they who sip of the cup find it so bitter, what will they do who drink its dregs? Psal 75:8. Solomon says, 'The king's wrath is as the roaring of a lion.' Prov 19: 12. What then is God's wrath? When God musters up all his forces, and sets himself in battalia against a sinner, how can his heart endure? Ezek 22: 14. Who is able to lie under mountains of wrath? God is the sweetest friend but the sorest enemy.

(1) The wrath of God shall seize upon every part of a sinner. Upon the body. The body, which was so tender that it could not bear heat or cold, shall be tormented in the wine press of God's wrath. Those eyes which before could behold amorous objects, shall be tormented with the sight of devils. The ears, which before were delighted with music, shall be tormented with the hideous shrieks of the damned. The wrath of God shall seize upon the soul of a reprobate. Ordinary fire cannot touch the soul. When the martyrs' bodies were consuming, their souls triumphed in the flames; but God's wrath burns the soul. The memory will be tormented to remember what means of grace have been abused. The conscience will be tormented with self-accusations. The sinner will accuse himself for presumptuous sins, for misspending his precious hours, and for resisting the Holy Ghost.

(2) The wrath of God is without intermission. Hell is an abiding place, but no resting place; there is not a minute's rest. Outward pain has some abatement. If it be the stone or colic, the patient has sometimes ease; but the torments of the damned have no intermission; he who feels God's wrath never says, 'I have ease.'

(3) The wrath of God is eternal. So says the text. 'Everlasting fire.' No tears can quench the flame of God's anger; no, though we could shed rivers of tears. In all pains of this life men hope for cessation - the suffering will not continue long; either the tormentor dies or the tormented; but the wrath of God is always feeding upon the sinner. The terror of natural fire is, that it consumes what it burns; but what makes the fire of God's wrath terrible is, that it does not consume what it burns. Sic morientur damnati ut semper vivunt [Those that are lost will so die as to remain always alive]. Bernard. The sinner will ever be in the furnace. After innumerable millions of years the wrath of God is as far from ending as it was at the beginning. If all the earth and sea were sand, and every thousand years a bird should come and take away a grain, it would be a long while ere that vast heap of sand were emptied; but if, after all that time, the damned might come out of hell, there would be some hope; but this word 'Ever' breaks the heart.

How does it consist with God's justice to punish sin, which perhaps was committed in a moment, with eternal fire?

On account of the heinous nature of sin. Consider the Person offended; it is Crimen laesae majestatis [a charge of the highest treason]. Sin is committed against an infinite majesty, therefore it is infinite, and the punishment must be infinite. Because the nature of man is but finite, and a sinner cannot at once bear infinite wrath, therefore he must be satisfying in enmity what he cannot satisfy at once.

(4) While the wicked lie scorching in the flames of wrath, they have none to commiserate them. It is some ease of grief to have some to condole with us; but the wicked have wrath and no pity shown them. Who will pity them? God will not. They derided his Spirit, and he will now laugh at their calamity. Prov 1: 26. The saints will not pity them. They persecuted them upon earth, therefore they will rejoice to see God's justice executed on them. 'The righteous shall rejoice when he sees the vengeance.' Psa 58: 10.

(5) The sinner under wrath has no one to speak a good word for him. If an elect person sins, he has one to intercede for him. 'We have an advocate, Jesus Christ the righteous.' I John 2: 1. Christ will say, 'It is one of my friends, one for whom I have shed my blood; Father, pardon him.' But the wicked who die in sin have none to solicit for them; they have an accuser, but no advocate; Christ's blood will not plead for them; they slighted Christ and refused to come under his government, therefore Christ's blood cries against them.

[3] God's wrath is just. The Greek word for vengeance signifies justice. The wicked shall drink a sea of wrath, but not one drop of injustice, It is just that God's honour be repaired, and how can that be but by punishing offenders? He who infringes the king's laws deserves the penalty. Mercy goes by favour, punishment by desert. 'To us belongeth confusion of face.' Dan 9: 8. Wrath is that which belongs to us as we are simmers; it is due to us as any wages that are paid.

Use one. For information. (1) God is justified in condemning sinners at the last day. They deserve wrath, and it is no injustice to give them that which they deserve. If a malefactor deserves death, the judge does him no wrong in condemning him.

(2) See what a great evil sin is, which exposes a person to God's wrath for ever. You may know the lion by his paw; and you may know what an evil sin is by the wrath and curse it brings. When you see a man drawn upon a hurdle to execution, you conclude he is guilty of some capital crime that brings such a punishment; so when a man lies under the torrid zone of God's wrath, and roars out in flames, you must say, 'How horrid an evil sin is!' They who now see no evil in swearing, or Sabbath breaking, will see it looks black in the glass of hell-torments.

(3) See here a handwriting upon the wall; that which may check a sinner's mirth. He is now brisk and frolicsome, he chants to the sound of the viol, and invents instruments of music (Amos 6: 5); he drinks 'stolen waters,' and says, 'they are sweet;' but let him remember that the wrath and curse of God hang over him, which will shortly, if he repent not, be executed on him. Dionysus thought, as he sat at table, that he saw a naked sword hang over his head; but the sword of God's

justice hangs over a sinner, and when the slender thread of life is cut asunder it falls upon him. 'Rejoice, O young man, in thy youth; and let thy heart cheer thee in the days of thy youth... but know thou, that for all these things God will bring thee into judgement.' Eccl 11: 9. For a drop of pleasure thou must drink a sea of wrath. Your pleasure cannot be so sweet as wrath is bitter. The delights of the flesh cannot countervail the horror of conscience. Better want the devil's honey than be stung with the wrath of God. The garden of Eden, which signifies pleasure, had a flaming sword placed at the east end of it. Gen 3: 24. The garden of carnal and sinful delight is surrounded with the flaming sword of God's wrath.

Use two. For reproof. The stupidity of sinners is reproved who are no more affected with the curse and wrath of God which is due to them. 'None considereth in his heart.' Isa 44: IS. If they were in debt and the sergeant was about to arrest them, they would be affected with that; but though the fierce wrath of God is ready to arrest them, they remember it not. Though a beast has no shame, he has fear: he is afraid of fire; but sinners are worse than brutish, for they fear not the 'fire of hell' till they are in it. Most have their consciences asleep, or seared; but when they shall see the vials of God's wrath dropping, they will cry out as Dives, 'Oh! I am tormented in this flame!' Luke 16: 24.

Use three. For exhortation. (1) Let us adore God's patience, who has not brought this wrath and curse upon us all this while. We have deserved wrath, yet God has not given us our desert. We may all subscribe to Psa 103: 8, 'The Lord is slow to anger;' and to ver 10, 'He has not rewarded us according to our iniquities.' God has deferred his wrath, and given us space to repent. Rev 2: 21. He is not like a hasty creditor, who requires the debt, and gives no time for payment; he shoots off his warning-piece, that he may not shoot off his murdering-piece. 'The Lord is long suffering to usward, not willing that any perish.' 2 Pet 3: 9. God adjourns the assizes, to see if sinners will turn; he keeps off the storm of his wrath: but if men will not be warned, let them know that long forbearance is no forgiveness.

(2) Let us labour to prevent the wrath we have deserved. How careful are men to prevent poverty or disgrace! O labour to prevent God's eternal wrath, that it may not only be deferred, but removed.

What shall we do to prevent and escape the wrath to come?

[1] By getting an interest in Jesus Christ. Christ is the only screen to stand betwixt us and the wrath of God; he felt God's wrath that they who believe in him should never feel it. 'Jesus which delivered us from the wrath to come.' I Thess 1: 10. Nebuchadnezzar's fiery furnace was a type of God's wrath, and that furnace did not singe the garments of the three children, nor had 'the smell of fire passed upon them.' Dan 3: 27. Jesus Christ went into the furnace of his Father's wrath; and the smell of the fire of hell shall never pass upon those that believe in him.

[2] If we would prevent the wrath of God, let us take heed of those sins which will provoke it.

Edmund, successor of Anselm, had a saying, 'I had rather leap into a furnace of fire, than willingly commit a sin against God.' There are several fiery sins we must take heed of, which will provoke the fire of God's wrath. The fire of rash anger. Some who profess religion cannot bridle their tongue; they care not what they say in their anger; they will even curse their passions. James says, 'The tongue is set on fire of hell;' chap 3: 6. Oh! take heed of a 'fiery tongue,' lest it bring thee to 'fiery torment.' Dives begged a drop of water to cool his tongue. Cyprian says he had offended most in his tongue, and now that was most set on fire. Take heed of the fire of malice. Malice is a malignant humour, whereby we wish evil to others; it is a vermin that lives on blood; it studies revenge. Caligula had a chest where he kept deadly poisons for those against whom he had malice. The fire of malice brings men to the fiery furnace of God's wrath. Take heed of the sin of uncleanness. 'Whoremongers and adulterers God will judge.' Heb 13: 4. Such as burn in uncleanness are in great danger to burn one day in hell. Let one fire put out another; let the fire of God's wrath put out the fire of lust.

(3) To you who have a well-grounded hope that you shall not feel this wrath, which you have deserved, let me exhort you to be very thankful to God, who has given his Son to save you from this tremendous wrath. Jesus has delivered you from wrath to come. The Lamb of God was scorched in the fire of God's wrath for you. Christ felt the wrath which he did not deserve, that you might escape the wrath which you have deserved. Pliny observes, that there is nothing better to quench fire than blood. Christ's blood has quenched the fire of God's wrath for you. 'Upon me be thy curse,' said Rebekah to Jacob. Gen 27: 13. So said Christ to God's justice, 'Upon me be the curse, that my elect may inherit the blessing.' Be patient under all the afflictions which you endure. Affliction is sharp, but it is not wrath, it is not hell. who would not willingly drink in the cup of affliction that knows he shall never drink in the cup of damnation? Who would not be willing to bear the wrath of man that knows he shall never feel the wrath of God?

Christian, though thou mayest feel the rod, thou shalt never feel the bloody axe. Augustine once said, 'Strike, Lord, where thou wilt, if sin be pardoned.' So say, 'Afflict me, Lord, as thou wilt in this life, seeing I shall escape the wrath to come.'

4. THE WAY OF SALVATION

4.1 Faith

What does God require of us, that we may escape his wrath and curse due to us for our sin?

Faith in Jesus Christ, repentance unto life, with the diligent use of all the outward means, whereby Christ communicateth to us the benefits of redemption.

I begin with the first, faith in Jesus Christ. 'Whom God has set forth to be a propitiation through faith in his blood.' Rom 3: 25. The great privilege in the text is, to have Christ for a propitiation; which is not only to free us from God's wrath, but to ingratiate us into his love and favour. The means of having Christ to be our propitiation is, 'Faith in his blood.' There is a twofold faith, Fides quae creditur [the faith which is believed], which is 'the doctrine of faith;' and Fides qua creditur [the faith by which we believe], which is 'the grace of faith.' The act of justifying faith lies in recumbency; we rest on Christ alone for salvation. As a man that is ready to drown catches hold on the bough of a tree, so a poor trembling sinner, seeing himself ready to perish, catches hold by faith on Christ the tree of life, and is saved. The work of faith is by the Holy Spirit; therefore faith is called the 'fruit of the Spirit.' Gal 5: 22. Faith does not grow in nature, it is an outlandish plant, a fruit of the Spirit. This grace of faith is sanctissimum humani pectoris bonum [the most hallowed possession of the human heart]; of all others, the most precious rich faith, and most holy faith, and faith of God's elect: hence it is called 'precious faith.' 2 Pet 1: 1. As gold is most precious among metals, so is faith among the graces. Faith is the queen of the graces; it is the condition of the gospel. 'Thy faith has saved thee,' not thy tears. Luke 7: 50. Faith is the 'vital artery of the soul' that animates it. 'The just shall live by his faith.' Hab 2: 4. Though unbelievers breathe, they want life. Faith, as Clemens Alexandrinus calls it, is a mother grace; it excites and invigorates all the graces; not a grace stirs till faith sets it to work. Faith sets repentance to work; it is like fire to the still; it sets hope to work. First we believe the promise, then we hope for it. If faith did not feed the lamp of hope with oil, it would soon die. It sets love to work. 'Faith which worketh by love.' Gal 5: 6. Who can believe in the infinite merits of Christ, and his heart not ascend in a fiery chariot of love? It is a catholicon, or remedy against all troubles; a sheet anchor cast into the sea of God's mercy to keep us from sinking in despair. Other graces have done worthily; thou, O faith, excellest them all. In heaven love will be the chief grace; but while we are here love must give place to faith. Love takes possession of glory, but faith gives a title to it. Love is the crowning grace in heaven, but faith is the conquering grace upon earth. 'This is the victory that overcometh the world, even our faith.' I John 5: 4. Faith carries away the garland from all the other graces. Other graces help to sanctify us, but faith only has the honour to justify us. 'Being justified by faith.' Rom 5: 1.

How comes faith to be so precious?

Not that it is a more holy quality, or has more worthiness than other graces, but respectu objecti [with respect to its object], 'as it lays hold on Christ the blessed object,' and fetches in his fulness. John 9: 36. Faith in itself considered, is but manus mendica, 'the beggar's hand;' but as this hand receives the rich alms of Christ's merits, so it is precious, and challenges a superiority over the rest of the graces.

Use one. Of all sins, beware of the rock of unbelief 'Take heed lest there be in any of you an evil heart of unbelief' Heb 3: 12. Men think, as long as they are not drunkards or swearers, it is no great matter to be unbelievers. This is the gospel sin, it dyes your other sins in grain.

(1) Unbelief is a Christ-reproaching sin. It disparages Christ's infinite merit as if it could not save; it makes the wound of sin to be broader than the plaister of Christ's blood. This is a high contempt offered to Christ, and is a deeper spear than that which the Jews thrust into his side.

(2) Unbelief is an ungrateful sin. Ingratus vitandus est ut dirum selus, tellus ipsa foedius nihil creat [The ungrateful man is to be avoided like a fearful crime; the world herself produces nothing more shameful]. Ingratitude is a prodigy of wickedness; and unbelief is being ungrateful for the richest mercy. Suppose a king, to redeem a captive, should part with his crown of gold, and when he had done this should say to the redeemed man, 'All I desire of thee in lieu of my kindness, is to believe that I love thee.' If he should say 'No, I do not believe any such thing, or that thou carest at all for me;' I appeal to you whether this would not be odious ingratitude? So is the case here. God has sent his Son to shed his blood; he requires us only to believe in him, that he is able and willing to save us. No, says unbelief, his blood was not shed for me, I cannot persuade myself that Christ has any purpose of love to me. Is not this horrid ingratitude? This enhances a sin, and makes it of a crimson colour.

(3) Unbelief is a leading sin. It is the breeder of sin. Qualitas malae vitae initium summit ab infidelitate [A life of wickedness has unbelief as its point of origin]. Unbelief is a root sin, and the devil labours to water this root, that the branches may be fruitful. It breeds hardness of heart; therefore they are put together. Mark 16: 14. Christ upbraids them with their unbelief and hardness of heart. Unbelief breeds the stone of the heart. He who believes not in Christ, is not affected with his sufferings, he melts not in tears of love. Unbelief freezes the heart; first it defiles and then hardens. Unbelief breeds profaneness. An unbeliever will stick at no sin, neither at false weights, nor false oaths. He will swallow down treason. Judas was first an unbeliever, and then a traitor. John 6: 64. He who has no faith in his heart, will have no fear of God before his eyes.

(4) Unbelief is a wrath procuring sin. It is inimica salutis [an enemy of salvation]. Bernard. John 3: IS. Jam condemnatus est [he is already condemned], dying so, he is as sure to be condemned as if he were so already. 'He that believeth not on the Son of God, the wrath of God abideth on him.' John 3: 36. He who believes not in the blood of the Lamb, must feel the wrath of the Lamb. The Gentiles that believe not in Christ will be damned as well as the Jews who blaspheme him. And if unbelief be so fearful and damnable a sin, shall we not be afraid to live in it?

Use two. Above all graces set faith to work on Christ. 'That whosoever believeth in him should not perish.' John 3: 15. 'Above all, taking the shield of faith.' Eph 6: 16. Say as queen Esther, 'I will go in unto the king: and if I perish, I perish.' She had nothing to encourage her; she ventured against law, yet the golden sceptre was held forth to her. We have promises to encourage our faith. 'Him that comes unto me, I will in no wise cast out.' John 6: 37. Let us then advance faith by a holy recumbency on Christ's merits. Christ's blood will not justify without believing; they are both put together in the text, 'Faith in his blood.' The blood of God, without faith in Christ, will not save. Christ's sufferings are the plaister to heal a sin-sick soul, but this plaister must be applied by faith. It is not money in a rich man's hand, though offered to us, that will enrich us, unless we receive it. So Christ's virtues or benefits will do us no good unless we receive them by the hand of faith. Above all graces set faith on work. It is a faith most acceptable to God upon many accounts.

(1) Because it is a God-exalting grace. It glorifies God. Abraham 'was strong in faith, giving glory to God.' Rom 4: 20. To believe that there is more mercy in God and merit in Christ than sin in us, and that Christ has answered all the demands of the law, and that his blood has fully satisfied for us, is in a high degree to honour God. Faith in the Mediator brings more glory to God than martyrdom, or the most heroic act of obedience.

(2) Faith in Christ is acceptable to God because it is a self-denying grace; it makes a man go out of himself, renounce all self-righteousness, and wholly rely on Christ for justification. It is very humble, it confesses its own indigence, and lives wholly upon Christ. As the bee sucks sweetness from the flower, so faith sucks all its strength and comfort from Christ.

(3) Faith is a grace acceptable to God, because by faith we present a righteousness to him which best pleases him; we bring the righteousness of Christ into court, which is called the righteousness of God. 2 Cor 5: 21. To bring Christ's righteousness, is to bring Benjamin with us. A believer may say, Lord, it is not the righteousness of Adam, or of the angels, but of Christ who is God-Man, that I bring before thee. The Lord cannot but smell a sweet savour in Christ's righteousness.

Use three. Let us try our faith. There is something that looks like faith, and is not. Pliny says there is a Cyprian stone which is in colour like a diamond, but it is not of the right kind; so there is a spurious faith in the world. Some plants have the same leaf with others, but the herbalist can distinguish them by the root and taste; so something may look like true faith, but it may be distinguished several ways: -

(1) True faith is grounded upon knowledge. Knowledge carries the torch before faith. There is a knowledge of Christ's orient excellencies. Phil 3: 8. He is made up of all love and beauty. True faith is a judicious intelligent grace, it knows whom it believes, and why it believes. Faith is seated as well in the understanding as in the will. It has an eye to see Christ, as well as a wing to fly to him. Such therefore as are veiled in ignorance, or have only an implicit faith to believe as the church believes, have no true and genuine faith.

(2) Faith lives in a broken heart. 'The father cried out with tears, Lord, I believe.' Mark 9: 24. True faith is always in a heart bruised for sin. They, therefore, whose hearts were never touched for sin, have no faith. If a physician should tell us there was a herb that would help us against all infections, but it always grows in a watery place; if we should see a herb like it in colour, leaf, smell, blossom, but growing upon a rock, we should conclude that it was the wrong herb. So

saving faith always grows in a heart humbled for sin, in a weeping eye and a tearful conscience. If, therefore, there be a show of faith, but it grows upon the rock of a hard impenitent heart, it is not the true faith.

(3) True faith is at first nothing but an embryo, it is minute and small; it is full of doubts, temptations, fears; it begins in weakness. It is like the smoking flax. Matt 12: 20. It smokes with desires, but does not flame with comfort; it is at first so small, that it is scarce discernible. They who, at the first dash, have a strong persuasion that Christ is theirs, who leap out of sin into assurance, have a false and spurious faith, The faith which comes to its full stature on its birth-day is a monster. The seed that sprung up suddenly withered. Matt 13: 5, 6.

(4) Faith is a refining grace, it consecrates and purifies. Moral virtue may wash the outside, but faith washes the inside. 'Purifying their hearts by faith.' Acts 15: 9. Faith makes the heart a temple with this inscription, 'Holiness to the Lord.' They whose hearts have legions of lust in them, were never acquainted with the true faith. For one to say he has faith, and yet live in sin, is, as if one should say he was in health when his vitals are perished. Faith is a virgin grace, it is joined with sanctity. 'Holding the mystery of the faith in a pure conscience.' I Tim 3: 9. The jewel of faith is always put in the cabinet of a pure conscience. The woman that touched Christ by faith, fetched a healing and cleansing virtue from him.

(5) True faith is obediential. 'The obedience of faith.' Rom 16: 26. Faith melts our will into the will of God. If God commands duty, though cross to flesh and blood, faith obeys. 'By faith Abraham obeyed.' Heb 11: 8. It not only believes the promise, but obeys the command. It is not having a speculative knowledge that will evidence you to be believers. The devil has knowledge; but that which makes him a devil is that he has no obedience.

(6) True faith is increasing. 'From faith to faith,' i.e. from one degree of faith to another. Rom 1: 17. Faith does not lie in the heart, as a stone in the earth, but as seed that grows. Joseph of Arimathaea was a disciple of Christ, but was afraid to confess him; afterwards he went boldly to Pilate and begged the body of Jesus. John 19: 38. A Christian's increase in faith is known two ways: -

By steadfastness. He is a pillar in the temple of God, 'Rooted and built up in him; and established in the faith.' Col 2: 7. Unbelievers are sceptics in religion; they are unsettled; they question every truth; but when faith is on the increasing hand, it does stabilire animum [strengthen the spirit], it corroborates a Christian. He is able to prove his principles; he holds no more than he will die for; as that martyr woman said, 'I cannot dispute for Christ, but I can burn for him.' An increasing faith is not like a ship in the midst of the sea, that fluctuates, and is tossed upon the waves; but like a ship at anchor, which is firm and steadfast.

A Christian's increase in faith is known by his strength. He can do that now which he could not do before. When one is man-grown, he can do that which he was not able to do when he was a child; he can carry a heavier burden: so a growing Christian can bear crosses with more patience.

But I fear I have no faith, it is so weak!

If you have faith, though but in its infancy, be not discouraged. For, (1) A little faith is faith, as a spark of fire is fire. (2) A weak faith may lay hold on a strong Christ; as a weak hand can tie the knot in marriage as well as a strong one. She, in the gospel, who but touched Christ, fetched virtue from him. (3) The promises are not made to strong faith, but to true. The promise does not say, he who has a giant faith, who can believe God's love through a frown, who can rejoice in affliction, who can work wonders, remove mountains, stop the mouth of lions, shall be saved, but whosoever believes, be his faith never so small. A reed is but weak, especially when it is bruised; yet a promise is made to it. 'A bruised reed shall he not break.' Matt 12: 20. (4) A weak faith may be fruitful. Weakest things multiply most. The vine is a weak plant, but it is fruitful. The thief on the cross, who was newly converted, was but weak in grace; but how many precious clusters grew upon that tender plant! He chided his fellow-thief. 'Dost thou not fear God?' Luke 23: 40. He judged himself, 'We indeed suffer justly.' He believed in Christ, when he said, 'Lord.' He made a heavenly prayer, 'Remember me when thou comest into thy kingdom.' Weak Christians may have strong affections. How strong is the first love, which is after the first planting of faith! (5) The weakest believer is a member of Christ as well as the strongest; and the weakest member of the body mystic shall not perish. Christ will cut off rotten members, but not weak members. Therefore, Christian, be not discouraged. God, who would have us receive them that are weak in faith, will not himself refuse them. Rom 14: 1.

4.2 Repentance

'Then has God also to the Gentiles granted repentance unto life.' Acts 11: 18.

Repentance seems to be a bitter pill to take, but it is to purge out the bad humour of sin. By some Antinomian spirits it is cried down as a legal doctrine; but Christ himself preached it. 'From that time Jesus began to preach, and to say, Repent,' &c. Matt 4: 17. In his last farewell, when he was ascending to heaven, he commanded that 'Repentance should be preached in his name.' Luke 24: 47. Repentance is a pure gospel grace. The covenant of works would not admit of repentance; it cursed all that could not perform perfect and personal obedience. Gal 3: 10. Repentance comes in by the gospel; it is the fruit of Christ's purchase that repenting sinners shall be saved. It is wrought by the ministry of the gospel, while it sets before our eyes Christ crucified. It is not arbitrary, but necessary; there is no being saved without it. 'Except ye repent, ye shall all likewise perish.' Luke 13: 3. We may be thankful to God that he has left us this plank after shipwreck.

I. I shall show first the counterfeits of repentance.

[1] Natural softness and tenderness of spirit. Some have a tender affection, arising from their constitution, whereby they are apt to weep and relent when they see any object of pity. These are not repenting tears: for many weep to see another's misery, who cannot weep at their own sin.

[2] Legal terrors. A man who has lived in a course of sin, at last is made sensible; he sees hell ready to devour him, and is filled with anguish and horror; but after a while the tempest of conscience is blown over, and he is quiet. He then concludes he is a true penitent, because he has felt some bitterness in sin, but this is not repentance. Judas had some trouble of mind. If anguish and trouble were sufficient for repentance, then the damned would be most penitent, for they are most in anguish of mind. There may be trouble of mind where there is no grieving for the offence against God.

[3] A slight superficial sorrow. When God's hand lies heavy upon a man, as when he is sick or lame, he may vent a sigh or tear, and say, 'Lord, have mercy;' yet this is not true repentance. Ahab did more than all this. 'He rent his clothes, and fasted, and lay in sackcloth, and went softly.' I Kings 21: 27. His clothes were rent, but not his heart. The eye may be watery, and the heart flinty. An apricot may be soft without, but it has a hard stone within.

[4] God motions rising in the heart. Every good motion is not repentance. Some think if they have motions in their hearts to break off their sins, and become religious, it is repentance. As the devil may stir up bad motions in the godly, so the Spirit of God may stir up good motions in the wicked. Herod had many good thoughts and inclinations stirred up in him by John Baptist's preaching, yet he did not truly repent, for he still lived in incest.

[5] Vows and resolutions. What vows and solemn protestations do some make in their sickness, that if God should recover them they will be new men, but afterwards they are as bad as ever! 'Thou saidst, I will not transgress;' here was a resolution: but for all this, she ran after her idols. 'Under every green tree thou wanderest, playing the harlot.' Jer 2: 20.

[6] Leaving off some gross sin. (1) A man may leave off some sins, and keep others. Herod reformed many things that were amiss, but kept his Herodias. (2) An old sin may be left to entertain a new one. A man may leave off riot and prodigality, and turn covetous; which is merely to exchange one sin for another.

These are the counterfeits of repentance. Now, if you find that yours is a counterfeit repentance, and you have not repented aright, mend what you have done amiss. As in the body, if a bone be set wrong, the surgeon has no way but to break it again, and set it aright; so you must do by repentance; if you have not repented aright, you must have your heart broken again in a godly manner, and be more deeply afflicted for sin than ever.

II. This brings me to show wherein repentance consists. It consists in two things: humiliation and transformation.

[1] Humiliation. 'If their uncircumcised hearts be humbled.' Lev 26: 4l. There is, as the schoolmen say, a twofold humiliation, or breaking of the heart. (1) Attrition; as when a rock is broken in pieces. This is done by the law, which is a hammer to break the heart. (2) Contrition; as when ice is melted into water. This is done by the gospel, which is as a fire to 'melt the heart.' Jer 23: 9. The sense of abused kindness causes contrition.

[2] Transformation, or change. 'Be ye transformed by the renewing of your mind.' Rom 12: 2. Repentance works a change in the whole man. As when wine is put into a glass of water, it runs into every part of the water, and changes its colour and taste; so true repentance does not rest in one part, but diffuses and spreads itself into every part.

(1) Repentance causes a change in the mind. Before, a man liked sin well, and said in defence of it, as Jonah, 'I do well to be angry;' chap 4: 9; or I did well to swear, and break the Sabbath. When he becomes penitent, his judgement is changed, he looks upon sin as the greatest evil. The Greek word for repentance signifies after-wisdom; when, having seen how deformed and damnable a thing sin is, we change our mind. Paul, before conversion, verily thought he ought to do many things contrary to the name of Jesus (Acts 26: 9); but, when he became a penitent, he was of another mind. 'I count all things but loss for the excellency of the knowledge of Christ Jesus.' Phil 3: 8. Repentance causes a change of judgement.

(2) Repentance causes a change in the affections, which move under the will as the commander-in-chief. It metamorphoses the affections. It turns rejoicing in sin into sorrowing for sin; it turns boldness in sin into holy shame; it turns the love of sin into hatred. As Ammon hated Tamar more than ever he loved her (2 Sam 13: 15), so the true penitent hates sin more than ever he loved it. 'I hate every false way.' Psa 119: 104.

(3) Repentance works a change in the life. Though repentance begins at the heart, it does rest there, but goes into the life. It begins at the heart. 'O Jerusalem, wash thy heart.' Jer 4: 14. If the spring be corrupt, no pure stream can run from it. But though repentance begins at the heart, it does not rest there, but changes the life. What a change did repentance make in Paul! It changed a persecutor into a preacher. What a change did it make in the jailer! Acts 16: 33. He took Paul and Silas, and washed their stripes, and set meat before them. What a change did it make in Mary Magdalene! She who before kissed her lovers with wanton embraces, now kisses Christ's feet; she that used to curl her hair, and dress it with costly jewels, now makes it a towel to wipe Christ's feet; her eyes that used to sparkle with lust, and with impure glances to entice her lovers, now become fountains of tears to wash her Saviour's feet; her tongue that used to speak vainly and loosely, now is an instrument set in tune to praise God. This change of life has two things in it: -

[1] The terminus a quo, a breaking off sin. 'Break off thy sins by righteousness.' Dan 4: 27. This breaking off sin must have three qualifications. (1) It must be universal, a breaking off all sin. One disease may kill as well as more. One sin lived in, may damn as well as more. The real

penitent breaks off secret, gainful, habitual sins; he takes the sacrificing knife of mortification, and runs it through the heart of his dearest lusts. (2) Breaking off sin must be sincere; it must not be out of fear, but upon spiritual grounds; as from antipathy and disgust, and a principle of love to God. If sin had not such evil effects, a true penitent would forsake it out of love to God. The best way to separate things that are frozen, is by fire. When sin and the heart are frozen together, the best way to separate them is by the fire of love. Shall I sin against a gracious Father, and abuse that love which pardons me? (3) The breaking off sin must be perpetual, so as never to have to do with sin any more. 'What have I to do any more with idols?' Hos 14: 8. Repentance is a spiritual divorce, which must be till death.

[2] Change of life has in it terminus ad quem, a returning unto the Lord. It is called 'Repentance towards God.' Acts 20: 21. It is not enough, when we repent, to leave old sins; but we must engage in God's service; as when the wind leaves the west, it turns into a contrary corner. The repenting prodigal not only left his harlots, but arose and went to his father. Luke 15: 18. In true repentance the heart points directly to God, as the needle to the north pole.

Use. Let us all set upon this great work of repentance; let us repent sincerely and speedily: let us repent of all our sins, our pride, rash anger, and unbelief. 'Without repentance, no remission.' It is not consistent with the holiness of God's nature to pardon a sinner while he is in the act of rebellion. O meet God, not with weapons, but tears in your eyes. To stir you up to a melting penitent frame: -

(1) Consider what there is in sin, that you should continue in the practice of it. It is the 'accursed thing.' Josh 7: 11. It is the spirits of mischief distilled. It defiles the soul's glory; it is like a stain to beauty. It is compared to a plague-sore. I Kings 8: 38. Nothing so changes one's glory into shame as sin. Without repentance sin tends to final damnation. Peccatum transit actu, manet reatu [The moment of sin passes, the guilt remains]. Sin at first shows its colour in the glass, but afterwards it bites like a serpent. Those locusts in Rev 9: 7, are an emblem of sin: 'On their heads were crowns like gold, and they had hair as the hair of women, and their teeth were as the teeth of lions, and there were stings in their tails.' Sin unrepented of ends in a tragedy. It has the devil for its father, shame for its companion, and death for its wages. Rom 6: 23. What is there in sin then, that men should continue in it? Say not it is sweet. Who would desire the pleasure which kills?

(2) Repentance is very pleasing to God. No sacrifice like a broken heart. 'A broken and a contrite heart, O God, thou wilt not despise.' Psa 51: 17. Augustine caused this sentence to be written over his bed when he was sick. When the widow brought empty vessels to Elisha, the oil was poured into them. 2 Kings 4: 6. Bring God the broken vessel of a contrite heart, and he will pour in the oil of mercy. Repenting tears are the joy of God and of angels. Luke 15: 7. Doves delight to be about the waters; and surely God's Spirit, who once descended in the likeness of a dove, takes great delight in the waters of repentance. Mary stood at Jesus' feet weeping. Luke 7: 38.

She brought two things to Christ, tears and ointment; but her tears were more precious to Christ than her ointment.

(3) Repentance ushers in pardon. Therefore they are joined together. 'Repentance and remission.' Luke 24: 47. Pardon of sin is the richest blessing; it is enough to make a sick man well. 'The inhabitant shall not say, I am sick; the people that dwell therein shall be forgiven their iniquity.' Isa 33: 24. Pardon settles upon us the richer charter of the promises. Pardoning mercy is the sauce that makes all other mercies relish the sweeter; it sweetens our health, riches, and honour. David had a crown of pure gold set upon his head. Psa 21: 3. That which David most blessed God for, was not that God had set a crown of gold upon his head, but that he had set a crown of mercy upon his head. 'Who crowneth thee with mercies.' Psa 103: 4. What was this crown of mercy? You may see in ver 3: 'Who forgiveth all thine iniquities.' David more rejoiced that he was crowned with forgiveness than that he wore a crown of pure gold. Now, what is it that makes way for pardon of sin but repentance? When David's soul was humbled and broken, the prophet Nathan brought him good news. 'The Lord has put away thy sin.' 2 Sam 12: 13.

But my sins are so great, that if I should repent, God would not pardon them!

God will not go from his promise. 'Return, thou backsliding Israel, saith the Lord, and I will not cause mine anger to fall upon you, for I am merciful.' Jer 3: 12. If thy sins are as rocks, yet upon thy repentance, the sea of God's mercy can drown them. 'Wash you, make you clean.' Isa 1: 16. Wash in the lever of repentance. 'Come now, and let us reason together, saith the Lord: though your sins be as scarlet, they shall be as white as snow;' ver 18. Manasseh was a crimson sinner; but when he humbled himself greatly, the golden sceptre of mercy was held forth. When his head was a fountain to weep for sin, Christ's side was a fountain to wash away sin. It is not the greatness of sin, but impenitence, that destroys. The Jews, who had a hand in crucifying Christ, upon their repentance found the blood they had shed was a sovereign balm to heal them. When the prodigal came home to his father, he had the robe and the ring put upon him, and his 'father kissed him.' Luke 15: 20, 22. If you break off your sins, God will become a friend to you; all that is in God shall be yours; his power shall be yours, to help you; his wisdom shall be yours, to counsel you; his Spirit shall be yours, to sanctify you; his promises shall be yours, to comfort you; his angels shall be yours, to guard you; his mercy shall be yours, to save you.

(4) There is much sweetness in repenting tears. The soul is never more enlarged and inwardly delighted than when it can melt kindly for sin. Weeping days are festival days. The Hebrew word to repent, nicham, signifies consolari, 'to take comfort.' 'Your sorrow shall be turned into joy.' John 16: 20. Christ turns the water of tears into wine. David, who was the great mourner in Israel, was the sweet singer. And the joy which a true penitent finds, is a pre-libation and foretaste of the joy of paradise. The wicked man's joy turns to sadness: the penitent's sadness turns to joy. Though repentance seems at first to be thorny and bitter, yet of this thorn a Christian gathers grapes. All which considerations may open a vein of godly sorrow in our souls, that we

may both weep for sin, and turn from it. If ever God restores comfort, it is to his mourners. Isa 57: 18. When we have wept, let us look up to Christ's blood for pardon. Say, as that holy man, Iava, Domine, lacrimas meas: 'Lord, wash my tears in thy blood.' We drop sin with our tears, and need Christ's blood to wash them. This repentance must be not for a few days only, like the mourning for a friend, which is soon over, but it must be the work of our lives; the issue of godly sorrow must not be stopped till death. After sin is pardoned, we must repent. We run afresh upon the score, 'we sin daily, therefore must repent daily.' Some shed a few tears for sin; and when, like the widow's oil, they have run awhile, they cease. Many, if the plaister of repentance begin to smart a little, pluck it off; whereas the plaister of repentance must still lie on, and not be plucked off till death, when, as all other tears, so these of godly sorrow shall be wiped away.

What shall we do to obtain a penitential frame of heart?

Seek to God for it. It is his promise to give a 'heart of flesh' (Ezek 36:26); and to pour on us a spirit of mourning. Zech 12: 10. Beg God's 'Holy Spirit.' 'He causeth his wind to blow, and the waters flow.' Psa 147: 18. When the wind of God's Spirit blows upon us, then the waters of repentant tears will flow from us.

4.3 The Word

The third way to escape the wrath and curse of God, and obtain the benefit of redemption by Christ, is the diligent use of ordinances, in particular, 'the word, sacraments, and prayer.'

I begin with the best of these ordinances.

The 'word... which effectually worketh in you that believe.' I Thess 2:13.

What is meant by the word's working effectually?

The word of God is said to work effectually when it has the good effect upon us for which it was appointed by God; when it works powerful illumination and thorough reformation. 'To open their eyes, and turn them from the power of Satan unto God.' Acts 26: 18. The opening of their eyes denotes illumination; and turning them from Satan to God denotes reformation.

How is the word to be read and heard that it may become effectual to salvation.

This question consists of two branches.

How may the word be read effectually?

That we may so read the word that it may conduce effectually to our salvation,

(1) Let us have a reverend esteem of every part of canonical Scripture. 'More to be desired are they than gold.' Psa 19: 10. Value the book of God above all other books. It is a golden epistle, indited by the Holy Ghost, and sent us from heaven. More particularly to raise our esteem, the Scripture is a spiritual glass, to dress our souls by. It shows us more than we can see by the light of natural conscience. This may discover gross sins; but the glass of the word shows us heart-sins, vain thoughts, unbelief, &c. It not only shows us our spots, but washes them away. The Scripture is a magazine out of which we may fetch spiritual artillery to fight against Satan. When our Saviour was tempted by the devil, he fetched armour and weapons from Scripture; 'it is written.' Matt 4: 4, 7. The holy Scripture is a panacea, or universal medicine for the soul; it gives a recipe to cure deadness of heart, Psa 119: 50; pride, I Pet 5: 5; and infidelity, John 3: 36. It is a physic garden where we may gather a herb or antidote to expel the poison of sin. The leaves of Scripture, like the leaves of the tree of life, are for the 'healing of the nations.' Rev 22: 2. Should not this cause a reverential esteem of the word?

(2) If we would have the written word effectual to our souls, let us peruse it with 'intenseness of mind.' 'Search the Scriptures.' John 5: 39. The Greek word, ereunate, signifies to search as for a 'vein of silver.' The Bereans 'searched the Scriptures daily.' Acts 17: 11. The word anakrinontes signifies to make a curious and critical search. Apollo was mighty in the Scriptures. Acts 18: 24. Some gallop over a chapter in haste and get no good by it. If we would have the word effectual and saving, we must mind and observe every passage of Scripture. That we may be diligent in the perusal of Scripture, consider that the word written is norma cultus [the only standard of conduct], the rule and platform by which we are to square our lives. It contains in it all things needful to salvation; what duties we are to do, and what sins we are to avoid. Psa 19: 7. God gave Moses a pattern how he would have the tabernacle made; and he was to go exactly according to the pattern. Exod 25: 9. The word is the pattern God has given us in writing, for modelling our lives. How careful, therefore, should we be in pursuing and looking over this pattern!

As the written word is our pattern, so it will be our judge. 'The word that I have spoken, the same shall judge him at the last day.' John 12: 48. We read of the opening of the books. Rev 20: 12. One book which God will open is the book of the Scripture, and will judge men out of it. He will say, 'Have you lived according to the rule of this word?' The word has a double work - to teach, and to judge.

(3) If we would have the written word effectual, we must bring faith to the reading of it; believe it to be the word of the eternal Jehovah. It comes with authority, and shows its commission from heaven. 'Thus saith the Lord.' It is of divine inspiration. 2 Tim 3: 16. The oracles of Scripture must be surer to us than a voice from heaven. 2 Pet 1: 18, 19. Unbelief enervates the virtue of Scripture, and renders it ineffectual. First men question the truth of the Scripture, and then fall away from it.

(4) If we would have the written word effectual to salvation, we must delight in it as our spiritual cordial. 'Thy words were found, and I did eat them, and thy word was the joy and rejoicing of my heart.' Jer 15: 16. All true solid comfort is fetched out of the word. The word, as Chrysostom says, is a spiritual garden, and the promises are the fragrant flowers or spices in this garden. How should we delight to walk among these beds of spices! Is it not a comfort, in all dubious perplexed cases, to have a counsellor to advise us? 'Thy testimonies are my counsellors.' Psa 119: 24, is it not a comfort to find our evidences for heaven? And where should we find them but in the word? I Thess 1: 4, 5. The word written is a sovereign elixir, or comfort, in an hour of distress. 'This is my comfort in my affliction, for thy word has quickened me.' Psa 119: 50. It can turn all our 'water into wine.' How should we take a great complacence and delight in the word! They only who come to the word with delight, go from it with success.

(5) If we would have the Scripture effectual and saving, we must be sure, when we have read the word, to hide it in our hearts. 'Thy word have I hid in my heart.' Psa 119: 11. The word, locked up in the heart, is a preservative against sin. Why did David hide the word in his heart? 'That I might not sin against thee.' As one would carry an antidote about him when he comes near a place infected, so David carried the word in his heart as a sacred antidote to preserve him from the infection of sin. When the sap is hid in the root, it makes the branches fruitful; when the seed is hid in the ground, the corn springs up; so, when the word is hid in the heart, it brings forth good fruit.

(6) If we would have the written word effectual, let us labour not only to have the light of it in our heads, but its power in our hearts. Let us endeavour to have it copied out, and written a second time in our hearts. 'The law of his God is in his heart.' Psa 37: 31. The word says, 'Be clothed with humility.' 1 Pet 5: 5. Let us be low and humble in our own eyes. The word calls for sanctity. Let us labour to partake of the divine nature, and to have something conceived in us which is of the Holy Ghost. 2 Pet 1: 4. When the word is thus copied out into our hearts, and we are changed into its similitude, it is made effectual to us, and becomes a savour of life.

(7) When we read the holy Scriptures let us look up to God for a blessing. Let us beg the Spirit of wisdom and revelation, that we may see the 'deep things of God.' Eph 1: 17, I Cor 2: 10. Pray God that the same Spirit that wrote the Scripture would enable us to understand it. Pray that God would give us the 'savour of his knowledge,' that we may relish a sweetness in the word we read. 2 Cor 2: 14. David tasted it as 'sweeter than the honeycomb.' Psa 19: 10. Let us pray that God would not only give us his word as a rule of holiness, but his grace as a principle of holiness

How may we hear the word that it may be effectual and saving to our souls?

(1) Give great attention to the word preached. Let nothing pass without taking special notice of it. 'All the people were very attentive to hear him.' Luke 19: 48. They hung upon his lips. 'Lydia, a seller of purple, which worshipped God, heard us, whose heart the Lord opened, that she attended unto the things which were spoken of Paul.' Acts 16: 14. Give attention to the word, as

to a matter of life and death. For this purpose have a care to banish vain impertinent thoughts, which will distract yell, and take you off from the work in hand. These fowls will be coming to the sacrifice, therefore we must drive them away. Gen 15: 2. An archer may take a right aim; but if one stand at his elbow, and jog him when he is going to shoot, he will not hit the mark. Christians may have good aims in hearing; but take heed of impertinent thoughts which will jog and hinder you in God's service. Banish dullness. The devil gives many hearers a sleepy sop, so that they cannot keep their eyes open at a sermon. They eat so much on the Lord's-day that they are more fit for the pillow and couch than the temple. Frequent and customary sleeping at a sermon shows high contempt and irreverence of the ordinance. It gives a bad example to others; it makes your sincerity to be called in question; it is the devil's seedtime. 'While men slept, his enemy came and sowed tares.' Matt 13: 25 O shake off drowsiness, as Paul shook off the viper! Be serious and attentive in hearing the word. 'For it is not a vain thing for you, it is your life.' Deut 32: 47. When people do not mind what God speaks to them in his word, God as little minds what they say to him in prayer.

(2) If you would have the word preached effectual, come with a holy appetite to the word. I Pet 2: 2. The thirsting soul is the thriving soul. In nature one may have an appetite and no digestion; but it is not so in religion. Where there is a great appetite for the word, there is for the most part good digestion. Come with hungering of soul after the word, and desire it, that it may not only please you but profit you. Look not at the garnishing of the dish more than at the meat - at eloquence and rhetoric more than solid matter. It argues both a wanton palate and surfeited stomach to feed on salads and dainties rather than on wholesome food.

(3) If you would have the preaching of the word effectual, come to it with tenderness upon your heart. 'Because thy heart was tender.' I Chron 22: 5. If we preach to hard hearts, it is like shooting against a brazen wall, the word does not enter. It is like setting a gold seal upon marble, which takes no impression. O come to the word preached with a melting frame of heart! It is the melting wax that receives the stamp of the seal; so, when the heart is in a melting frame, it will better receive the stamp of the preached word. When Paul's heart was melted and broken for sin, he cried, 'Lord, what wilt thou have me to do?' Acts 9: 6. Come not hither with hard hearts. Who can expect a crop when the seed is grown UPON stony ground?

(4) If you would have the word effectual, receive it with meekness. 'Receive with meekness the ingrafted word.' James 1: 21. Meekness is a submissive frame of heart to the word - a willingness to hear the counsels and reproofs of the word. Contrary to this meekness is fierceness of spirit, whereby men are ready to rise up in rage against the sword. Proud men, and guilty, cannot endure to hear of their faults. Proud Herod put John in prison. Mark 6: 17. The guilty Jews, being told of their crucifying Christ, stoned Stephen. Acts 7: 59. To tell men of sin, is to hold a glass to one that is deformed, who cannot endure to see his own face. Contrary to meekness is stubbornness of heart, whereby men are resolved to hold fast their sins, let the word say what it will. 'We will burn incense unto the queen of heaven.' Jer 44: 17. O take heed of this! If you

would have the word preached effectually, lay aside fierceness and stubbornness, receive the word with meekness. By meekness the word preached comes to be ingrafted. As a good scion that is grafted in a bad stock changes the nature of the fruit and makes it taste sweet, so, when the word is ingrafted into the soul, it sanctifies it, and makes it bring forth the sweet fruit of righteousness.

(5) Mingle the word preached with faith. 'The word preached did not profit them, not being mixed with faith.' Heb 4: 2. If you leave out the chief ingredient in a medicine, it hinders the operation; do not leave out the ingredient of faith. Believe the word, and so believe it as to apply it. When you hear Christ preached, apply him to yourselves. This is to put on the Lord Jesus. Rom 13: 14. When you hear a promise spoken, apply it. This is to suck the flower of the promise, and turn it to honey.

(6) Be not only attentive in hearing, but retentive after hearing. 'We ought to give the more earnest heed to the things which we have heard, lest at any time we should let them slip;' lest we should let them run out as water out of a sieve. Heb 2: 1. If the ground retain not the seed sown into it, there can be no good crop. Some have memories like leaking vessels: the sermons they hear are presently gone, and there is no good done. If meat does not stay and digest in the stomach, it will not nourish. Satan labours to steal the word out of the mind. 'When they have heard, Satan comes immediately, and taketh away the word that was sown.' Mark 4: 15. Our memories should be like the chest of the ark, where the law was put.

(7) Reduce your hearing to practice. Live on the sermons you hear. 'I have done thy commandments.' Psa 119: 166. Rachel was not content that she was beautiful, but her desire was to be fruitful. What is a knowing head without a fruitful heart? 'Filled with the fruits of righteousness.' Phil 1: 11. It is obedience that crowns hearing. That hearing will never save the soul which does not reform the life.

(8) Beg of God that he will accompany his word with his presence and blessing. The Spirit must make all effectual. Ministers may prescribe physic, but it is God's Spirit must make it work. 'He has his pulpit in heaven that converts souls.' Augustine. 'While Peter yet spake, the Holy Ghost fell on all them which heard.' Acts 10: 44. It is said, the alchemist can draw oil out of iron. God's Spirit can produce grace in the most obdurate heart.

(9) If you would have the word work effectually to your salvation, make it familiar to you. Discourse of what you have heard when you come home. 'My tongue shall speak of thy word.' Psa 119: 172. One reason why some people get no more good by what they hear, is that they never speak to one another of what they have heard; as if sermons were such secrets that they must not be spoken of again; or as if it were a shame to speak of matters of salvation. 'They that feared the Lord spake often one to another... and a book of remembrance was written.' Mal 3: 16.

Use one. Take heed, as you love your souls, that the word become not ineffectual to you. There are some to whom the word preached is ineffectual. (1) Such as censure the word; who, instead of judging themselves, judge the word. (2) Such as live in contradiction to the word. Isa 30: 9. (3) Such as are more hardened by the word. 'They made their hearts as an adamant stone.' Zech 7: 12. And when men harden their hearts wilfully, God hardens them judicially. 'Make their ears heavy.' Isa 6: 10. The word to these is ineffectual. Would it not be sad, if a man's meat did not nourish him; nay, if it should turn to poison? O take heed that the word preached be not ineffectual and to no purpose!

Use two. Consider three things: -

(1) If the word preached does us no good, there is no other way by which we can be saved. This is God's institution, and the main engine he uses to convert souls. 'If they hear not Moses and the prophets, neither will they be persuaded though one rose from the dead.' Luke 16: 31. If an angel should come to you out of heaven, and preach of the excellency of the glorified estate, and the joys of heaven, and that in the most pathetic manner - if the word preached does not persuade, neither would you be wrought upon by such an oration from heaven. If a damned spirit should come from hell, and preach to you in flames, and tell you what a place hell is, and roar out the torments of the damned, it might make you tremble, but it would not convert, if the preaching of the word will not do it.

(2) To come to the word, and not be savingly wrought upon, is that which the devil is pleased with. He cares not though you hear frequently, if it be not effectually; he is not an enemy to hearing, but profiting. Though the minister holds out the breasts of the ordinances to you, he cares not as long as you do not suck the sincere milk of the word. The devil cares not how many sermon-pills you take, so long as they do not work upon your conscience.

(3) If the word preached be not effectual to men's conversion, it will be effectual to their condemnation. The word will be effectual one way or other; if it does not make your hearts better, it will make your chains heavier. We pity those who have not the word preached, but it will be worse with those who are not sanctified by it. Dreadful is their case who go loaded with sermons to hell. But I will conclude with the apostle, I am 'persuaded better things of you, and things that accompany salvation.' Heb 6: 9.

4.4 Baptism

'Go ye, therefore, and teach all nations, baptising them in the name of the Father, and of the Son, and of the Holy Ghost; teaching them,' Matt 28: 19.

I. The way whereby Christ communicates to us the benefits of redemptions, is, in the use of the sacraments.

What are the sacraments in general?

They are visible signs of invisible grace.

Is not the word of God sufficient to salvation? What need then is there of sacraments?

We must not be wise above what is written. It is God's will that his church should have sacraments; and it is God's goodness thus to condescend to weak capacities. 'Except ye see signs, ye will not believe.' John 4: 48. To strengthen our faith, God confirms the covenant of grace, not only by promises but by sacramental signs.

What are the sacraments of the New Testament?

Two: Baptism and the Lord's Supper.

Are there no more? The Papists tell us of five more, viz., confirmation, penance, matrimony, orders, and the extreme unction.

(1) There were but two sacraments under the law, therefore there are no more now. I Cor 10: 2, 3, 4.

(2) These two sacraments are sufficient; the one signifying our entrance into Christ, and the other, our growth and perseverance in him.

II. The first sacrament is baptism. 'Go ye, therefore, and teach all nations, baptising them in the name of the Father, and of the Son, and of the Holy Ghost; teaching them,' 'Go, teach all nations;' the Greek word is 'Make disciples of all nations.' If it be asked, how should we make them disciples? It follows, 'Baptising them and teaching them.' In a heathen nation, first teach, and then baptise them; but in a Christian church, first baptise, and then teach them.

What is baptism?

In general, it is a matriculation, or visible admission of children into the congregation of Christ's flock. More particularly, 'Baptism is a sacrament, wherein the washing or sprinkling with water, in the name of the Father, Son, and Holy Ghost, does signify and seal our ingrafting into Christ, and partaking of the benefits of the covenant of grace, and our engagement to be the Lord's.'

What is meant by the parent when he presents his child to be baptised?

The parent, in presenting the child to be baptised, (1) Makes a public acknowledgement of original sin; that the soul of his child is polluted, therefore needs washing from sin by Christ's blood and Spirit; both which washings are signified by the sprinkling of water in baptism. (2) The parent by bringing his child to be baptised, solemnly devotes it to the Lord, and enrols it in God's family; and truly it is a great satisfaction to a religious parent to have given up his child to the Lord in baptism. How can a parent look with comfort on that child who was never dedicated to God?

What is the benefit of baptism?

The party baptised has, (1) An entrance into the visible body of the church. (2) He has a right sealed to the ordinances, which is a privilege full of glory. Rom 9: 4. (3) The child baptised is under a more special providential care of Christ, who appoints the tutelage of angels to be the infant's life-guard.

Is this all the benefit?

No! To such as belong to the election, baptism is a 'seal of the righteousness of faith,' a laver of regeneration, and a badge of adoption. Rom 4: 11.

How does it appear that children have a right to baptism?

Children are parties in the covenant of grace. The covenant was made with them. 'I will establish my covenant between me and thee, and thy seed after thee, for an everlasting covenant, to be a God unto thee, and to thy seed after thee.' Gen 17: 7. 'The promise is to you and to your children.' Acts 2: 39. The covenant of grace may be considered either, (1) More strictly, as an absolute promise to give saving grace; and so none but the elect are in covenant with God. Or, (2) More largely, as a covenant containing in it many outward glorious privileges, in which respects the children of believers do belong to the covenant of grace. The promise is to you and to your seed. The infant seed of believers may as well lay a claim to the covenant of grace as their parents; and having a right to the covenant, they cannot justly be denied baptism, which is its seal. It is certain the children of believers were once visibly in covenant with God, and received the seal of their admission into the church; where now do we find this covenant interest, or church membership of infants, repealed or made void? Certainly Jesus Christ did not come to put believers and their children into a worse condition than they were in before. If the children of believers should not be baptised, they are in worse condition now than they were in before Christ's coming.

[1] Objections. The Scripture is silent herein and does not mention infant baptism.

Though the word infant baptism is not in Scripture, yet the thing is. Mention is not made in Scripture of woman's receiving the sacrament; but who doubts but the command, 'Take, eat, this is my body,' concerns them? Does not their faith need strengthening as well as others? So the word Trinity is not to be found in Scripture, but there is that which is equivalent to it. 'There are Three that bear record in heaven, the Father, the Word, and the Holy Ghost; and these Three are one.' I John 5: 7. So, though the word infant baptism is not mentioned in Scripture, the practice of baptising infants may be drawn from Scripture by undeniable consequence.

How is that proved?

The Scripture mentions whole families baptised; as the household of Lydia, Crispus, and the jailer. 'He was baptised, he and all his.' Acts 16: 33. Wherein we must rationally imagine there were some little children. If it be said, there is no mention here made of children; I answer, neither are servants named; and yet it cannot be supposed but that, in so great a family, there were some servants.

But infants are not capable of the end of baptism; for baptism signifies the washing away of sin by the blood of Christ. Infants cannot understand this; therefore what benefit can baptism be to them?

Neither could the child that was to be circumcised understand circumcision; yet the ordinance of circumcision was not to be omitted or deferred. Though an infant understand not the meaning of baptism it may partake of the blessing of baptism. The little children that Christ took in his arms, understood not Christ's meaning, but they had Christ's blessing. 'He put his hands upon them and blessed them.' Mark 10: 16.

But what benefit can the child have of baptism if it understand not the nature of baptism?

It may have a right to the promise sealed up, which it shall have an actual interest in when it comes to have faith. A legacy may be of use to the child in the cradle; though it now understand not the legacy, yet when it is grown up to years, it is fully possessed of it. But it may be further objected: -

The party to be baptised is to be engaged to God; but how can the child enter into such an engagement?

The parents can engage for it, which God is pleased to accept as equivalent to the child's personal engagement.

If baptism comes in the room of circumcisions, and the males only were circumcised, what warrant is there for baptising females? Gen 17: 10.

Females were included, and were virtually circumcised in the males. What is done to the head is done to the body; the man being the head of the woman. I Cor 11: 3. What was done to the male sex was interpretatively done to the female.

[2] Having answered these objections, I come now to prove by argument, infant baptism.

(1) If children during their infancy are capable of grace, they are capable of baptism; but children in their infancy are capable of grace, therefore they are capable of baptism. I prove the minor, that they are capable of grace, thus: if children in their infancy may be saved, then they are capable of grace; but children in their infancy may be saved; which is thus proved: that if the kingdom of heaven belongs to them, they may be saved; but the kingdom of heaven may belong

to them, as it is clear from, 'Of such is the kingdom of God' (Mark 10: 14); who then can forbid that the seal of baptism should be applied to them?

(2) If infants may be among the number of God's servants, there is no reason why they should be shut out of God's family; but infants may be in the number of God's servants, because God calls them his servants. 'He shall depart from thee, and his children with him, for they are my servants.' Lev 25: 41. Therefore children in their infancy, being God's servants, why should they not have baptism, which is the tessera, the mark or seal which God sets upon his servants?

(3) 'But now are they (your children) holy.' I Cor 7: 14. Children are not called holy, as if they were free from original sin; but in the judgement of charity they are to be esteemed holy, and true members of the church of God, because their parents are believers. Hence that excellent divine, Mr Hildersam, says, 'that the children of the faithful as soon as they are born, have a covenant holiness, and so a right and title to baptism, which is the token of the covenant.'

(4) From the opinion of the fathers and the practice of the church. The ancient fathers were strong asserters of infant baptism, as Irenaeus, Basil, Lactantius, Cyprian, and Augustine. It was the practice of the Greek church to baptise her infants. Erasmus says that infant baptism has been used in the church of God for above fourteen hundred years. And Augustine, in his book against Pelagius, affirms that it has been the custom of the church in all ages to baptise infants. Yea, it was an apostolic practice. Paul affirms that he baptised the whole house of Stephanus. I Cor 1: 16.

Having seen Scripture arguments for infant baptism, let us consider whether the practice of those who delay the baptising of children till riper years, be warrantable. For my part, I cannot gather it from Scripture. Though we read of adult persons, and grown up to years of discretion, in the apostles' times, being baptised, yet they were such as were converted from heathenish idolatry to the true orthodox faith; but that in a Christian church the children of believers should be kept unbaptised for several years, I know neither precept nor example for it in Scripture, but it is wholly apocryphal. The baptising of persons, grown up to maturity, we may argue against ab effectu, from the ill consequence of it. They dip the persons they baptise over head and ears in cold water, and naked; which, as it is indecent, so it is dangerous, and has often been the occasion of chronic disease, yea, and of death itself; and so is a plain breach of the sixth commandment. How far God has given up many persons, who are for deferring baptism, to other vile opinions and vicious practices, is evident, if we consult history; especially if we read the doings of the Anabaptists in Germany.

Use one. See the riches of God's goodness, who will not only be the God of believers, but takes their seed into covenant with them. 'I will establish my covenant between me and thee, and thy seed after thee, to be a God unto thee and to thy seed.' Gen 17: 7. A father counts it a great privilege, not only to have his own name, but his child's name put in a will.

Use two. Those parents are to be blamed who forbid little children to be brought to Christ; and withhold from them this ordinance. By denying their infants baptism, they exclude them from membership in the visible church, so that their infants are sucking pagans. Such as deny their children baptism, make God's institutions under the law more full of kindness and grace to children than they are under the gospel; which, how strange a paradox it is, I leave you to judge.

Use three. For exhortation. (1) Let us who are baptised, labour to find the blessed fruits of it in our own souls; not only to have the signs of the covenant, but the grace of the covenant. Many glory in their baptism. The Jews gloried in their circumcision, because of their royal privileges; to them belonged the adoption, and the glory, and the covenants. Rom 9: 4. But many of them were a shame and reproach to their circumcision. 'For the name of God is blasphemed among the Gentiles through you.' Rom 2: 24. The scandalous Jews, though circumcised, were, in God's account, as heathens. 'Are ye not as children of the Ethiopians to me? saith the Lord.' Amos 9: 7. Alas! what is it to have the name of Christ, and want his image? What is baptism of water without the baptism of the Spirit? Many baptised Christians are no better than heathens. O let us labour to find the fruits of baptism, that Christ is formed in us (Gal 4: 19); that our nature is changed; that we are made holy and heavenly. This is to be baptised into Jesus. Rom 6: 3. Such as live unsuitable to their baptism, may go with baptismal-water on their faces, and sacramental bread in their mouths, to hell.

(2) Let us labour to make a right use of our baptism. Let us use it as a shield against temptations. Satan, I have given up myself to God by a sacred vow in baptism; I am not my own, I am Christ's; therefore I cannot yield to thy temptations, for I should break my oath of allegiance which I made to God in baptism. Luther tells us of a pious woman, who, when the devil tempted her to sin, answered, Satan, baptizata sum, 'I am baptised;' and so beat back the tempter.

Let us use it as a spur to holiness. By remembering our baptism, let us be stirred up to make good our baptismal engagements; renouncing the world, flesh, and devil, let us devote ourselves to God and his service. To be baptised into the name of the Father, Son, and Holy Ghost, implies a solemn dedication of ourselves to the service of all the Three Persons in the Trinity. It is not enough that our parents dedicate us to God in baptism, but we must dedicate ourselves to him; this is called living to the Lord. Rom 14: 8. Our life should be spent in worshipping God, in loving God, in exalting God; we should walk as becomes the gospel. Phil 1: 27. We should shine as stars in the world, and live as earthly angels.

Let us use it as an argument to courage. We should be ready to confess that Holy Trinity, into whose name we were baptised. With the conversion of the heart must go the confession of the tongue. 'Whosoever shall confess me before men, him shall the Son of man also confess before the angels of God.' Luke 12: 8. Peter openly confessed Christ crucified. Acts 4:10. Cyprian, a man of a brave spirit, was like a rock, whom no waves could shake; like an adamant, whom no sword could cut. He confessed Christ before the pro-consul, and suffered himself to be proscribed; yea, chose death rather than betray the truths of Christ. He that dare not confess the Holy Trinity, shames his baptism, and God will be ashamed to own him at the day of judgement.

Use four. See the fearfulness of the sin of apostasy! It is renouncing our baptism. It is damnable perjury to go away from God after a solemn vow. 'Demas has forsaken me.' 2 Tim 4:10. He turned renegado, and afterwards became a priest in an idol-temple, says Dorotheus. Julia the apostate, Gregory Nazianzen observes, bathed himself in the blood of beasts offered in sacrifice to heathen gods; and so, as much as in him lay, washed off his former baptism. The case of such as fall away after baptism is dreadful. 'If any man draw back.' Heb 10: 38. The Greek word to draw back, alludes to a soldier that steals away from his colours; so, if any man steal away from Christ, and run over to the devil's side, 'my soul shall have no pleasure in him;' that is, I will be severely avenged on him; I will make my arrows drunk with his blood. If all the plagues in the Bible can make that man miserable, he shall be so.

4.5 The Lord's Supper

'And as they did eat, Jesus took bread,' &c. Mark 14: 22.

Having spoken to the sacrament of baptism, I come now to the sacrament of the Lord's Supper. The Lord's Supper is the most spiritual and sweetest ordinance that ever was instituted. Here we have to do more immediately with the person of Christ. In prayer, we draw nigh to God; in the sacrament, we become one with him. In prayer, we look up to Christ; in the sacrament, by faith, we touch him. In the word preached, we hear Christ's voice; in the sacrament, we feed on him.

What names and titles in Scripture are given to the sacrament?

It is called, Mensa Domini, 'The Lord's table.' I Cor 10: 21. The Papists call it an altar, not a table. The reason is, because they turn the sacrament into a sacrifice, and pretend to offer up Christ corporally in the mass. It being the Lord's table, shows with what reverence and solemn devotion we should approach these holy mysteries. The Lord takes notice of the frame of our hearts when we come to his table. 'The king came in to see the guests.' Matt 22: 11. We dress ourselves when we come to the table of some great monarch; so, when we are going to the table of the Lord, we should dress ourselves by holy meditation and heart consideration. Many think it is enough to come to the sacrament, but mind not whether they come in 'due order.' I Chron 15: 13. Perhaps they had scarce a serious thought before where they were going: all their dressing was by the glass, not by the Bible. Chrysostom calls it, 'The dreadful table of the Lord:' and so it is to such as come unworthily. The sacrament is called Coena Domini, the Lord's supper - to import, it is a spiritual feast. I Cor 11: 20. It is a royal feast. God is in this cheer: Christ, in both natures, God and man, is the matter of this supper. It is called a 'communion.' 'The bread which we break, is it not the communion of the body of Christ?' I Cor 10: 16. The sacrament being called a communion, shows: -

(1) That this ordinance is for believers only, because none else can have communion with Christ in these holy mysteries. Communio fundatur in unione [Communion is based upon union]. Faith only gives us union with Christ, and by virtue of this we have communion with him in his body and blood. None but the spouse communicates with her husband; a stranger may drink of his cup, but she only has his heart, and communicates with him in a conjugal manner; so strangers may drink of the cup, but believers only drink of Christ's blood, and have communion with him.

(2) The sacrament being a communion, shows that it is symbolum amoris [a symbol of love], a bond of that unity and charity which should be among Christians. 'We being many are one body.' I Cor 10: 17. As many grains make one bread, so many Christians are one body. A sacrament is a love-feast. The primitive Christians, as Justin Martyr notes, had their holy salutations at the blessed supper, in token of that dearness of affection which they had to each other. It is a communion, therefore - there must be love and union. The Israelites did eat the Passover with bitter herbs; so must we eat the sacrament with bitter herbs of repentance, but not with bitter hearts of wrath and malice. The hearts of the communicants should be knit together with the bond of love. 'Thou braggest of thy faith' says Augustine, 'but show me thy faith by thy love to the saints.' For, as in the sun, light and heat are inseparable, so faith and love are twisted together inseparably. Where there are divisions, the Lord's supper is not properly a communion but a disunion.

What is the Lord's supper?

It is a visible sermon, wherein Christ crucified is set before us; or, it is a sacrament of the New Testament, wherein by receiving the holy elements of bread and wine, our communion with Christ is signified and sealed up to us; or it is a sacrament divinely instituted, wherein by giving and receiving bread and wine, Christ's death is showed forth, and the worthy receivers by faith are made partakers of his body and blood, and all the benefits flowing from thence.

For further explaining the nature of the Lord's supper, I shall refer to its institution.

'Jesus took bread.' Here is the master of the feast, or the institutor of the sacrament. The Lord Jesus took bread. He only is fit to institute a sacrament who is able to give virtue and blessing to it.

'He took bread.' His taking the bread was one part of his consecration of the elements, and setting them apart for a holy use. As Christ consecrated the elements, so we must labour to have our hearts consecrated before we receive these holy mysteries in the Lord's supper. How unseemly is it to see any come to these holy elements, having hearts leavened with pride, covetousness, or envy? These, with Judas, receive the devil in the sop, and are no better than crucifiers of the Lord of glory.

'And blessed it.' This is another part of the consecration of the element. Christ blessed it. He blesseth and it shall be blessed. He looked up to heaven for a benediction upon this newly-founded ordinance.

'And brake it.' The bread broken, and the wine poured out, signify to us the agony and ignominy of Christ's sufferings, the rending of Christ's body on the cross, and the effusion of blood which was distilled from his blessed side.

'And gave it to them.' Christ's giving the bread, denotes giving himself and all his benefits to us freely. Though he was sold, yet he was given. Judas sold Christ, but Christ gave himself to us.

'He gave it to them;' that is, to the disciples. This is children's bread. Christ does not cast these pearls before swine. Whether Judas was present at the supper is controverted. I incline to think he was not, for Christ said to the disciples, 'This is my blood, which is shed for you.' Luke 22: 20. He knew his blood was never shed effectually and intentionally for Judas. In eating the passover, he gave Judas a sop, which was a bit of unleavened bread dipped in a sauce made with bitter herbs; Judas having received the sop, went out immediately. John 13: 30. Suppose Judas was there, he received the elements, but not the blessing.

'Take, eat.' This expression of eating denotes four things; (1) The near mystic union between Christ and his saints. As the meat which is eaten incorporates with the body, and becomes one with it, so, by eating Christ's flesh, and drinking his blood spiritually, we partake of his merits and graces, and are mystically 'one with them.' 'I in them.' John 17: 23. (2) 'Take, eat.' Eating shows the infinite delight the believing soul has in Christ. Eating is grateful and pleasing to the palate; so feeding on Christ by a lively faith is delicious. Nullus animae suavior cibus [The soul knows no sweeter food]. Lactantius. No such sweet feeding as on Christ crucified. This is a 'feast of fat things, and wines on the lees well refined.' (3) 'Take, eat.' Eating denotes nourishment. As meat is delicious to the palate, so it is nourishing to the body; so eating Christ's flesh and drinking his blood, is nutritive to the soul. The new creature is nourished at the table of the Lord to everlasting life. 'Whose eateth my flesh, and drinketh my blood, has eternal life.' John 6: 54. (4) 'Take, eat,' shows the wisdom of God, who restores us by the same means by which we fell. We fell by taking and eating the forbidden fruit, and we are recovering again by taking and eating Christ's flesh. We died by eating the tree of knowledge, and we live by eating the tree of life.

'This is my body.' These words, Hoc est corpus meum, have been much controverted between us and the Papists. 'This is my body;' that is, by a metonymy; it is a sign and figure of my body. The Papists hold transsubstantiation - that the bread, after consecration, is turned into the very substance of Christ's body. We say, we receive Christ's body spiritually; they say, they receive Christ's body carnally; which is contrary to Scripture. Scripture affirms, that the heavens must receive Christ's body 'until the times of the restitution of all things.' Acts 3: 21. Christ's body cannot be at the same time in heaven and in the host. Aquinas says, 'It is not possible by any miracle, that a body should be locally in two places at once.' Besides, it is absurd to imagine that the bread in the sacrament should be turned into Christ's flesh, and that his body which was hung before, should be made again of bread. So that, 'This is my body,' is, as if Christ had said, 'This is a sign and representation of my body.'

'And he took the cup.' The cup is put by a metonymy of the subject for the adjunct, for the wine in the cup. It signifies the blood of Christ shed for our sins. The taking of the cup denotes the redundancy of merit in Christ, and the fulness of our redemption by him. He not only took the bread, but the cup.

'And when he had given thanks.' Christ gave thanks that God had given these elements of bread and wine to be signs and seals of man's redemption by Christ. Christ's giving thanks shows his philanthropy, or love to mankind, who did so rejoice and bless God that lost man was now in a way of recovery, and that he should be raised higher in Christ than ever he was in innocence.

'He gave the cup to them.' Why then dare any withhold the cup? This is to pollute and curtail the ordinance, and alter it from its primitive institution. Christ and his apostles administered the sacrament in both kinds, the bread and the cup. I Cor 11: 24, 25. The cup was received in the ancient church for the space of 1400 years, as is confessed by two Popish councils. Christ says expressly, 'Drink ye all of this.' He does not say, 'Eat ye all of this;' but 'Drink ye all;' as foreseeing the sacrilegious impiety of the church of Rome, in keeping back the cup from the people. The Popish council of Constance speaks plainly but impudently, 'That although Christ instituted and administered the sacrament in both kinds, the bread and the wine, yet the authority of the holy canons, and the customs of the mother church, think good to deny the cup to the laity.' Thus, as the Popish priests make Christ but half a Saviour, so they administer to the people but half a sacrament. The sacrament is Christ's last will and testament 'This is my blood of the New Testament.' Now, to alter or take away any thing from a man's will and testament, is great impiety. What is it to alter and mangle Christ's last will and testament? Sure it is a high affront to Christ.

What are the ends of the Lord's supper?

(1) It is an ordinance appointed to confirm our faith. 'Except ye see signs ye will not believe.' John 4: 48. Christ sets the elements before us, that by these signs our faith may be strengthened. As faith comes by hearing, so it is confirmed by seeing Christ crucified. The sacrament is not only a sign to represent Christ, but a seal to confirm our interest in him.

But the Spirit confirms faith, therefore not the sacrament.

This is not good logic. The Spirit confirms faith, therefore not the sacrament, is, as if one should say, 'God feeds our bodies, therefore bread does not feed us;' whereas, God feeds us by bread, so the Spirit confirms our faith by the use of the sacrament.

(2) The end of the sacrament is to keep up the 'memory of Christ's death.' 'This do ye in remembrance of me.' I Cor 11: 25. If a friend gives us a ring at his death, we wear it to keep up the memory of our friend; much more ought we to keep the memorial of Christ's death in the sacrament. His death lays a foundation for all the magnificent blessings which we receive from him. The covenant of grace was agreed on in heaven, but sealed upon the cross. Christ has sealed all the articles of peace in his blood. Remission of sin flows from Christ's death. 'This is my blood of the New Testament, which is shed for many, for the remission of sins.' Matt 26: 28. Consecration, or making us holy, is the fruit of Christ's death. 'How much more shall the blood of Christ purge your conscience?' Heb 9: 14. Christ's intercession is made available to us by virtue of his death. He could not have been admitted an advocate if he had not been first a sacrifice. Our entering into heaven is the fruit of his blood. Heb 10: 19. He could not have prepared mansions for us, if he had not first purchased them by his death: so that we have great cause to commemorate his death in the sacrament.

In what manner are we to remember the Lord's death in the sacrament?

It is not only an historical remembrance of Christ's death and passion. Judas remembered his death and betrayed him; and Pilate remembered his death and crucified him: but our remembering his death in the sacrament must be, [1] A mournful remembrance. We should not be able to look on Christ crucified with dry eyes. 'They shall look on him whom they have pierced, and mourn over him.' Zech 12: 10. O Christian, when thou lookest on Christ in the sacrament, remember how often thou hast crucified him! The Jews did it but once, thou often. Every oath is a nail with which thou piercest his hands; every unjust sinful action is a spear with which thou woundest his heart. Oh, remember Christ with sorrow, to think thou shouldst make his wounds bleed afresh! [2] It must be a joyful remembrance. 'Abraham rejoiced to see my day.' John 8: 56. When a Christian sees a sacrament-day approaching, he should rejoice. This ordinance of the supper is an earnest of heaven; it is the glass in which we see him whom our souls love, it is the chariot by which we are carried up to Christ. When Jacob saw the wagons and the chariots which were to carry him to his son Joseph, his spirit revived. Gen 45: 27. God has appointed the sacrament on purpose to cheer and revive a sad heart. When we look on our sins we have cause to mourn; but when we see Christ's blood shed for our sins we rejoice. In the sacrament our wants are supplied, our strength is renewed; there we meet with Christ, and does not this call for joy? A woman that has been long debarred from the society of her husband is glad of his presence. At the sacrament the believing spouse meets with Christ; he saith to her, 'All I have is thine; my love is thine, to pity thee; my mercy is thine, to save thee.' How can we think in the sacrament on Christ's blood shed, and not rejoice? Sanguis Christi clavis paradisi; 'Christ's blood is the key which opens heaven,' else we had been all shut out.

(3) The end of the sacrament is to work in us an endeared love to Christ. When Christ bleeds for us, well may we say, 'Behold how he loved us!' Who can see Christ die and not be 'sick of love?' That is a heart of stone which Christ's love will not melt.

(4) The end of the sacrament is the mortifying of corruption. To see Christ crucified for us is a means to crucify sin in us. His death, like the water of jealousy, makes the thigh of sin to rot. Numb 5: 27. How can a wife endure to see the spear which killed her husband? How can we endure those sins which made Christ veil his glory and lose his blood? When the people of Rome saw Caesar's bloody robe, they were incensed against them that slew him. Sin has rent the white robe of Christ's flesh and dyed it of a crimson colour. The thoughts of this should make us seek to be avenged on our sins.

(5) Another end is the augmentation and increase of all the graces, hope, zeal, and patience. The word preached begets grace, the Lord's supper nourishes it. The body by feeding increases strength, so the soul by feeding on Christ sacramentally. Cum defecerit virtus mea calicem salutarem accipiam. Bernard. 'When my spiritual strength begins to fail, I know a remedy,' says Bernard, 'I will go to the table of the Lord; there will I drink and recover my decayed strength.' There is a difference between dead stones and living plants. The wicked, who are stones, receive no spiritual increase; but the godly, who are plants of righteousness, being watered with Christ's blood, grow more fruitful in grace.

Why are we to receive this holy supper?

(1) Because it is an incumbent duty. 'Take, eat.' And observe, it is a command of love. If Christ had commanded us some great matter, would we not have done it? 'If the prophet had bid thee do some great thing, wouldest thou not have done it?' 2 Kings 5: 13. If Christ had enjoined us to have given him thousands of rams, or to have parted with the fruit of our bodies, would we not have done it? Much more when he only says, 'Take,' and 'Eat.' Let my broken body feed you, let my blood poured out save you. 'Take,' and 'Eat.' This is a command of love, and shall we not readily obey?

(2) We are to celebrate the Lord's supper, because it is provoking Christ to stay away. 'Wisdom has furnished her table.' Prov 9: 2. So Christ has furnished his table, set bread and wine (representing his body and blood) before his guests, and when they wilfully turn their backs upon the ordinance, he looks upon it as slighting his love, and it makes the fury rise up in his face. 'For I say unto you, that none of those men which were bidden shall taste of my supper.' Luke 14: 24. I will shut them out of my kingdom, I will provide them a black banquet, where weeping shall be the first course, and gnashing of teeth the second.

Should the Lord's supper be often administered?

Yes. 'As often as ye eat this bread.' I Cor 11: 26. The ordinance is not to be celebrated once in a year, or once only in our lives, but often. A Christian's own necessities may make him come often hither. His corruptions are strong, therefore he had need come often hither for an antidote to expel the poison of sin. His graces are weak. Grace is like a lamp, which if it be not often fed with oil is apt to go out. Rev 3: 2. How then do they sin against God who come but very seldom to this ordinance! Can they thrive who for a long time forbear their food? Others there are who wholly forbear, which is a great contempt offered to Christ's ordinance. They tacitly say, Let Christ keep his feast to himself. What a cross-grained piece is a man! He will eat when he should not, and he will not eat when he should. When God says, 'Eat not of this forbidden fruit;' then he will be sure to eat: when God says, 'Eat of this bread, and drink of this cup;' then he refuses to eat.

Are all to come promiscuously to this holy ordinance?

No; for that were to make the Lord's table an ordinary. Christ forbids to 'cast pearls before swine.' Matt 7: 6. The sacramental bread is children's bread, and it is not to be cast to the profane. As, at the giving of the law God set bounds about the mount that none might touch it, so God's table should be guarded, that the profane should not come near. Exod 19: 12. In primitive times, after sermon was done, and the Lord's supper was about to be celebrated, an officer stood up and cried, 'Holy things for holy men;' and then several of the congregation departed. 'I would have my hand cut off,' says Chrysostom, 'rather than I would give Christ's body and blood to the profane.' The wicked do not eat Christ's flesh, but tear it; they do not drink his blood, but spill it. These holy mysteries in the sacraments are tremenda hysteria, mysteries that the soul is to tremble at. Sinners defile the holy things of God, they poison the sacramental cup. We read that the wicked are to be set at Christ's feet, not at his table. Psa 110: 1.

That we may receive the supper of the Lord worthily, and that it may become efficacious: -

I. We must solemnly prepare ourselves before we come. We must not rush upon the ordinance rudely and irreverently, but come in due order. There was a great deal of preparation for the passover, and the sacrament comes in the room of it. 2 Chron 30: 18, 19. This solemn preparation for the ordinance consists: -

[1] In examining ourselves. [2] In dressing our souls before we come, which is by washing in the water of repentance and by exciting the habit of grace into exercise. [3] In begging a blessing upon the ordinance.

[1] Solemn preparation for the sacrament consists in self-examination. 'But let a man examine himself, and so let him eat.' I Cor 11: 28. It is not only a counsel, but a charge: 'Let him examine himself. ' As if a king should say, 'Let it be enacted.' These elements in the supper having been consecrated by Jesus Christ to a high mystery, represent his body and blood; therefore there must be preparation; and if preparation, there must be first self-examination. Let us be serious in examining ourselves, as our salvation depends upon it. We are curious in examining other things; we will not take gold till we examine it by the touchstone; we will not take land before we examine the title; and shall we not be as exact and curious in examining the state of our souls?

What is required for this self-examination?

There must be a solemn retirement of the soul. We must set ourselves apart, and retire for some time from all secular employment, that we may be more serious in the work. There is no casting up accounts in a crowd; nor can we examine ourselves when we are in a crowd of worldly business. We read, that a man who was in a journey might not come to the Passover, because his mind was full of secular cares, and his thoughts were taken up about his journey. Num 9: 13. When we are upon self-examining work, we had not need to be in a hurry, or have any distracting thoughts, but to retire and lock ourselves up in our closets, that we may be more intent upon the work.

What is self-examination?

It is the setting up a court of conscience and keeping a register there that by a strict scrutiny a man may see how matters stand between Got and his soul. It is a spiritual inquisition, a heart-anatomy, whereby a man takes his heart in pieces, as a watch, and sees what is defective therein. It is a dialogue with one's self 'I commune with my own heart.' Psa 77: 6. David called himself to account, and put interrogatories to his own heart. Self-examination is a critical enquiry or search. As the woman in the parable lighted a candle and searched for her lost groat, so conscience is the candle of the Lord. Luke 15: 8. Search with this candle what thou can't find wrought by the Spirit in thee.

What is the rule by which we are to examine ourselves?

The rule or measure by which we must examine ourselves is the Holy Scripture. We must not make fancy, or the good opinion which others have of us, a rule to judge of ourselves. As the goldsmith brings his gold to the touchstone, so we must bring our hearts to a Scripture touchstone. 'To the law and to the testimony.' Isa 8: 20. What says the word? Are we divorced from sin? Are we renewed by the Spirit? Let the word decide whether we are fit communicants or not. We judge of colours by the sun, so we must judge of the state of our souls by the sunlight of Scripture.

What are the principal reasons for self-examination before we approach the Lord's supper?

(1) It is a duty imposed: 'Let him examine himself.' The passover was not to be eaten raw. Exod 12: 9. To come to such an ordinance slightly, without examination, is to come in an undue manner, and is like eating the passover raw.

(2) We must examine ourselves before we come, because it is not only a duty imposed, but opposed. There is nothing to which the heart is naturally more averse than self-examination. We may know that duty to be good which the heart opposes. But why does the heart so oppose it? Because it crosses the tide of corrupt nature, and is contrary to flesh and blood. The heart is guilty; and does a guilty person love to be examined? The heart opposes it; therefore the rather set upon it; for that duty is good which the heart opposes.

(3) Because self-examination is a needful work. Without it, a man can never tell how it is with him, whether he has grace or not; and this must needs be very uncomfortable. He knows not, if he should die presently what will become of him, to what coast he shall sail, whether to hell or heaven; as Socrates said, 'I am about to die, and the gods know whether I shall be happy or miserable.' How needful, therefore, is self-examination; that a man by search may know the true state of his soul, and how it will go with him to eternity!

Self-examination is needful, with respect to the excellence of the sacrament. Let him eat de illo pane, 'of that bread,' that excellent bread, that consecrated bread, that bread which is not only the bread of the Lord, but the bread the Lord. I Cor 11: 28. Let him drink de illo poculo, 'of that cup;' that precious cup, which is perfumed and spiced with Christ's love; that cup which holds the blood of God sacramentally. Cleopatra put a jewel in a cup which contained the price of a kingdom: this sacred cup we are to drink of, enriched with the blood of God, is above the price of a kingdom; it is more worth than heaven. Therefore, coming to such a royal feast, having a whole Christ, both his divine and human nature to feed on, how should we examine ourselves beforehand, that we may be fit guests for such a magnificent banquet!

Self-examination is needful, because God will examine us. That was a sad question, 'Friend, how camest thou in hither, not having a wedding garment?' Matt 22: 12. Men are loath to ask themselves the question, 'O my soul! art thou a fit guest for the Lord's table?' Are there not some sins thou hast to bewail? Are there not some evidences for heaven that thou hast to get?' Now, when persons will not ask themselves the question, then God will bring the question to them, How came you in hither to my table, not prepared? How came you in hither, with an unbelieving or profane heart? Such a question will cause a heart-trembling. God will examine a man, as the chief captain would Paul, with scourging. Acts 22: 24. It is true that the best saint, if God should weigh him in the balance, would be found wanting: but, when a Christian has made an impartial search, and has laboured to deal uprightly between God and his own soul, Christ's merits will cast in some grains of allowance into the scales.

Self-examination is needful, because of secret corruption in the heart, which will not be found out without searching. There are in the heart plangendae tenebrae, Augustine, 'hidden pollutions.' It is with a Christian, as with Joseph's brethren, who, when the steward accused them of having the cup, were ready to swear they had it not; but upon search it was found in one of their sacks. Little does a Christian think what pride, atheism, uncleanness is in his heart till he searches it. If there be therefore such hidden wickedness, like a spring running under ground, we had need examine ourselves, that finding out our secret sin, we may be humbled and repent. Hidden sins, if not searched out, defile the soul. If corn lie long in the chaff, the chaff defiles the corn; so sins long hidden defile our duties. Needful therefore it is, before we come to the holy supper, to search out these hidden sins, as Israel searched for leaven before they came to the passover.

Self-examination is needful, because without it we may easily have a cheat put upon us. 'The heart is deceitful above all things.' Jer 17: 9. Many a man's heart will tell him he is fit for the Lord's table. As when Christ asked the sons of Zebedee, 'Are ye able to drink of the cup that I shall drink of?' Matt 20: 22. Can ye drink such a bloody cup of suffering? 'They say unto him, We are able.' So the heart will suggest to a man, he is fit to drink of the sacramental cup, he has on the wedding-garment. Grande profundum est homo. Augustine. 'The heart is a grand impostor.' As a cheating tradesmen will put one off with bad wares, so the heart will put a man off with seeming grace, instead of saving. A tear or two shed is repentance, a few lazy desires are faith, just as blue and red flowers growing among corn, look like good flowers, but are beautiful weeds only. The foolish virgins' vessels looked as if they had oil in them, but they had none. Therefore, to prevent a cheat, that we may not take false grace instead of true, we had need make a thorough search of our hearts before we come to the Lord's table.

Self-examination is needful, because of the false fears which the godly are apt to nourish in their hearts, which make them go sad to the sacrament. As they who have no grace, for want of examining, presume, so they who have grace, for want of examining, are ready to despair. Many of God's children look upon themselves through the black spectacles of fear. They fear Christ is not formed in them, they fear they have no right to the promise; and these fears in the heart cause tears in the eye; whereas, would they but search and examine, they might find they had grace. Are not their hearts humbled for sin? What is this but the bruised reed? Do not they weep after the Lord? What are these tears but seeds of faith? Do they not thirst after Christ in an ordinance? What is this but the new creature crying for the breast? Here are, you see, seeds of grace; and, would Christians examine their hearts, they might see there is something of God in them, and so their false fears would be prevented, and they might approach with comfort to the holy mysteries in the Eucharist.

Self-examination is needful with respect to the danger of coming unworthily without it. He 'shall be guilty of the body and blood of the Lord.' I Cor 11: 27. Par facit quasi Christum trucidaret [It is as if he were butchering Christ]. Grotius. God reckons with him as with a crucifier of the Lord Jesus. He does not drink Christ's blood, but sheds it; and so brings that curse upon him, as when the Jews said, 'His blood be upon us and our children.' Than the virtue of Christ's blood, nothing is more comfortable; than the guilt of it, nothing is more formidable.

(4) We must examine ourselves before the sacrament, on account of the difficulty of the work. Difficulty raises a noble spirit. Self-examination is difficult, because it is an inward work, it lies with the heart. External acts of devotion are easy; to lift up the eye, to bow the knee, to read over a few prayers, is as easy as for the Papists to tell over a few beads; but to examine a man's self, to take the heart in pieces, to make a Scripture-trial of our fitness for the Lord's supper, is not easy. Reflexive acts are hardest. The eye cannot see itself but by a glass; so we must have the glass of the word and conscience to see our own hearts. It is easy to spy the faults of others; but it is hard to find out our owns. Self-examination is difficult, with regard to self-love. As ignorance blinds, so self-love flatters. What Solomon says of love, 'Love covereth all sins,' is most true of self-

love. Prov 10: 12. A man looking upon himself in the flattering glass of self-love, his virtues appear greater than they are, and his sins less. Self-love makes a man rather excuse himself, than examine himself; self-love makes one think the best of himself; and he who has a good opinion of himself, does not suspect himself; and not suspecting himself, he is not forward to examine himself. The work, therefore, of self- examination being so difficult, requires the more impartiality and industry. Difficulty should be a spur to diligence.

(5) We must examine ourselves before we come, because of the benefit of self-examination. The benefit is great whatever way it terminates. If, upon examination, we find that we have no grace in truth, the mistake is discovered, and the danger prevented; if we find that we have grace, we may take the comfort of it. He who, upon search, finds that he has the minimum quod sit, the least degree of grace, he is like one that has found his box of evidences; he is a happy man; he is a fit guest at the Lord's table; he is heir to all the promises; he is as sure to go to heaven as if he were in heaven already.

What must we examine?

(1) Our sins. Search if any dead fly spoils sweet ointment. When we come to the sacrament, as the Jews did before the passover, we should search for leaven, and having found it we should burn it. Let us search for the leaven of pride. This sours our holy things. Will a humble Christ be received into a proud heart? Pride keeps Christ out. Intus existens prohibet alienum [Its presence within blocks the entrance of any other]. To a proud man Christ's blood has no virtue; it is like a cordial put into a dead man's mouth, which loses its virtue. Let us search for the leaven of pride, and cast it away. Let us search for the leaven of avarice. The Lord's supper is a spiritual mystery, to represent Christ's body and blood; what should an earthly heart do here? The earth puts out the fire; so earthliness quencheth the fire of holy love. The earth is elementum gravissimum [the heaviest of the elements], it cannot ascend. A soul belimed with earth cannot ascend to heavenly cogitations. 'Covetousness, which is idolatry.' Col 3: 5. Will Christ come into the heart where there is an idol? Search for this leaven before you come to this ordinance. How can an earthly heart converse with that God which is a spirit? Can a clod of earth kiss the sun? Search for the leaven of hypocrisy. 'Beware ye of the leaven of the Pharisees, which is hypocrisy.' Luke 12: 1. Aquinas describes it as simulatio virtutis: hypocrisy is 'the counterfeiting of virtue.' The hypocrite is a living pageant, he only makes a show of religion; he gives God his knee, but no heart; and God gives him bread and wine in the sacrament, but no Christ. Oh, let us search for this leaven of hypocrisy and burn it!

(2) We must examine our graces. I shall instance one only - our knowledge.

We are to examine whether we have knowledge, or we cannot give God a reasonable service. Rom 12: 1. Knowledge is a necessary requisite in a communicant; without it there can be no fitness for the sacrament. A person cannot be fit to come to the Lord's table who has no goodness; but without knowledge the mind is not good. Prov 19: 2. Some say they have good hearts, though they want knowledge; as if one should say, his eye is good, but it wants sight. Under the law, when the plague of leprosy was in a man's head, the priest was to pronounce him unclean. The ignorant person has the plague in his head, he is unclean; ignorance is the womb of lust. 1 Pet 1: 14. Therefore it is requisite, before we come, to examine what knowledge we have in the main fundamentals of religion. Let it not be said of us, that 'unto this day the vail is upon their heart.' 2 Cor 3: 15. In this intelligent age, we cannot but have some insight into the mysteries of the gospel. I rather fear, we are like Rachel, who was fair and well-sighted, but barren: therefore,

Let us examine whether our knowledge be rightly qualified. Is it influential. Does our knowledge warm our heart? Claritas intellectu parit ardorem in effectu [Clearness in the understanding breeds zeal in the doing]. Saving knowledge not only directs but quickens; it is the light of life. John 8: 12. Is our knowledge practical? We hear much; do we love the truths we know? That is the right knowledge which not only adorns the mind, but reforms the life.

[2] This solemn preparation for the sacrament consists in dressing our souls before we come. This soul-dress is in two things:

(1) Washing in the lever of repenting tears. To come to this ordinance with the guilt of any sin unrepented of makes way for further hardening of the heart, and gives Satan fuller possession of it. 'They shall look on me whom they have pierced, and they shall mourn for him.' Zech 12: 10. The cloud of sorrow must drop into tears. We must grieve as for the pollution, so for the unkindness in every sin which is against Christ's love who died for us. When Peter thought of Christ's love in calling him out of his unregeneracy to make him an apostle, and to carry him up to the mount of transfiguration, where he saw the glory of heaven in a vision, and then of his denying Christ, it broke his heart: 'he wept bitterly.' Matt 26: 75. To think, before we come to a sacrament, of sins against the bowel-mercies of God the Father, the bleeding wounds of God the Son, the blessed inspirations of God the Holy Ghost, is enough to fill our eyes with tears, and put us into a holy agony of grief and compunction. We must be distressed for sin, be divorced from it. Before the serpent drinks it casts up its poison; in this we must be wise as serpents. Before we drink of the sacramental cup we must cast up the poison of sin by repentance. Ille vere plangit commissa, qui non committit plangenda. Augustine. 'He truly bewails the sins he has committed who does not commit the sins he has bewailed.'

(2) The soul-dress is the exciting and stirring up the habit of grace into a lively exercise. 'I put thee in remembrance, that thou stir up the gift of God which is in thee,' that is, the gifts and graces of the Spirit. 2 Tim 1: 6. The Greek word to stir up, signifies to blow up grace into a flame. Grace is often like fire in the embers, which needs blowing up. It is possible that even a good man may not come so well disposed to this ordinance, because he has not before taken pains with his heart to come in due order, to stir up grace into vigorous exercise; and though he does not eat and drink damnation, yet he does not receive consolation in the sacrament.

[3] A solemn preparation for the sacrament consists in begging a blessing upon the ordinance. The efficacy of the sacrament depends upon the co-operation of the Spirit, and a word of blessing. In the institution, Christ blessed the elements: 'Jesus took bread and blessed it.' The sacrament will do us good no farther than it is blessed to us. We ought, before we come, to pray for a blessing, that it may not only be a sign to represent, but a seal to conform, and an instrument to convey Christ and all his benefits to us. We are to pray that this great ordinance may be poison to our sins, and food to our graces. As with Jonathan, when he tasted the honeycomb, 'and his eyes were enlightened;' so by receiving this holy Eucharist, our eyes may be enlightened to 'discern the Lord's body.' I Sam 14: 27. Thus should we implore a blessing upon the ordinance before we come. The sacrament is like a tree hung full of fruit, but none of this fruit will fall unless shaken by the hand of prayer.

II. That the sacrament may be effectual to us, there must be a right participation of it, which consists in four things. [1] When we draw nigh to God's table in a humble sense of our unworthiness. We do not deserve one crumb of the bread of life; we are poor indigent creatures, who have lost our glory, and are like a vessel that is shipwrecked; we smite on our breasts, as the publican, 'God be merciful to us sinners.' This is partaking of the ordinance aright. It is part of our worthiness to see our unworthiness.

[2] We rightly partake when at the Lord's table we are filled with breathing of soul and inflamed desires after Christ, which nothing can quench but his blood. 'Blessed are they which thirst.' Matt 5: 6. They are blessed not only when they are filled, but while they are thirsting.

[3] A right participation of the supper is, when we receive it in faith. Without faith we get no good. What is said of the word preached, it 'did not profit them, not being mixed with faith,' is true of the sacrament. Heb 4: 2. Christ turned stones into bread: unbelief turns the bread into stones, that do not nourish. We partake aright when we come in faith. Faith has a twofold act, an adhering, and an applying. By the first we go over to Christ, by the second we bring Christ over to us. Gal 2: 20. This is the grace we must set to work. Acts 10: 43. Philo calls it, fides oculata [the eye of faith]: it is the eagle-eye that discerns the Lord's body; it causes a virtual contact, it touches Christ. Christ said to Mary, 'Touch me not,' &c. John 20: 17. She was not to touch him with the hands of her body; but he says to us, 'Touch me,' touch me with the hand of your faith. Faith makes Christ present to the soul. The believer has a real presence in the sacrament. The body of the sun is in the firmament, but the light of the sun is in the eye. Christ's essence is in heaven, but he is in a believer's heart by his light and influence. 'That Christ may dwell in your hearts by faith.' Eph 3: 17. Faith is the palate which tastes Christ. I Pet 2: 3. It causes the bread of life to nourish. Crede et manducasti [Believe and thou hast fed]. Augustine. Faith makes us one with Christ. Eph 1: 23. Other graces make us like Christ, faith makes us members of Christ.

[4] We partake aright of the sacrament when we receive it in love.

(1) Love to Christ. Who can see Christ pierced with a crown of thorns, sweating in his agony,

bleeding on the cross, but his heart must needs be endeared in love to him? How can we but love him who has given his life a ransom for us? Love is the spiced wine and juice of the pomegranate which we must give to Christ. Cant 8: 2. Our love to this superior and blessed Jesus must exceed our love to other things; as the oil runs above the water. Though we cannot, with Mary, bring our body ointment to anoint his body, we do more than this, whence bring him our love, which is sweeter to him than all ointments and perfumes.

(2) Love to the saints. This is a love-feast. Though we must eat it with the bitter herbs of repentance, yet not with the bitter herbs of malice. Were it not sad if all the meat we eat should turn to bad humours? He who comes in malice to the Lord's table turns all he eats to his hurt. 'He eateth and drinketh damnation to himself.' I Cor 11: 29. 'Come in love.' It is with love as with fire which you keep all the day upon the hearth, but upon special occasions make larger. We must have love to all; but to the saints, who are our fellow-members here, we must draw out the fire of our love larger; and must show the largeness of our affections to them, by prizing their persons, by choosing their company, by doing all offices of love to them, by counselling them in their doubts, comforting them in their fears, and supplying them in their wants. Thus one Christian may be an Ebenezer to another, and as an angel of God to him. The sacrament cannot be effectual to him who does not receive it in love. If a man drinks poison and then takes a cordial, the cordial will do him little good, so he who has the poison of malice in his soul, the cordial of Christ's blood will do him no good; come therefore in love and charity.

Use one. From the whole doctrine of this sacrament learn how precious should a sacrament be to us. It is a sealed deed to make over the blessings of the new covenant to us. A small piece of wax put to a parchment is made the instrument to confirm a rich conveyance or lordship to another; so these elements in the sacrament of bread and wine, though in themselves of no great value, yet being consecrated to be seals to confirm the covenant of grace to us, are of more value than all the riches of the Indies.

Use two. The sacrament being such a holy mystery, let us come to it with holy hearts. There is no receiving a crucified Christ but into a consecrated heart. Christ in his conception lay in a pure virgin's womb, and, at his death, his body was wrapped in clean linen, and put into a new virgin tomb, never yet defiled. If Christ would not lie in an unclean grave, surely he will not be received into an unclean heart. 'Be ye clean that bear the vessels of the Lord.' Isa 52: 11. If they who carried the vessels of the Lord were to be holy, they who are to be the vessels of the Lord, and are to hold Christ's blood and body, ought to be holy.

Use three. Christ's body and blood in the sacrament are a most sovereign elixir or comfort to a distressed soul. Having poured out his blood, God's justice is fully satisfied. There is in the death of Christ enough to answer all doubts. What if sin is the poison, the flesh of Christ is an antidote against it! What if sin be red as scarlet, is not Christ's blood of a deeper colour, and can wash away sin? If Satan strikes us with his darts of temptation, here is a precious balm out of Christ's wounds to heal us. Isa 53: 5. What though we feed upon the bread of affliction, so long as in the sacrament we feed upon the bread of life? Christ received aright sacramentally, is a universal medicine for healing, and a universal cordial for cheering our distressed souls.

4.6 Prayer

'But I give myself unto prayer.' Psa 109: 4.

I shall not here expatiate upon prayer, as it will be considered more fully in the Lord's prayer. It is one thing to pray, and another thing to be given to prayer: he who prays frequently, is said to be given to prayer; as he who often distributes alms, is said to be given to charity. Prayer is a glorious ordinance, it is the soul's trading with heaven. God comes down to us by his Spirit, and we go up to him by prayer.

What is prayer?

It is an offering up of our desires to God for things agreeable to his will, in the name of Christ.

'Prayer is offering up our desires;' and therefore called making known our requests. Phil 4: 6. In prayer we come as humble petitioners, begging to have our suit granted. It is 'offering up our desires to God.' Prayer is not to be made to any but God. The Papists pray to saints and angels, who know not our grievances. 'Abraham be ignorant of us.' Isa 63: 16. All angel-worship is forbidden. Col 2: 18, 19. We must not pray to any but whom we may believe in. 'How shall they call on him in whom they have not believed?' Rom 10: 14. We cannot believe in an angel, therefore we must not pray to him.

Why must prayer be made to God only?

(1) Because he only hears prayer. 'Oh thou that hearest prayer.' Psa 65: 2. Hereby God is known to be the true God, in that he hears prayer. 'Hear me, O Lord, hear me, that this people may know that thou art the Lord God.' I Kings 18: 37.

(2) Because God only can help. We may look to second causes, and cry, as the woman did, 'Help, my lord, O king.' And he said, 'If the Lord do not help thee, whence shall I help thee?' 2 Kings 6: 26, 27. If we are in outward distress, God must send from heaven and save; if we are in inward agonies, he only can pour in the oil of joy; therefore prayer is to be made to him only.

We are to pray 'for things agreeable to his will.' When we pray for outward things, for riches or children, perhaps God sees these things not to be good for us; and our prayers should comport with his will. We may pray absolutely for grace; 'For this is the will of God, even your sanctification.' I Thess 4: 3. There must be no strange incense offered. Exod 30: 9. When we pray for things which are not agreeable to God's will, it is offering strange incense.

We are to pray 'in the name of Christ.' To pray in the name of Christ, is not only to mention Christ's name in prayer, but to pray in the hope and confidence of his merits. 'Samuel took a sucking lamb and offered it,' &c. I Sam 7: 9. We must carry the lamb Christ in the arms of our faith, and so shall we prevail in prayer. When Uzziah would offer incense without a priest, God was angry, and struck him with leprosy. 2 Chron 26: 16. When we do not pray in Christ's name, in the hope of his mediation, we offer up incense without a priest; and what can we expect but to meet with rebukes, and to have God answer us by terrible things?

What are the several parts of prayer?

(1) There is the confessors part, which is the acknowledgement of sin. (2) The supplicatory part, when we either deprecate and pray against some evil, or request the obtaining of some good. (3) The congratulatory part, when we give thanks for mercies received, which is the most excellent part of prayer. In petition, we act like men; in giving thanks, we act like angels.

What are the several sorts of prayer?

(1) There is mental prayer, in the mind. I Sam 1: 13. (2) Vocal. Psa 77: 1. (3) Ejaculatory, which is a sudden and short elevation of the heart to God. 'So I prayed to the God of heaven.' Neh 2: 4. (4) Inspired prayer, when we pray for those things which God puts into our heart. The Spirit helps us with sighs and groans. Rom 8: 26. Both the expressions of the tongue, and the impressions of the heart, so far as they are right, are from the Spirit. (5) Prescribed prayer. Our Saviour has set us a pattern of prayer. God prescribed a set form of blessing for the priests. Numb 6: 23. (6) Public prayer, when we pray in the audience of others. Prayer is more powerful when many join and unite their forces. Vis unita fortior [A united force is stronger]. Matt 18: 19. (7) Private prayer; when we pray by ourselves. 'Enter into thy closet.' Matt 6: 6.

That prayer is most likely to prevail with God which is rightly qualified. That is a good medicine which has the right ingredients; and that prayer is good, and most likely to prevail with God, which has these seven ingredients in it: -

[1] It must be mixed with faith. 'But let him ask in faith.' James 1: 6. Believe that God hears, and will in due time grant, believe his love and truth; believe that he is love, and therefore will not deny you; believe that he is truth, and therefore will not deny himself. Faith sets prayer to work. Faith is to prayer what the feather is to the arrow; it feathers the arrow of prayer, and makes it fly swifter, and pierce the throne of grace. The prayer that is faithless is fruitless.

[2] It must be a melting prayer. 'The sacrifices of God are a broken spirit.' Psa 51: 17. The incense was to be beaten to typify the breaking of the heart in prayer. Oh! says a Christian, I cannot pray with such gifts and elocution as others; as Moses said, 'I am not eloquent;' but can't

thou weep? Does thy heart melt in prayer? Weeping prayer prevails. Tears drop as pearls from the eye. Jacob wept and made supplication; and 'had power over the angel.' Hosea 12: 4.

[3] Prayer must be fired with zeal and fervency. 'Effectual fervent prayer availeth much.' James 5: 16. Cold prayer, like cold suitors, never speed. Prayer without fervency, is like a sacrifice without a fire. Prayer is called a 'pouring out of the soul,' to signify vehemence. I Sam 1: 15. Formality starves prayer. Prayer is compared to incense. 'Let my prayer be set forth as incense.' Psa 141: 2. Hot coals were to be put to the incense, to make it odoriferous and fragrant; so fervency of affection is like coals to the incense; it makes prayer ascend as a sweet perfume. Christ prayed with strong cries. Heb 5: 7. Clamor iste penetrat nubes [Such a cry pierces the clouds]. Luther. Fervent prayer, like a powder engine set against heaven's gates, makes them fly open. To cause holy fervour and ardour of soul in prayer, consider, (1) Prayer without fervency is no prayer; it is speaking, not praying. Lifeless prayer is no more prayer than the picture of a man is a man. One may say as Pharaoh, 'I have dreamed a dream.' Gen 41: 15. It is dreaming, not praying. Life and fervency baptise a duty, and give it a name. (2) Consider in what need we stand of those things which we ask in prayer. We come to ask the favour of God; and if we have not his love all we enjoy is cursed to us. We pray that our souls may be washed in Christ's blood; if he wash us not we have no part in him. John 13: 8. When will we be in earnest, if not when we are praying for the life of our souls? (3) It is only fervent prayer that has the promise of mercy affixed to it. 'Ye shall find me, when ye shall search for me with all your heart.' Jer 29: 13. It is dead praying without a promise; and the promise is made only to ardency. The a tiles among the Romans, had their doors always standing open, that all who had petitions might have free access to them; so God's heart is ever open to fervent prayer.

[4] Prayer must be sincere. Sincerity is the silver thread which must run through the whole duties of religion. Sincerity in prayer is when we have gracious holy ends; when our prayer is not so much for temporal mercies as for spiritual. We send out prayer as our merchant ship, that we may have large returns of spiritual blessings. Our aim in it is, that our hearts may be more holy, that we may have more communion with God and that we may increase our stock of grace. The prayer which wants a good aim, wants a good issue.

[5] The prayer that will prevail with God must have a fixedness of mind. 'My heart is fixed, O God.' Psa 57: 7. Since the fall the mind is like quicksilver, which will not fix; it has principium motus, but non quietus [a principle of restlessness, not of peace]. The thoughts will be roving and dancing up and down in prayer, just as if a man who is travelling to a certain place should run out of the road, and wander he knows not whither. In prayer we are travelling to the throne of grace, but how often do we, by vain cogitations, turn out of the road! This is rather wandering than praying.

How shall we cure these vain impertinent thoughts, which distract us in prayer, and, we fear, hinder its acceptance?

(1) Be very apprehensive in prayer of the infiniteness of God's majesty and purity. His eye is upon us in prayer, and we may say as David, 'Thou tellest my wanderings.' Psa 56: 8. The thoughts of this would make us hoc agere, mind the duty we are about. If a man were to deliver a petition to an earthly prince, would he at the same time be playing with a feather? Set yourselves, when you pray, as in God's presence. Could you but look through the keyhole of heaven, and see how devout and intent the angels are in their worshipping God, surely you would be ready to blush at your vain thoughts and vile impertinences in prayer.

(2) If you would keep your mind fixed in prayer, keep your eye fixed. 'Unto thee lift I up mine eyes, O thou that dwellest in the heavens.' Psa 123: 1. Much vanity comes in at the eye. When the eye wanders in prayer, the heart wanders. To think to keep the heart fixed in prayer, and yet let the eye gaze, is as if one should think to keep his house safe, and yet let the windows be open.

(3) If you would have your thoughts fixed in prayer, get more love to God. Love is a great fixer of the thoughts. He who is in love cannot keep his thoughts off the object. He who loves the world has his thoughts upon the world. Did we love God more, our minds would be more intent upon him in prayer. Were there more delight in duty, there would be less distraction.

(4) Implore the help of God's Spirit to fix your minds, and make them intent and serious in prayer. The ship without a pilot rather floats than sails. That our thoughts do not float up and down in prayer, we need the blessed Spirit to be our pilot to steer us. Only God's Spirit can bound the thoughts. A shaking hand may as well write a line steadily, as we can keep our hearts fixed in prayer without the Spirit of God.

(5) Make holy thoughts familiar to you in your ordinary course of life. David was often musing on God. 'When I am awake, I am still with thee.' Psa 139: 18. He who gives himself liberty to have vain thoughts out of prayer, will scarcely have other thoughts in prayer.

(6) If you would keep your mind fixed on God, watch your hearts, not only after prayer, but in prayer. The heart will be apt to give you the slip, and have a thousand vagaries in prayer. We read of angels ascending and descending on Jacob's ladder; so in prayer you shall find your hearts ascending to heaven, and in a moment descending upon earthly objects. O Christians, watch your hearts in prayer. What a shame is it to think, that when we are speaking to God our hearts should be in the fields, or in our counting-houses, or one way or other, running upon the devil's errand!

(7) Labour for larger degrees of grace. The more ballast the ship has the better it sails; so the more the heart is ballasted with grace, the steadier it will sail to heaven in prayer.

[6] Prayer that is likely to prevail with God must be argumentative. God loves to have us plead with him, and use arguments in prayer. See how many arguments Jacob used in prayer. 'Deliver me, I pray thee, from the hand of my brother.' Gen 32: 11. The arguments he used are from God's

command 'Thou saidst to me, Return to thy country;' ver 9; as if he had said, I did not take this journey of my own head, but by thy direction; therefore thou canst not but in honour protect me. And he uses another argument. 'Thou saidst, I will surely do thee good;' ver 12. Lord, wilt thou go back from thy own promise? Thus he was argumentative in prayer; and he got not only a new blessing, but a new name. 'Thy name shall be called no more Jacob, but Israel: for as a prince hast thou power with God, and hast prevailed;' ver 28. God loves to be overcome with strength of argument. Thus, when we come to God in prayer for grace, let us be argumentative. Lord, thou callest thyself the God of all grace; and whither should we go with our vessel, but to the fountain? Lord, thy grace may be imparted, yet not impaired. Has not Christ purchased grace for poor indigent creatures? Every drachm of grace costs a drop of blood. Shall Christ die to purchase grace for us, and shall not we have the fruit of his purchase? Lord, it is thy delight to milk out the breast of mercy and grace, and wilt thou abridge thyself of thy own delight? Thou hast promised to give thy Spirit to implant grace; can truth lie? can faithfulness deceive? God loves thus to be overcome with arguments in prayer.

[7] Prayer that would prevail with God, must be joined with reformation. 'If thou stretch out thy hands toward him; if iniquity be in thy hand, put it far away.' Job 11: 13, 14. Sin, lived in, makes the heart hard, and God's ear deaf. It is foolish to pray against sin, and then sin against prayer. 'If I regard iniquity in my heart, the Lord will not hear me.' Psa 66: 18. The loadstone loses its virtue when bespread with garlic; so does prayer when polluted with sin. The incense of prayer must be offered upon the altar of a holy heart.

Thus you see what is the prayer which is most likely to prevail with God.

Use one. It reproves (1) Such as pray not at all. It is made the note of a reprobate, that he calls not upon God. Psa 14: 4. Does he think to have an alms who never asks it? Do they think to have mercy from Cod who never seek it? Then God would befriend them more than he did his own Son. Christ offered up prayers with strong cries. Heb 5: 7. None of God's children are born dumb. Gal 4: 6.

(2) It reproves such as have left off prayer, which is a sign that they never felt the fruit and comfort of it. He that leaves off prayer leaves off to fear God. 'Thou castest off fear, and restrainest prayer before God.' Job 15: 4. A man that has left off prayer, is fit for any wickedness. When Saul had given over inquiring after God he went to the witch of Endor.

Use two. Be persons given to prayer. 'I give myself,' says David, 'to prayer.' Pray for pardon and purity. Prayer is the golden key that opens heaven. The tree of the promise will not drop its fruit unless shaken by the hand of prayer. All the benefits of Christ's redemption are handed over to us by prayer.

I have prayed a long time for mercy, and have no answer. 'I am weary of crying.' Ps 69: 3.

(1) God may hear us when we do not hear from him; as soon as prayer is made, God hears it, though he does not presently answer. A friend may receive our letter, though he does not presently send us an answer. (2) God may delay prayer, yet he will not deny it.

Why does God delay an answer to prayer?

(1) Because he loves to hear the voice of prayer. 'The prayer of the upright is his delight.' Prov 15: 8. You let the musician play a great while ere you throw him down money, because you love to hear his music. Cant 2: 14.

(2) God may delay prayer when he will not deny it, that he may humble us. He has spoken to us long in his word to leave our sins, but we would not hear him; therefore he lets us speak to him in prayer and seems not to hear us.

(3) He may delay to answer prayer when he will not deny it, because he sees we are not yet fit for the mercy we ask. Perhaps we pray for deliverance when we are not fit for it; our scum is not yet boiled away. We would have God swift to deliver, and we are slow to repent.

(4) God may delay to answer prayer, that the mercy we pray for may be more prized, and may be sweeter when it comes. The longer the merchant's ships stay abroad, the more he rejoices when they come home laden with spices and jewels; therefore be not discouraged, but follow God with prayer. Though God delays, he will not deny. Prayer vincit invincibilem [conquers the invincible], it overcomes the Omnipotent. Hos 12: 4. The Syrians tied their god Hercules fast with a golden chain, that he should not remove. The Lord was held by Moses' prayer as with a golden chain. 'Let me alone;' why, what did Moses? he only prayed. Exod 32: 10. Prayer ushers in mercy. Be thy case never so sad, if thou canst but pray thou needest not fear. Psa 10: 17. Therefore give thyself to prayer.

End

Printed in Great Britain
by Amazon

40805844R00119